MW00763343

A Year in the Psalms

365 Daily Devotions from 52 Psalms

Brenton Cox

CROSSBOOKS
PUBLISHING

CrossBooks™
A Division of LifeWay
1663 Liberty Drive
Bloomington, IN 47403
www.crossbooks.com
Phone: 1-866-879-0502

©2010 Brenton Cox. All rights reserved.

No part of this book may be reproduced, stored in a retrieval system, or
transmitted by any means without the written permission of the author.

First published by CrossBooks 9/21/2010

ISBN: 978-1-6150-7178-4 (sc)
Library of Congress Control Number: 2010930997

Unless otherwise indicated, Scripture quotations are from the HOLY BIBLE, NEW
INTERNATIONAL VERSION. Copyright 1973, 1978, 1984 by International Bible Society.
Used by permission of Zondervan. All rights reserved.

Scripture quotations marked KJV are taken from The Holy Bible, King James Version.

Scripture quotations marked LB are taken from The Living Bible, copyright 1971 by Tyndale
House Publishers, Wheaton, IL.

Scripture quotations marked THE MESSAGE are taken from THE MESSAGE. Copyright 1993,
1994, 1995, 1996. Used by permission of NavPress Publishing Group.

Scripture quotations marked NASB are taken from the New American Standard Bible, copyright
1960, 1962, 1963, 1968, 1971 by The Lockman Foundation.

Scripture quotations marked NKJV are taken from the Holy Bible, New King James Version
copyright 1982 by Thomas Nelson.

Scripture quotations marked NLT are taken from the Holy Bible, New Living Translation,
copyright 1996, 2004. Used by permission of Tyndale House Publishers, Inc., Wheaton, Illinois
60189. All rights reserved.

Scripture quotations marked NRSV are taken from the New Revised Standard Version Bible,
copyright 1989 by Division of Christian Education of the National Council of Churches of Christ
in the United States.

Scripture quotations marked TEV are taken from The Bible in Today's English Version, copyright
1976 by American Bible Society.

Printed in the United States of America

This book is printed on acid-free paper.

To Mildred Guy
friend and saint
who encouraged me to write this book

Contents

Introduction

It is a worthy goal for a Christian to read through the Bible in a year. Such a survey provides an overview of God's plan of redemption in the Scriptures. What does one do the next year? Return to the Bible with a slower pace. Seek an in-depth understanding of each portion of God's Word. There are many plans for reading through the Bible in a year. There are fewer resources to help the Christian return to the Bible and linger in certain sections for an extended period of time. This book was born from that need. The reader is invited to spend a year in the Psalms.

In the arrangement of this book, a different group of psalms is considered each month. Some of these units reflect different literary types of psalms (such as penitential psalms, personal laments, psalms of trust, and psalms of praise). Other units reflect themes that run through the Psalms (such as the character of God, fear, and the hope of a Messiah). Within these units, one week is devoted to each psalm. This allows time to dig deeper into its meaning and to reflect upon its application. In this way the reader studies 52 psalms that are somewhat representative of the 150 psalms in the book. (Two weeks are devoted to the massive Psalm 119, but Psalms 42 and 43 are a unit and are considered in one week.)

Much of the material in this book was first preached in a yearlong series of sermons at First Baptist Church, Manchester, Tennessee. During 2006, I asked our congregation to spend a year with me in the Psalms. I wanted us to immerse ourselves in these songs so that we could know them better and be changed by them. I learned a lot as I preached through this book, and I am grateful to our congregation for their support. This year, I invite you to spend a year with me in the Psalms.

January

How to Have a Fresh Start in Life

At the beginning of a new year, many people long for a new beginning in life. You may feel some dissatisfaction with who you are. You may feel shame or remorse about some things you have done in the past. You may wonder, "Is it really possible to change? Can a person get a clean slate and make a new beginning?" The Psalms answer that question with a resounding "yes!" You can have a fresh start in life. The penitential psalms tell you how.

David wrote most of the penitential psalms. In them, he shares how he experienced change and how he came to a new joy in life. This month we will examine five penitential psalms that describe a five-step process for starting over in life.

January 1-7
Psalm 38: Confess Your Sin to God

January 1

My guilt has overwhelmed me,
like a burden too heavy to bear
(Psalm 38:4).

David wrote Psalm 38 as a prayer asking God for mercy. "O Lord, do not rebuke me in your anger or discipline me in your wrath" (v. 1). David was hurting when he wrote this psalm: "For your arrows have pierced me, and your hand has come down upon me" (v. 2). He was hurting physically: "There is no health in my body" (v. 3). He was also hurting emotionally: "My guilt has overwhelmed me like a burden too heavy to bear" (v. 4). In today's terminology, we would say that David was depressed: "Even the light has gone from my eyes" (v. 10). Depression had left David withdrawn and unable to communicate: "I have become like a man who does not hear, whose mouth can offer no reply" (v. 14).

David knew the reason for his predicament. He said it was "because of my sinful folly" (v. 5). He had acted as a fool. He had sinned and, as a consequence, he was wracked with guilt. Certainly not all sickness is caused by sin and guilt. The book of Job makes that abundantly clear. However, some illness does come from guilt. Certainly not all depression is caused by sin, but some emotional anguish is. David's was, and he knew it.

You will never have a fresh start in life until you deal with the sin in your life. Perhaps you have been dancing around some sin issues in your life. The first step in a fresh start is to confess your sin, both past and present.

January 2

All my longings lie open before you, O Lord;
my sighing is not hidden from you
(Psalm 38:9).

How do you respond when someone asks, "How are you doing?" If you are like most of us, you respond, "Fine." We may be dealing with marital conflict, financial setback, and physical pain, but we still say, "Fine." We often play similar games with God. Our prayers are formal and superficial. The difference between pretending to be fine with people and pretending to be fine with God is that God knows the truth. He knows our deepest longings.

One of David's greatest strengths was that he was honest with God. He understood that God knew the depth of his soul, and he talked openly to God about his deepest feelings. David poured out his doubts and complaints and fears and sins to God.

God knows *your* deepest longings today—both good and bad. He understands your sighs. You will not make much progress in your spiritual life until you learn to be honest with God in your prayers. Your fresh start in life depends on a frank, honest dialogue with God about your deepest feelings and problems.

January 3

I confess my iniquity;
I am troubled by my sin
(Psalm 38:18).

This is the key verse in Psalm 38. This verse explains confession, which is the first step in a fresh start in life. We will spend the next several days exploring what it means.

Confession first involves taking responsibility for your sin. Note the words "I" and "my" in verse 18. David does not excuse or rationalize his folly. He does not bring up mitigating or extenuating circumstances. He doesn't protest, "I was provoked" or "I was seduced." Doubtless there were external factors involved in David's sin. There always are. Reviewing them only attempts to lessen or shift responsibility. God knows all the factors. If you want a fresh start, you must take personal responsibility for the course of your life, for the things you have done or said or thought. Will you say with David, "*I confess my iniquity*"?

January 4

I confess my iniquity;
I am troubled by my sin
(Psalm 38:18).

Confession involves telling your sin. The word "confess" means, "to report, declare, reveal, admit." Confession is not just *feeling* responsibility and guilt. Confession involves *verbalizing* this responsibility and guilt. To whom must you confess your sin? To God. Pray as David did in this psalm. You may be thinking, "God already knows all about my sin, so why do I need to tell him?" Confession is agreement with God concerning his commandments.

You should also confess your sins to those who have been directly harmed by your sin. Perhaps you have cheated your employer or you have not been considerate of your spouse. Tell that person, even if he or she already knows. Confession begins the process of forgiveness in your life.

January 5

I confess my iniquity;
I am troubled by my sin
(Psalm 38:18).

Confession involves being troubled by your sin. Almost every verse in the Psalms contains two lines. The second line often restates the first line in different words. This is called *parallelism*, and it is the predominant feature of Hebrew wisdom poetry. The best commentary on the first line of a verse in the Psalms is often the second line of the verse. Thus, Psalm 38:18 says that confessing sin (the first line of the verse) involves being troubled by sin (the second line).

In order to have a fresh start in life, you need to experience the weight of your sin. You need to see the holiness of God and be bothered by your offense against him. You need to be broken as David was. Much modern counsel ignores this step, but it cannot be bypassed. God wants you to feel better about your sin, but you cannot feel better until you have felt bad. Many people have no joy in forgiveness because they have felt no pain in confession.

The apostle Paul wrote a stinging letter to the church at Corinth that caused them great sorrow, but it also brought them to repentance. Later Paul wrote them again, "Even if I caused you sorrow by my letter, I do not regret it…. For you became sorrowful as God intended and so were not harmed in any way by us. Godly sorrow brings repentance that leads to salvation and leaves no regret" (2 Cor. 7:8-10).

January 6

I confess my iniquity;
I am troubled by my sin
(Psalm 38:18).

The process of confession applies to past sin as well as present sin. Why dig up sins from the distant past and relive unpleasant memories? Because without confession there is no forgiveness, no healing, no hope of moving into the future.

On September 22, 1998, Daniel Crocker confessed to a murder he committed nineteen years earlier. No one had tracked him down. Crocker's confession came from the conviction God had placed on his heart. When he was nineteen years old, Crocker had been on a three-day LSD high when he killed nineteen-year-old Tracy Fresquez after meeting her briefly at a convenience store. Few clues were left behind. Not long after the murder, Crocker realized he had to make serious changes in his life. He turned to Christ and soon became involved in church and Bible study. Later he married a woman from his church and they started a family. He and his wife came to the consensus that he needed to confess his crime. So, at age thirty-eight, he said goodbye to his wife and two children and surrendered to a prosecutor. Why did he turn himself in? He had read Proverbs 28:13: "He who conceals his sins does not prosper, but whoever confesses and renounces them finds mercy."[1] Are there unconfessed sins from your past that are blocking you from prosperity and mercy? Why not confess them today?

---

1   Raymond McHenry, *McHenry's Stories for the Soul* (Peabody, MA: Hendrickson, 2001), 54-55.

January 7

Come quickly to help me,
O Lord my Savior
(Psalm 38:22).

The first step in a journey is always the toughest. Confession is the toughest step in your spiritual life. The verses we have studied this week have been challenging. If during this week you have faced up to the sin issues in your life, if you have been so troubled by your sin that you have taken personal responsibility for it and honestly admitted it to God, you have taken the hardest step in a fresh start in life.

Understand that God wants to help you through this process. David ends Psalm 38 with a prayer for God's help as he makes a fresh start. Because of your faith in Jesus Christ, God stands in a relationship of authority and deliverance in your life. He is your Lord and Savior. Isn't it comforting to know that he is on your side? Why don't you pray the prayer in verse 22 right now?

January 8-14
Psalm 51: Ask God for Cleansing

January 8

Have mercy on me, O God,
according to your unfailing love;
according to your great compassion
blot out my transgressions
(Psalm 51:1).

The second step in having a fresh start in life is to ask God for cleansing. The title of Psalm 51 explains that David wrote this psalm after the prophet Nathan had confronted him about his adultery with Bathsheba (2 Samuel 11-12). David also had Bathsheba's husband killed to cover up his sin. David certainly needed a fresh start! The good news is you can have a fresh start no matter what you have done. It is never too late, and your sin is never so bad that you cannot be forgiven.

For those who, like David, have failed royally, this is a difficult concept. A Christian woman who has aborted a child, a Christian man who has betrayed his spouse, or a Christian leader who has disgraced his calling and brought shame to his church, may struggle with the reality of cleansing. Notice the basis of David's request for mercy: "according to your unfailing love; according to your great compassion." God never stops loving you, no matter what you do. God's nature is to express compassion. God can "blot out" your transgressions—removing them from your record. This will happen only when you ask him to do so.

January 9

Have mercy on me, O God,
according to your unfailing love;
according to your great compassion
blot out my transgressions.
Wash away all my iniquity
and cleanse me from my sin
(Psalm 51:1-2).

You may be thinking that your record is not as bad as David's. You may never have committed adultery or murder. Sin is still the major issue in your life. There are three main words for sin in the Old Testament, and all three of them are found in Psalm 51:1-2.

The first word is "transgression." It means "to step over the line, to rebel against the authority of God." Perhaps you tell your boss some half-truths even though you know God's Word says, "Do not lie." That is transgression, stepping over the line in willful disobedience.

The second word is "iniquity." It means "to bend or twist." It refers to crookedness, perversion, or error. It denotes a bending of God's purposes. Perhaps you gossip about someone while explaining that you are "simply expressing your concern." That is iniquity, twisting God's purposes.

The third word is "sin." It means "to miss the mark or fall short of God's will and purpose." Perhaps you fail to share your faith or exercise your spiritual gifts in his service. That is sin, missing the mark of God's will. Will you ask God to blot out your transgressions, wash away your iniquity, and cleanse you from your sin?

January 10

For I know my transgressions,
and my sin is always before me.
Against you, you only, have I sinned
and done what is evil in your sight,
so that you are proved right when you speak
and justified when you judge
(Psalm 51:3-4).

After David introduces the theme of this psalm in verses 1-2 (Ask God for cleansing), he backs up in verses 3-4 and reviews the first step in a fresh start (Confess your sin to God). It will be worthwhile for us to review confession from these verses.

David takes personal responsibility for his sin: "I know my transgressions." David does not mention the role of Bathsheba. It is not pertinent here.

David acknowledges being troubled by his sin: "My sin is always before me."

David admits his sin to God: "Against you, you only, have I sinned." What does that mean? Had David not sinned against Uriah? He had killed him! Certainly your sin harms others. You may rightly say you have sinned against another person (Luke 15:18). However, sin is preeminently an offense against God. He is the Holy One, the one you have disobeyed. People excuse some types of sin by saying, "It's not hurting anyone." It is hurting God. It is thumbing your nose at him. David admits God is right to judge him. When you really confess your sin, you do not whine that you are being treated unfairly. You do not ask, "But what about my feelings?" When you really confess your sin, you recognize God's judgment is right.

January 11

Cleanse me with hyssop, and I will be clean;
wash me, and I will be whiter than snow
(Psalm 51:7).

In verse 7 David returns to the theme of this psalm, asking God for cleansing. The three requests introduced in verses 1-2 (blot out, wash away, cleanse) are repeated in reverse order in verses 7-9.

David prays, "Cleanse me with hyssop." Hyssop was a small plant with hairy stems and leaves. When dipped in a liquid, drops of the liquid would cling to the tiny hairs until it was shaken. Hyssop was used as a "paintbrush" to sprinkle blood on the doorposts at Passover (Ex. 12:22). The priests sprinkled blood on the altar and the temple furnishings to purify them. David is asking for that kind of cleansing in his life. Jesus died on the cross to shed his blood for your sins. When you ask him for cleansing, your heart is sprinkled with his blood to cleanse you from a guilty conscience (Heb. 10:22). You can be cleansed from your guilt if you will ask God.

If you are having trouble accepting such cleansing, repeat this verse as you stand in the shower with water flowing over you. Visualize your guilt washing off you as drops of water swirl down the drain. The cleansing of God is just as real.

January 12

Let me hear joy and gladness;
let the bones you have crushed rejoice
(Psalm 51:8).

In the movie, *The Shawshank Redemption*, a man breaks out of prison during a severe thunderstorm. He uses a rock to knock a hole in the prison sewer line, timing his blows to coincide with the claps of thunder so that he will not be heard. Then he lowers himself through the hole and crawls through one hundred yards of blackness and raw human sewage. Finally, he comes out the end of the pipe and plops into a pool of waste. He stands to his feet and strips off his shirt. He turns his face toward the skies and lets the pouring rain wash away the stench from his body. He is standing in filth, but a smile is on his face because he is free, and he is being washed clean.

This is an image of what David is experiencing in this psalm and what you can experience in your life. Ask God to cleanse you so that you may hear joy and gladness again.

January 13

Create in me a pure heart, O God,
and renew a steadfast spirit within me.
Do not cast me from your presence
or take your Holy Spirit from me.
Restore to me the joy of your salvation
and grant me a willing spirit to sustain me
(Psalm 51:10–12).

The first nine verses of this psalm deal with the past, but the last seven look to the future. God wants to remove the stain of sin, but he also wants to change you so that you do not bring such pain upon yourself again.

Ask God to give you a new heart (v. 10). The word "create" means to make a new thing out of nothing. Only God can do that. God can change you on the inside. God can give you a heart transplant: "I will give you a new heart and put a new spirit in you. I will remove from you your heart of stone and give you a heart of flesh" (Ezek. 36:26).

Ask God for the help of the Holy Spirit (v. 11). Your sin grieves the Holy Spirit who lives within you (Eph. 4:30). Confession brings cleansing which restores that fellowship.

Ask God to restore to you the joy of his salvation (v. 12). You cannot lose your salvation, but you can lose the joy of salvation. God wants you to live with joy. This process can restore your joy. You cannot ask for joy until you have confessed your sin and been cleansed. People often want the result without the process. You cannot start this psalm in verse 12. Move through the entire process, and the result will be joy in your life.

January 14

Then I will teach transgressors your ways,
and sinners will turn back to you
(Psalm 51:13).

David promises he will tell others how to have a fresh start in life. God has a redemptive purpose even in your failure. After you have experienced God's forgiveness, you are to share your experience with others. Nothing communicates the power of God like a first-hand testimony. When you testify to God's mercy, "sinners will turn back" to God.

This psalm is a model for how to return to God. Many people want to "rededicate" their lives to God or make a new commitment to him. Rededication or recommitment will not be effective unless it involves confession and cleansing. When you feel prompted to rededicate your life to Christ, ask yourself, "What is the specific sin in my life that I need to confess to Christ?" If you say, "There is no specific sin in my life," then you must be in the center of God's will with no need for rededication. Rededication always involves the need for confession of transgression, iniquity, or sin. Think about it!

January 15–21
Psalm 130: Trust God to Forgive You

January 15

Out of the depths I cry to you, O LORD;
O Lord, hear my voice.
Let your ears be attentive to my cry for mercy
(Psalm 130:1-2).

Psalm 130 introduces the third step in how to have a fresh start in life, but first it reviews the steps we have already studied. Verses 1-2 are largely a review of the first step: confess your sin to God.

Have you ever been down in the dumps? That is not such a bad place to be! When you are down, you are more likely to look up. Jesus said, "Blessed are the poor in spirit, for theirs is the kingdom of heaven. Blessed are those who mourn, for they will be comforted" (Matt. 5:3-4). Recognizing the poverty of your spiritual condition is the first and biggest hurdle to spiritual renewal. If you have become aware of your spiritual need, take heart! You are well on your way to the kingdom of heaven!

January 16

If you, O LORD, kept a record of sins,
O Lord, who could stand?
But with you there is forgiveness;
therefore you are feared
(Psalm 130:3-4).

Verses 3-4 review the second step in how to have a fresh start: ask God for cleansing. The natural tendency is to try to bargain with God about your sins: "If you will forgive me, I promise to go to church, tithe, and never do this again." However, you have nothing to offer God. You have no bargaining power. Your only option is to ask God for cleansing. When you do, he freely forgives.

Some people think the result of free forgiveness will be presumption: "If God freely forgives, why not sin all we want and just ask him to forgive us again?" Such thinking indicates a person has not been through the process of being troubled by sin and feeling its weight. Verse 4 indicates that the result of forgiveness will be a fear of the Lord. When you understand the cost of your forgiveness, you will be awed at his unfathomable greatness. Do you have a healthy fear of the Lord that comes from a sense of really being forgiven?

January 17

I wait for the Lord, my soul waits,
and in his word I put my hope
(Psalm 130:5).

In verses 5-6, we come to the heart of this psalm, the third step in a fresh start: trust God to forgive you. There are many people who confess their sin and ask God for cleansing, but do not feel they have been forgiven. They continue to carry a load of guilt and shame. You must trust that you have been forgiven even when you do not feel forgiven. This is a process that may take some time.

What is the psalmist waiting for in verse 5? He is not waiting for forgiveness. That is already present in verse 4. You do not wait for forgiveness; it is instantaneous. You must wait for renewed intimacy with the Lord. To put it another way, you must wait for your feelings to catch up with the facts of forgiveness. Feelings often lag behind facts. You are forgiven immediately, but you may not feel good immediately. If a woman has an abortion, then is troubled by it, takes responsibility for it, confesses it, and asks for cleansing, is she forgiven immediately? Yes. Will she feel okay immediately? Maybe not. She must trust God has forgiven her. The word "wait" is translated "trust" in Isaiah 25:9. It is translated "hope" in Psalm 37:9 and Isaiah 40:31. "Wait" indicates the element of time. "Trust" indicates the element of perseverance. "Hope" indicates the element of anticipation.

January 18

I wait for the Lord, my soul waits,
and in his word I put my hope
(Psalm 130:5).

A Christian must often live contrary to his or her feelings. Feelings are not dependable as a guide for your life. You must live by faith and not by feelings. How do you trust that God has forgiven you when you do not feel forgiven? The latter part of verse 5 gives the answer: "In his word I put my hope." If you recite the promises of God in his Word, your feelings will eventually change. If you have confessed your sin repeatedly and still feel unforgiven, try claiming the promises of God. Say to God: "I do not feel forgiven. I still battle shame and guilt, but you say, 'With you there is forgiveness.' I choose to believe that I am forgiven based not on my feelings but on your Word." Do this repeatedly and your faith will change your feelings.

January 19

My soul waits for the Lord
more than watchmen wait for the morning,
more than watchmen wait for the morning
(Psalm 130:6).

Experiencing the forgiveness of God and renewed intimacy with him will be a process in your life. It will take time. You must not grow tired of waiting. You must not give up. Imagine a guard on a city wall in the long hours of the night, waiting and trusting and hoping for daybreak. My dad was a night watchman for a copper mining company in Tennessee. Throughout the night he would drive from one mine site to another. When he had checked everything at one mine, he would radio a report, and then sit in his patrol car until it was time to drive to the next mine. He often told me how hard it was to stay awake on dark nights. He would rejoice when the eastern sky began to lighten, because it would be far easier to stay awake. The Bible says you are to wait for the Lord and for the feeling of forgiveness with that kind of anticipation.

January 20

O Israel, put your hope in the LORD,
for with the LORD is unfailing love
and with him is full redemption
(Psalm 130:7).

Some churches hold watch night services on New Year's Eve. They watch and wait for the New Year to come. Some trace the origin of these services to the West Indies. Slaves were to be freed there on August 1, 1830. Thousands of slaves never went to bed the night before. They sent watchmen to the hills to catch the first rays of dawn. You must hold onto God with that kind of hope and anticipation.

Many people are on the right track in their Christian discipleship. They just give up too soon because they do not see evidence of change or do not feel they are making progress. Stay the course! Put your hope in the Lord, for with him there is full redemption.

January 21

He himself will redeem Israel
from all their sins
(Psalm 130:8).

Psalm 130 ends with a prophecy that God will personally redeem his people from all their sins. About one thousand years after those words were written, God fulfilled this prophecy through his Son. Jesus was God in human flesh. Jesus died in order to satisfy the death penalty for our sins. "In him we have redemption through his blood, the forgiveness of sins, in accordance with the riches of God's grace" (Eph. 1:7). The object of our faith is the work of Jesus on the cross as he released us from the penalty of our sins. Reaffirm your faith in the death of Jesus Christ as the payment for your sins. Whenever you do not feel forgiven, revisit the cross of Christ in your mind. Meditate on what Christ has done for you there. That is the path to assurance of forgiveness.

January 22–28
Psalm 32: Receive God's Blessing

January 22

Blessed is he
whose transgressions are forgiven,
whose sins are covered
(Psalm 32:1).

The fourth step in having a fresh start is to receive God's blessing on your life. God's blessing is the joy of forgiveness. Psalm 32 celebrates the happiness, the exuberance, the joy of being forgiven. You may not be receiving the joy and blessing God wants you to have. You may be holding on to feelings of guilt, insecurity, shame, and self-deprecation when God wants you to experience liberation.

This psalm begins with the word "blessed." It means "happiness that comes from God." This is the second psalm that begins with a beatitude or statement of blessing. Psalm 1 begins, "Blessed is the man who does not walk in the counsel of the wicked." The greatest happiness is to avoid sin. That's the theme of Psalm 1. However, we do not always do that. The second greatest happiness is to be forgiven of sin. That's the theme of Psalm 32.

Are you happy? If not, one possible reason is that you have not dealt thoroughly with the sin in your life.

January 23

Blessed is he
whose transgressions are forgiven,
whose sins are covered
(Psalm 32:1).

We have learned that there are three main words in the Old Testament for sin ("transgression," "iniquity," and "sin"—found together in Psalm 51:1 and 32:5). There are also three main words for forgiveness, and they are all found in Psalm 32:1-2. These three words describe the basis for our joy. The first word is "forgiven." It means "carried away, removed, lifted." On the Day of Atonement, the Israelites were to choose two goats. One was a scapegoat. Sins were confessed over the head of that goat, and the priest laid his hands upon it. The scapegoat was sent away into the desert, carrying away the sins laid on it (Lev. 16:21-22). In the New Covenant, Jesus is our scapegoat, bearing away our sins.

When you have trusted God for forgiveness, your sin has been carried away from you. Visualize it leaving. That is the basis of your joy. In *The Pilgrim's Progress*, Pilgrim carried a burden on his back. When he came to the cross, the burden loosened from his shoulders. It fell to the ground and rolled into the empty tomb and was seen no more![2] Later Ralph E. Hudson wrote a refrain to Isaac Watts' hymn, *At the Cross*:

> At the cross, at the cross where I first saw the light,
> And the burden of my heart rolled away,
> It was there by faith I received my sight,
> And now I am happy all the day!

---

2   John Bunyan, *The Pilgrim's Progress* (Grand Rapids: Zondervan, 1967), 40.

January 24

Blessed is he
whose transgressions are forgiven,
whose sins are covered
(Psalm 32:1).

The second word for forgiveness in verse 1 is "covered". On the Day of Atonement, the second goat was slaughtered. Its blood was taken into the temple and sprinkled on the atonement cover (Lev. 16:15). The blood was a covering for the sin of Israel. In the New Covenant, the blood of Jesus covers or conceals our sin.

Later in this psalm David writes, "Then I acknowledged my sin to you and did not cover up my iniquity" (Ps. 32:5). Your natural tendency is to conceal your sin. When you cover your sin, God often uncovers it. However, when you uncover your sin in confession, God covers it with the blood of his Son! Rejoice that your sin is covered!

January 25

Blessed is the man
whose sin the LORD does not count against him
and in whose spirit is no deceit
(Psalm 32:2).

The third word for forgiveness, found in verse 2 of this psalm, is "count." God does not count your sins against you. That is a bookkeeping term. Paul loved this term. He quoted these verses in Romans 4:7-8. This word means to be justified or "square" with God. You can rejoice that you are in good standing with God! If you are beating yourself up after you have been forgiven, you are not being spiritual. There is no penance after forgiveness. There is only blessing. You must receive this blessing.

In the movie, *The Mission*, a man kills his brother in a quarrel over a woman. He regrets his action, and commits himself to become a missionary to a tribe in the interior of Brazil. To reach this tribe, he and his companions must climb a towering cliff. The man straps the armor of a soldier to his back, so that he will suffer as he climbs. Finally, someone takes a knife and cuts the rope securing the burden to his back. The armor clatters far down the face of the cliff. Rather than rejoicing in his freedom, he retreats down the precipice, retrieves his burden, and carries it back up the cliff. You may think you need to keep suffering for your sin after you have been forgiven. You do not. God wants you to experience his blessing. Receive it!

January 26

When I kept silent,
my bones wasted away
through my groaning all day long.
For day and night
your hand was heavy upon me;
my strength was sapped
as in the strength of summer.
Then I acknowledged my sin to you
and did not cover up my iniquity.
I said, "I will confess
my transgressions to the LORD"—
and you forgave
the guilt of my sin
(Psalm 32:3-5).

You cannot start by receiving God's blessing. Many people are praying for God's blessing in the New Year without ever dealing with their sin. That will not work. In verses 3-5 David backs up and reviews the process that led him to the point of joy and blessedness. He remembers when he did not confess his sin, when he kept silent. His refusal to deal with the sin in his life affected him physically ("my bones wasted away") and emotionally ("my strength was sapped"). The turning point came when he acknowledged and confessed his sin.

Perhaps you are experiencing physical and emotional suffering caused by sin in your life. You want to get rid of this pain and experience joy again. However, you can't move directly from the "point A" of sin's consequences to the "point C" of joy and blessing. You must go through the "point B" of confession—uncovering your sin. This "point B" brings a different kind of pain—the pain of repentance. It is a necessary step in the healing process and the path to joy.

January 27

Therefore let everyone who is godly pray to you
while you may be found;
surely when the mighty waters rise,
they will not reach him.
You are my hiding place;
you will protect me from trouble
and surround me with songs of deliverance.
I will instruct you and teach you in the way you should go;
I will counsel you and watch over you.
Do not be like the horse or the mule,
which have no understanding
but must be controlled by bit and bridle
or they will not come to you
(Psalm 32:6-9).

David says other people can learn from his experience. He encourages everyone to follow the process of confession and cleansing. If you do, you will find the blessing of God.

You will find God to be your hiding place (v. 7). This verse is the inspiration for Corrie Ten Boom's book and movie *The Hiding Place*. She tells how her family built a secret room in their home and hid Jews from the Nazis during World War Two. The Germans learned of their covert activity and sent Corrie and her sister to a prison camp. Even there they found God himself to be their refuge, their hiding place.

David warns that if you do not follow this process, you will not experience blessing. Instead, like a horse or mule with a bit in its mouth, God may lead you in places you do not want to go (v. 9).

January 28

Rejoice in the LORD and be glad, you righteous;
sing, all you who are upright in heart!
(Psalm 32:11).

When you think of your past, does God want you to feel bad about your failures or feel good about his forgiveness? He wants you to experience both emotions in their proper time. First, you must be grieved by the offense of your sin against God. This grief will lead you to confession and repentance. Then, you must accept the free forgiveness of God through the sacrifice of Jesus Christ. This produces gladness and joy. At this point you must not return to guilt or grief over confessed sin. Whenever you find yourself slipping into depression over past failures that you have already confessed, stop yourself. Realize that feeling comes from Satan and not from God. Make a conscious effort to rejoice in the Lord and be glad. Singing is one way to express that joy. By doing this repeatedly, you will win victory over your false guilt and be able to live with a continual sense of joy.

January 29—February 4
Psalm 25: Ask God to Guide You

January 29

To you, O LORD, I lift up my soul
(Psalm 25:1).

There are five steps to a fresh start in your life. This psalm introduces step five, the final step in the process. You should find yourself in one of these five steps. If you are excusing or rationalizing your sin, you have not begun the process. If you are bothered by your sin, you are at step one. If you have confessed your sin and desire to be clean, you are at step two. If you have asked for God's cleansing but you still don't feel forgiven, you are at step three. If you have trusted God to forgive you but you are not yet experiencing joy, you are at step four. If you have done all these things, you are ready for step five: turn to the future and ask God for guidance so that you will avoid repeating the pain of your past. You need to chart a new course, break the cycles of sin and grief, and learn a different way to live.

Psalm 25 tells how to do that. David wrote this psalm in the latter years of his life. He reflects back on the past and attempts to move beyond the sins of his youth. This psalm is an acrostic. Each verse begins with a successive letter of the Hebrew alphabet. There are 22 letters in the Hebrew alphabet, and there are 22 verses in this psalm. These verses explain how to experience God's guidance.

January 30

In you I trust, O my God.
Do not let me be put to shame,
nor let my enemies triumph over me.
No one whose hope is in you
will ever be put to shame,
but they will be put to shame
who are treacherous without excuse
(Psalm 25:2-3).

There are two challenges in this step. The first challenge is that you not revert to sin. You want to make better choices in the future and avoid the pain of discipline. You need more than forgiveness. You need to break the sin pattern. Some of you are in a cycle of gossip or pornography or adultery. You need to break that cycle.

The second challenge is that you not revert to shame. David mentions shame three times in these two verses. Shame is one of the devil's favorite tools. If he cannot draw you into sin, he will attempt to draw you back into shame. He will use the comments of other people to arouse shame you thought was conquered. You must ask God to help you not be sucked back into shame. You do not belong there anymore. You have been forgiven.

January 31

Show me your ways, O LORD,
teach me your paths;
guide me in your truth and teach me,
for you are God my Savior,
and my hope is in you all day long
(Psalm 25:4–5).

How do you avoid reverting to sin or shame? The way to meet these challenges is to ask God to guide you. Verses 4-5 contain a three-fold prayer. I hope you will learn to pray this psalm. This is a prayer I have written in my prayer notebook for many years as a husband and father and pastor.

The first line is a prayer for illumination: "Show me your ways, O Lord." Ask God to show you his ways. I want to know what choices would be best for me. I was repainting the inside of our house. It took a lot longer than I expected to prepare every room and paint every ceiling and wall. Near the end of the process, I was trying to decide whether to repaint the inside of a bedroom closet. Who really sees the inside of a closet? Later that day the sun shone through the bedroom window so that it struck the closet and illuminated the back wall. Years of scuff marks and scratches were painfully evident. My choice was clear. I knew I had to paint the closet. I want God to illuminate choices in my life in that way. I want the spotlight of his holiness to illuminate choices so that I can see his will clearly. Why don't you pray for God to show you his ways?

February 1

Show me your ways, O LORD,
teach me your paths;
guide me in your truth and teach me,
for you are God my Savior,
and my hope is in you all day long
(Psalm 25:4-5).

The second line is a prayer for instruction: "Teach me your paths." Ask God to teach you his paths. I want to learn how God would have me respond.

Notice the pronoun: *your* paths. Often we want God to bless *our* plans and directions in life. That does not work. This prayer focuses on God's ways rather than our ways.

Gary Thomas tells of a time when he and his wife prayed extensively about buying a house. They gave God many opportunities to close the door, but he seemed to bless the move. They bought the house. Five years later it was worth considerably less than what they paid for it. They wondered, "Why didn't God stop us? We gave him plenty of opportunities." One day as Gary's wife was praying, she sensed God saying, "Have you ever considered the possibility that I wanted you in that neighborhood to minister there rather than to bolster your financial equity?"[3]

Are you asking God to bless the paths that you have chosen in life, or are you asking him to teach you his paths?

---

3 Gary Thomas, "The Freedom of Surrender," *Discipleship Journal,* September-October 1996, 52.

February 2

Show me your ways, O LORD,
teach me your paths;
guide me in your truth and teach me,
for you are God my Savior,
and my hope is in you all day long
(Psalm 25:4-5).

The third petition is a prayer for direction: "Guide me in your truth." Ask God to guide you in his truth. The word "guide" means to step on something in order to bend it. In the Old Testament it often refers to bending a bow in order to string it. It is a prayer for our lives to be bent to the will of God. If you have been struggling with sinful habits, you got off track somewhere along the way. You need to ask God to bend you in the right direction so that you will not take those paths again.

The process of bending an object involves pressure. Your natural tendency is to resist pressure. Can you identify the pressure of God in any area of your life? Is the Holy Spirit gently pressuring you to reconstruct some friendships or to change some routines? Is he pushing you away from some activities that have gotten you in trouble in the past? Are you pushing back against his guidance? Why not yield to his pressure and cooperate with his good will for your life?

February 3

Good and upright is the LORD;
therefore he instructs sinners in his ways.
He guides the humble in what is right
and teaches them his way
(Psalm 25:8-9).

There are two conditions for receiving God's guidance in your life. The first is humility. Whom will God instruct in his ways? The sinner. Everyone is a sinner. Does this mean God instructs everyone? No, it means God instructs the person who recognizes he is a sinner. God does not guide only those who are perfect. He guides sinners! Praise the Lord! Verse 9 repeats the thought with the word "humble." You miss his paths when you think you know the way in life. You receive his guidance when you admit you do not know and you cry out to him.

I read of a runner who was blind. She wore a radio receiver in her ear, and her coach transmitted instructions to her. If she got near the edge of her lane, he would tell her to move back to the center. He would communicate when a runner was about to overtake her or when it was time to lean to the finish line. She was totally dependent on his direction step by step. When you have that same sense of humility and dependence upon your Coach, he is able to instruct you and teach you his way.

February 4

Who, then, is the man who fears the LORD?
He will instruct him in the way chosen for him.
He will spend his days in prosperity,
and his descendants will inherit the land.
The Lord confides in those who fear him;
he makes his covenant known to them.
(Psalm 25:12-14).

The second condition for receiving God's guidance is a fear of the Lord. The "friendship" (NLT, NASB) of the Lord is with those who fear him. To fear the Lord means to respect his holiness so that sin is not taken lightly.

You can know God's guidance in your life if you humble yourself before him and fear him. You will still fall into sin, but it will not be an enslaving pattern in your life. You cannot start by asking God for guidance in this New Year. You must start with step one. Let's review the five steps to a fresh start:

1. Confess your sin to God (see Psalm 38).
2. Ask God for cleansing (see Psalm 51).
3. Trust God to forgive you (see Psalm 130).
4. Receive God's blessing (see Psalm 32).
5. Ask God to guide you (see Psalm 25).

How long do these steps take? They can happen all at once, but for most of us this is a process that takes time. Start wherever you are and move forward.

February

What Is God Like?

Almost everyone in America believes in God. Several surveys have revealed that over 90 percent of the people in the United States claim a belief in some kind of Supreme Being. However, we have many different concepts of the nature of God. What is God really like? Who is qualified to describe God to us? Is not God himself most qualified to explain his nature? The Bible is God's revelation of himself to human beings. The Psalms especially focus on the revelation of God's character. This month we will look at four psalms that explain to us what God is like.

February 5–11
Psalm 75: God Is Judge

February 5

You say, "I choose the appointed time;
it is I who judge uprightly"
(Psalm 75:2).

Psalm 75 tells us that God judges. This is a neglected aspect of God's character today. In the nineteenth century, there was too little emphasis on the love of God. An incident from the ministry of Dwight L. Moody reveals the imbalance. Moody invited an English preacher named Harry Moorhouse to preach in his church while he was away. When he returned to town, Moody asked his wife how Moorhouse was received. "They liked him very much," she replied. "He preaches a little different from you. He preaches that God *loves* sinners." The next Sunday Moorhouse preached again. Moorhouse moved through the Bible from Genesis to Revelation, giving proof that God loves the sinner. Moody later noted that by the time the sermon was over, "two or three of my sermons were spoiled." "Moody's teaching that God hates the sinner as well as the sin lay shattered at his feet."[4] Moody rediscovered the love of God.

Today the pendulum has swung to the other extreme. Everyone knows of the love of God. Many do not believe in the judgment of God. I hear statements such as "I don't believe God would send anyone to hell" or "God is about love; he is not about condemning people and their lifestyles." Today we need to rediscover the concept of God as judge. Psalm 75 can help us do that. God says, "It is I who judge uprightly."

---

4 J. C. Pollock, *Moody* (New York: MacMillan, 1963), 72-73.

February 6

You say, "I choose the appointed time;
it is I who judge uprightly"
(Psalm 75:2).

God says he has appointed a time for judgment. Judgment Day has already been scheduled in God's appointment book. People may seem to get by with terrible actions. Terrorists are never caught. Child abuse cases are never solved. Evil may seem to go unpunished, but that is because the date God has set for judgment has not yet arrived. God is incredibly patient, but he does not forget. He cannot be mocked. Some will make it through life without receiving justice for their actions, but God has set a date for Judgment Day at the end of time. We must not despair. We must not take vengeance into our own hands. Our vengeance short-circuits the just judgment of God. We are not God, so we are not able to judge uprightly. We must trust God and wait for his appointed time.

February 7

To the arrogant I say, "Boast no more,"
and to the wicked, "Do not lift up your horns.
Do not lift up your horns against heaven;
do not speak with outstretched neck"
(Psalm 75:4-5).

Many people today think God is like my grandmother. In the summers, I stayed with her during the day while my mother worked. When my cousins came to stay for a week, we tended to get rowdy. My grandmother would threaten that she was going to report our behavior when my mother got home from work. She never followed through with her threats. She was just too soft. After a while, my cousins and I tended to laugh at her threats. Now I am sorry for the problems we caused her.

Many people think God is like my grandmother. They think God will not follow through with judgment. God warns them not to boast against heaven. They lift up their "horns" against God. The horn is a symbol of power in Psalms. An animal with horns is threatening. God is not impressed by our power or worried by our boasting. He always keeps his word. He will hold every person accountable.

February 8

*No one from the east or west
or from the desert can exalt a man.
But it is God who judges:
He brings one down, he exalts another
(Psalm 75:6-7).*

Asaph, who wrote Psalm 75, has been quoting God's own words about his character in the first part of this psalm. Now Asaph begins to apply the words of God. He rightly concludes that God alone can exalt or humble a person.

God exercises his judgment not only at Judgment Day but also within the course of history. No national or political leader rises to power apart from the permission of God. This does not mean that God approves the character or conduct of all leaders. Wicked leaders come to power and do the very opposite of God's good purposes. However, God permits these evil leaders to rule for a time to accomplish his purposes. He exalted the evil kings of Babylon and used them to judge his people Judah. Then, when their time was over, God exalted the Persian leader Cyrus in order to bring down the Babylonians. Evil may reign for a time, but no evil leader will rule forever. All of history is under the judgment of Almighty God. When wicked rulers are in power, rest in the knowledge that God is really in control.

February 9

*In the hand of the Lord is a cup
full of foaming wine mixed with spices;
he pours it out, and all the wicked of the earth
drink it down to its very dregs
(Psalm 75:8).*

Asaph shares an important word picture to describe the judgment of God. God's judgment is described as a cup of foaming wine that will be poured out on the earth. All the wicked will drink this cup. Here is the problem. It is not only terrorists and child abusers who deserve the cup of God's judgment. It is all of us. I have also broken his commandments. I am under his judgment. *All* the wicked of the earth will drink it.

Many people do not rush to accept God's offer of salvation in Jesus Christ because they do not comprehend their predicament. They think God's judgment will fall only on those who have committed some egregious sin. The Bible says, "Whoever keeps the whole law and yet stumbles at just one point is guilty of breaking it all" (James 2:10). The first step in being right with God is seeing that you are not right with God. *All* the wicked of the earth will drink the cup of God's wrath.

February 10

In the hand of the Lord is a cup
full of foaming wine mixed with spices;
he pours it out, and all the wicked of the earth
drink it down to its very dregs
(Psalm 75:8).

God loves sinners. God judges sin. How could he do both? This was God's dilemma. He solved the dilemma by taking the judgment on himself. He gave the cup of his wrath to his own Son! In the garden of Gethsemane the night before he was crucified, Jesus prayed, "My Father, if it is possible, may this cup be taken from me. Yet, not as I will, but as you will" (Matt. 26:39). What was this cup of which he spoke? It was the cup of God's wrath described in Psalm 75! Jesus recoiled from bearing the wrath of God. The second time he prayed, "My Father, if it is not possible for this cup to be taken away unless I drink it, may your will be done" (Matt. 26:42). Jesus submitted to the Father's plan. When the crowd came to arrest him, Jesus told Peter to put away his sword. He said, "Shall I not drink the cup the Father has given me?" (John 18:11). Jesus was arrested, beaten, and crucified. He drank the cup of God's wrath that was poured for you.

Jesus offers you another cup to drink, the cup of his blood. He said, "This cup is the new covenant in my blood; do this, whenever you drink it, in remembrance of (1 Cor. 11:25). There remains a cup of wrath for those who refuse the cup of grace (Rev. 14:9-10). You have a choice: you can drink the cup of God's wrath, or you can believe that Jesus has already drained that cup for you and you can drink the cup of his blood. Which cup will you drink?

February 11

I will cut off the horns of the wicked,
but the horns of the righteous will be lifted up
(Psalm 75:10).

Psalm 75 ends with a final warning from God of the reality of judgment. It is amazing that we continue to ignore God's warnings about the danger of disobeying his commands. In 1986 the Chernobyl nuclear disaster brought great devastation to parts of the Soviet Union. The winter 1991 issue of the *University of Pacific Review* reported that the accident was caused by two electrical engineers in the control room who were "playing around" with the machine. They were trying to see how long a turbine would "free wheel" when they took the power off. To perform the experiment, they had to manually override six separate computer-driven alarm systems. One by one the alarms would say, "Stop! Dangerous! Go no further!" One by one, rather than shutting down the experiment, they shut off the alarms and kept going. The result was the largest industrial accident ever to occur, with nuclear fallout measured around the world.[5] Over and over in Scripture, God warns us, "Stop! Dangerous! Go no further!" If we proceed past his loving warnings, we bring disaster on ourselves in the day of judgment.

---

5   Tom Tripp, *Leadership*, Fall 1993, 56.

February 12–18
Psalm 103: God Is Love

February 12

*He made his ways known to Moses,
his deeds to the people of Israel:
The LORD is compassionate and gracious,
slow to anger, abounding in love
(Psalm 103:7-8).*

God revealed this wonderful statement to Moses on Mount Sinai. It is one of the greatest descriptions of the nature of God in the Bible. It is frequently cited throughout the Old Testament. When the Israelites grumbled against Moses and Aaron in the desert and talked about stoning them, God threatened to destroy the entire nation and start over. Moses interceded for the people and quoted this statement to God, "reminding" him of his grace and love (Num. 14:18). When Joel warned the people of God's judgment coming as a locust plague, he assured them they could still be forgiven if they returned to God, quoting this passage as evidence of God's compassion (Joel 2:13). When the people of Nineveh repented and God spared them from judgment, Jonah became angry with God. He did not want his enemies, the people of Nineveh, to be spared. He said to God, "This is why I was so quick to flee to Tarshish. I knew that you are a gracious and compassionate God, slow to anger and abounding in love" (Jonah 4:2).

Some people think that the love of God is only a New Testament concept. That is not so. In all his dealings with human beings, God has always acted from a heart of love. Psalm 103 celebrates the amazing love of God.

February 13

He will not always accuse,
nor will he harbor his anger forever
(Psalm 103:9).

Once President Lincoln was asked how he was going to treat the rebellious southerners when they had finally been defeated and had returned to the Union. The questioner expected Lincoln would respond in vengeance, but he answered, "I will treat them as if they had never been away."[6] God is like that. If you return to him, he will treat you as if you had never been away.

Joe and Carol Farrone received a call from their son asking for help. It was the first time they had heard from him in years. They drove to a distant city to get him. They found him in terrible condition. They literally carried him to the car. He reeked of perspiration and vomit. They had to cover their noses and open the car windows for ventilation. Joe said, "I've heard so many sermons about the prodigal son in a stinking pigpen. Now here I am holding my nose and living out that very scene. But what really hit me was how thankful the prodigal's father must have felt."[7] God is like that. He longs to forgive you and welcome you back.

---

6 William Barclay, *The Gospel of Luke, The Daily Study Bible Series* (Philadelphia: Westminster Press, 1956), 213.
7 Margie Lewis, *The Hurting Parent* , rev. ed. (Grand Rapids: Zondervan, 1988), 90-91

February 14

He does not treat us as our sins deserve
or repay us according to our iniquities
(Psalm 103:10).

Sometimes people complain that God is not being fair with them. They think they deserve better in life than they are receiving. You do not want God to treat you fairly! The Bible says, "The wages of sin is death" (Rom. 6:23). Since you are a sinner, fairness would mean instant death for you! You do not deserve to live another moment! If God were nothing more than fair, you and I would be in hell right now. In his great mercy, God treats us far better than we deserve. He delays the consequences of our sin to give us the opportunity to repent and be spared what we deserve.

How can God delay the punishment we deserve and still be a just and fair God? That question is left unanswered until the New Testament. Paul explains God's ingenious plan that would allow him to both show mercy to us and preserve his justice:

> God presented [Jesus] as a sacrifice of atonement, through faith in his blood. He did this to demonstrate his justice, because in his forbearance he had left sins committed beforehand unpunished— he did this to demonstrate his justice at the present time, so as to be just and the one who justifies those who have faith in Jesus (Rom. 3:25-26).

God's sacrifice of his Son proves both his justice and his mercy.

February 15

For as high as the heavens are above the earth,
so great is his love for those who fear him
(Psalm 103:11).

David had spent many nights under the stars as a shepherd. He compared the vastness of God's love to the vastness of the night sky. Astronomers tell us that the closest star to us is 93 million miles away. The second closest star is 22 trillion miles, or four light years, away. That means the light from that star, traveling at 186,000 miles per second, takes four years to reach our eyes. Those are the closest stars to us! No one really knows how far the most distant star is from our planet. Some scientists suggest the farthest stars may be 10 to 20 billion light years away. The size of the universe is mind-boggling. Yet, God's love for you is bigger than that. You cannot grasp the enormity of his concern and care for you. The best measure we have of that vast love is when he sent his only Son to leave heaven, cross the vast expanse of the universe, and arrive on our planet as a human baby. "For God so loved the world that he gave his one and only Son, that whoever believes in him shall not perish but have eternal life" (John 3:16).

February 16

As a father has compassion on his children,
so the Lord has compassion on those who fear him
(Psalm 103:13).

From the vastness of the universe, David moves to the intimacy of family to illustrate God's compassion for us. Bob Benson tells about taking his teenage son to college 700 miles from home. Though he and his wife were excited for their son, their hearts ached with loneliness at the thought of being so far from their firstborn. Benson recalls,

> Somebody said you still have three at home—three fine kids—and there is still plenty of noise, plenty of ball games to go to, plenty of responsibilities, plenty of laughter, plenty of everything—except Mike. And in parental math, four minus one just doesn't equal plenty. And I was thinking about God. He sure has plenty of children—plenty of artists, plenty of singers, and carpenters, and candlestick makers, and preachers, plenty of everybody—except you, and all of them together can never take your place. And there will always be an empty spot in His heart—and a vacant chair at His table when you're not coming home. And if once in a while it seems he's crowding you a bit—try to forgive him. It may be one of those nights when He misses you so much He can hardly stand it.[8]

---

8 Bob Benson, *Come Share the Being* (Nashville: Impact Books, 1974), 67-68.

February 17

For he knows how we are formed,
he remembers that we are dust
(Psalm 103:14).

God knows everything about us. He formed us from the dust of the earth (Gen. 2:7). He knows the frailties of the human condition. He knows our weaknesses in body, mind, and spirit.

John Hinckley attempted to assassinate President Reagan. Later his parents wrote a book, *Breaking Points*, on their parental perspective of that terrible tragedy and the events that followed. Jack Hinckley, John's father, reflected on his thoughts as they prepared for their visit with him:

> What do you say, the first time you see your son after he has done the unthinkable? Why did you shoot the President, son? Of course, you don't. Instead, as we'd done a number of times on the phone since Monday, we told John we loved him: No amount of anger or revulsion could change that.[9]

God loves you. No amount of anger or revulsion at your sin can change that.

---

9   Jack Hinckley, Jo Ann Hinckley, and Elizabeth Sherrill, *Breaking Points* (New York: Berkley Books, 1985), 111.

February 18

But from everlasting to everlasting
the Lord's love is with those who fear him,
and his righteousness with their children's children—
with those who keep his covenant
and remember to obey his precepts
(Psalm 103:17-18).

These verses say that God loves those who fear him and keep his commandments. Does that mean God does not love those who do not fear him? No, the Bible tells us that God loves everyone, even the worst sinners (Rom. 5:8). However, God has especially bound himself to those who have entered into a covenant relationship with him. These are covenant terms in these verses. The word "love" refers to steadfast love in a covenant relationship. God has a special love for his children. He has committed himself to them and he promises nothing will separate them from his love.

On Sunday, August 16, 1987, Northwest Airlines flight 225 crashed just after taking off from Detroit, killing 155 people. There was one survivor: a four year old girl named Cecelia. Rescuers first thought she had not been on the plane. They assumed she was a passenger in one of the cars on the highway, but the flight register revealed her name. Cecelia survived because, as the plane was falling, her mother unbuckled her own seat belt, got down on her knees in front of her daughter, wrapped her arms and body around her, and would not let go. That is a picture of what God has promised his children. He wraps himself around you and will never let go. "For I am convinced that neither angels nor demons, neither the present nor the future, nor any powers, neither height nor depth, nor anything else in all creation, will be able to separate us from the love of God that is in Christ Jesus our Lord" (Rom. 8:38-39).

February 19–25
Psalm 90: God Is Eternal

February 19

Lord, you have been our dwelling place
throughout all generations.
Before the mountains were born
or you brought forth the earth and the world,
from everlasting to everlasting you are God
(Psalm 90:1-2).

Psalm 90 tells us God is eternal. God has always existed. He had no beginning. There has never been a time in the past when God did not exist. There will never be a time in the future when God ceases to exist. God is always the same. He does not grow or change.

The title of this psalm tells us that Moses wrote it. Moses had moved several times in his life. He had never really found a home. He was born and raised in Egypt, but that was not home. He fled to Midian where he lived forty years, but that was not home. He returned to Egypt and then led the Israelites into the desert of Sinai for forty more years, but that was not home. The people of Israel had never had a homeland. They had been transients throughout their existence. Perhaps you have moved a lot and you really do not have a place you call home. How do you find a sense of stability and permanence in life? Do what Moses did. He said, "Lord you have been our dwelling place through all generations." The Lord—not a place—can be your home, your reference point in life. He will always be there. He never changes.

February 20

Lord, you have been our dwelling place
throughout all generations.
Before the mountains were born
or you brought forth the earth and the world,
from everlasting to everlasting you are God
(Psalm 90:1-2).

Kids often ask where things came from. We answer, "God made everything." They counter with another question, "Where did God come from? Who made God?" God has always been here. Psalm 90 tells us God has been here "before the mountains were born." The eternity of God helps us understand where we came from. The eternal God created everything that exists out of nothing: "You brought forth the earth." The existence of an eternal God is the most sensible, logical explanation of the origin of our universe. Ask someone who believes in evolution one question: "Where did that come from?" If life arose from a primordial soup, where did the soup come from? If the soup came from dust and gases, where did the dust and gases come from?

When considering the origin of the universe, we are pushed back to one of three options: (1) something appeared out of nothing, or (2) matter and energy are eternal, or (3) an eternal, uncaused God created something out of nothing. It seems most logical to me to believe there was a first cause to our universe. The Bible says that first cause is the One True Living God who revealed himself to Israel.

February 21

You sweep men away in the sleep of death;
they are like the new grass of the morning—
though in the morning it springs up new,
by evening it is dry and withered
(Psalm 90:5-6).

In contrast to the eternal God, our lives on this earth pass very quickly. Often we act as if we will live forever, but our lives are brief. We are like grass that is green in the morning but at night is withered and brown. The reason for the brevity of our lives is because of our sins (vv. 7-11). God did not create us to live such short lives. Death entered our world as a penalty for sin. We are under the wrath of God.

Some have suggested that the background of this psalm is Numbers 20.[10] In that context, this was the fortieth year of the exile from Egypt. Only five of the thousands of adults who left Egypt remained alive— Joshua, Caleb, Moses, Aaron, and Miriam. Three events happened at that point in Moses' life. First, Miriam, Moses' sister, died. Second, God told Moses he would not enter the promised land. Third, Aaron, Moses' brother, died. Moses realized how fleeting life is. Perhaps you have recently experienced the death of a loved one, or you have been reminded of your own mortality. Will you, like Moses, anchor your life to the unchanging, eternal God?

---

10 James Montgomery Boice, *Psalms*, vol. 2 (Grand Rapids: Baker, 1996), 740.

February 22

Teach us to number our days aright,
that we may gain a heart of wisdom
(Psalm 90:12).

Because God is eternal and because our lives are so brief, this psalm suggests four prayers that we should pray. First, we should pray, "Teach us to number our days." That means we should ask God to help us be conscious of how brief and unpredictable our lives are so that we live wisely. It means to live in the present and not the future. We tend to put off a decision to follow Christ or serve him. We say, "I am going to follow Christ after I get out of school." Or, "After baseball season is over, we will get back in church." Or, "After the kids are grown I will teach Sunday School." Or, "After I retire I will get involved in missions." You do not know there will be an "after."

There are three reasons you should "number your days": First, you may die and never have the opportunity to do what you are planning to do in the future. Second, you are missing the blessing of serving God now. Third, you are becoming every day the kind of person you will always be. Pray this prayer: "Teach me to number my days."

February 23

Relent, O LORD! How long will it be?
Have compassion on your servants
(Psalm 90:13).

Because God is eternal and because our lives are brief, this psalm teaches us to pray a second prayer: "Have compassion on us." Like Moses we are going to die. We cannot change that fact. But God is also a compassionate God. He shows grace to his servants during our brief time on earth. He responds to our prayers. King Hezekiah became ill. God told Hezekiah he was going to die. Hezekiah turned his face to the wall and prayed. God told Isaiah to tell the king, "I have heard your prayers and seen your tears. I will add fifteen years to your life" (Isa. 38:5). Every day we live is a compassionate gift of God to us.

God's greatest act of compassion is not in extending our lives. His ultimate act of compassion was sending his Son Jesus to make a way through death for us. He has compassionately provided us a way to experience eternal life beyond death. For today and for eternity, you need to pray, "Have compassion on me."

February 24

Satisfy us in the morning with your unfailing love,
that we may sing for joy and be glad all our days.
Make us glad for as many days as you have afflicted us,
for as many years as we have seen trouble
(Psalm 90:14-15).

In view of the brevity of life, there is a third prayer we should pray: "Satisfy us with your unfailing love." When the Israelites came to the edge of the promised land, God told Moses that he would not be permitted to enter. Moses was allowed to climb Mount Nebo and see the land from a distance, but he would not enter it. He had waited forty years to enter the land, but his dream would not be fulfilled.

Life is full of disappointments. Hopes are dashed, plans are ruined, and dreams die. How do you respond to disappointment? Ask God to satisfy you with himself. Real satisfaction is never found in events of this life. Everything here is ultimately less than fulfilling. Real satisfaction is found only in a relationship to God. Joy is possible even amid the disappointments of life. Pray this prayer today: "Satisfy us in the morning with your unfailing love, that we may sing for joy and be glad all our days."

February 25

May your deeds be shown to your servants,
your splendor to their children.
May the favor of the Lord our God rest upon us;
establish the work of our hands for us—
yes, establish the work of our hands
(Psalm 90:16-17).

Because God is eternal and your life is brief, there is a fourth prayer you should pray: "Establish the work of our hands." You cannot make a mark on this world. You are like a flower that quickly fades. But God can establish the work of your hands. That is what happened with Moses. He died without a real home. He did not get to enter the promised land. Yet, thirty-four centuries after Moses wrote the words of this psalm, you are reading them today! His writings have formed civilizations and his influence continues to impact the lives of millions of people. God established the work of his hands. Would you commit your work to God? Would you ask him to enable your life to have an impact upon the lives of other people for the kingdom? Pray this prayer: "Establish the work of our hands."

February 26—March 4
Psalm 139: God Is Too Wonderful for Me

February 26

Such knowledge is too wonderful for me,
too lofty for me to attain
(Psalm 139:6).

J. B. Phillips wrote a book entitled, *Your God Is Too Small.*[11] Each chapter exposes a view of God that is too limited. Phillips describes the images of God as Grand Old Man, Second Hand God, Parental Hangover, Heavenly Bosom, God-In-A-Box, and Pale Galilean. Have experiences in your life—unanswered prayer or unexplained suffering—caused you to have a dwarfed view of God? If so, you need to read this psalm.

Psalm 139 explodes all of our tiny views of God. Psalm 139 is about the incredible greatness of God. This psalm describes God as omniscient (all knowing), omnipresent (present everywhere), and omnipotent (all powerful). David is overwhelmed with the greatness of God. He says, "Such knowledge is too wonderful for me." Each of us needs to come to that same enthrallment with the grandeur of God. Perhaps that will happen in your life this week!

---

11 J. B. Phillips, *Your God Is Too Small* (New York: Macmillan, 1961).

February 27

O LORD, you have searched me
and you know me.
You know when I sit and when I rise;
you perceive my thoughts from afar.
You discern my going out and my lying down;
you are familiar with all my ways.
Before a word is on my tongue
you know it completely, O LORD
(Psalm 139:1–4).

God is omniscient. David speaks of the omniscience of God not in abstract terms—"God knows everything"—but in a very personal way—"Lord, you have searched me and you know me." This word "search" is used in the book of Job to refer to digging for treasure. God uncovers my life. In Numbers this word refers to spying out the land. God has me under surveillance.

God knows my life in detail. He knows my every movement—when I sit down and when I rise up. He knows my thoughts. He knows what I am thinking right now. He is familiar with my ways—every habit and twitch. He knows what I am going to say before I say it.

February 28

You hem me in—behind and before;
you have laid your hand upon me
(Psalm 139:5).

How does it make you feel to know that God is omniscient? This truth should comfort you. Verse 5 may refer to the encircling protection of God. Have you ever been misunderstood? God knows! Have you ever been overlooked? God sees! Have you been the victim of a rumor? God understands! Have you ever been falsely accused? God knows everything. That is comforting.

The omniscience of God should also convict you. Verse 5 can mean "God lays siege to me." God knows your wicked thoughts, your secret sins, and your impure motives. He knows the lies you tell and the games you play. God knows what you are hiding from your parents, your spouse, or your boss. I have been a pastor for thirty years. I find it almost comical when people try to hide things from me. Once I went to visit a man who had attended our church a few times. When I drove up in the driveway, he was sitting in a chair under a tree. I noticed as I drove up that he got up from his chair, went over to the doghouse, and returned to his lawn chair. I thought perhaps he wanted to restrain the dog from jumping on me. He offered me a chair and we sat and talked. I happened to sit so that I could see directly in the doghouse. There was a tall can of beer sitting if front of the curious dog. The man had hidden his beer from me! God must think it comical when we try to hide our actions and words and thoughts. He knows everything. That is convicting.

March 1

Where can I go from your Spirit?
Where can I flee from your presence?
If I go to the heavens, you are there;
if I make my bed in the depths, you are there.
If I rise on the wings of the dawn,
if I settle on the far side of the sea
(Psalm 139:7-9).

God is omnipresent. He is everywhere. Again David states this truth in very personal terms. No matter where I go, I cannot escape God. No matter how high I go, God is there. No matter how low I go, God is there. ("Depths" translates the Hebrew word *sheol*. This could mean ocean depths, but the word usually refers to the grave, the realm of the dead.) No matter how far to the east I go ("wings of the dawn"), God is there. No matter how far west I go, God is there. The sea was an unknown western frontier to the Jews, but whatever was there, David knew God was there.

The omnipresence of God raises some questions. What does the Bible mean when it refers to distance from God (Isa. 59:2) or drawing near to God (James 4:8)? What does it mean when it promises God is with two or three gathered in his name (Matt. 18:20)? Is God with the believer and the non-believer? Is God in hell? Theologians explain that God is present at every point in space but present in different ways in different places. He is present in hell to punish. He is present in the non-Christian's life to convict. He is present in a gathering of believers to bless. When we say we are away from God, we mean he is not present to bless us.

March 2

If I rise on the wings of the dawn,
if I settle on the far side of the sea,
even there your hand will guide me,
your right hand will hold me fast.
If I say, "Surely the darkness will hide me
and the light become night around me,"
even the darkness will not be dark to you;
the night will shine like the day,
for darkness is as light to you
(Psalm 139:9-12).

How does it make you feel to know that God is omnipresent? It should comfort you, because God is always close at hand. If you are in a covenant relationship with God, his right hand holds you fast no matter what the circumstances of your life may be. Even at the loneliest times in your life, you are never alone.

The omnipresence of God should also convict you. You cannot get away from God. Adam tried to hide from God. Jonah tried to run. You cannot hide from God or run from him. These verses assert that darkness cannot hide you from God. Much crime and sin takes place after dark. People try to cover their sin. Even the darkness is not dark to God. You cannot escape the presence of God. That is hard for us to grasp. The cafeteria at Asbury Theological Seminary in Wilmore, Kentucky, had the following sign over a bowl of apples: "Take only one apple. God is watching you." Down the line in the dessert section was a plate of cookies. A student had hastily scrawled another sign: "Take as many cookies as you want. God is back watching the apples!"[12] Psalm 139 tells us that God is watching both the apples and the cookies!

---

12 "Campus Comedy," *Reader's Digest*, June 1992, 39.

March 3

For you created me in my inmost being;
you knit me together in my mother's womb.
I praise you because I am fearfully and wonderfully made;
your works are wonderful,
I know that full well
(Psalm 139:13-14).

God is omnipotent. That means God is all-powerful. God's power is revealed in his creative work. Again David is very personal. He does not talk about how God made the stars or the planets or the mountains or oceans. He says, "God made me."

God was at work in your mother's womb to knit you together. This is the foundation of the Christian opposition to abortion. It disrupts the wonderful work of God.

You are his handiwork, and his work is wonderful. This is why you are special, unique, and valuable. You are the craftsmanship of the omnipotent God. You have value not based upon what you can accomplish in life, but based upon who you are as God's creation. Even if you never become "successful," even if you become physically or mentally incapacitated, you have value because you are the work of God.

In the same way, you must treat all people with respect and kindness. Each individual—regardless of I.Q, race, income level, or lifestyle—is a person of worth and value, because all God's works are wonderful.

March 4

Your eyes saw my unformed body.
All the days ordained for me
were written in your book
before one of them came to be
(Psalm 139:16).

God had a plan for your life before you were born. All the days ordained for you were written in his book before one of them came to be.

How does this truth make you feel? It should comfort you. Your life has value and purpose. No matter the circumstances of your birth, you were no accident. God had a plan for you before you were born.

This truth should also convict you. You will not live forever. God has already set the end date for your life. That day is unknown to you, but it is already written on God's calendar. You must be ready to meet God.

This month our goal has been to learn what God is like. Our purpose is not just to learn facts about God but to actually know him. God is real, and you can have a relationship with him as you would with any other person. You can know God in a personal way through faith in Jesus Christ. Jesus prayed in John 17:3: "Now this is eternal life: that they may know you, the only true God, and Jesus Christ, whom you have sent."

March

Learn to Worship God

Most of us could grow in our understanding of worship. Psalms can help us do that. This month we will study the psalms of praise. This may be the most important group of psalms in the entire book. In Hebrew, the title of the book we call Psalms is *Tehillim*, or "Praises."

Praise means to express approval or admiration. It means to commend the worth of an object or person. Praise expresses the worth of God in your life. The value of praise is that it orders your priorities in life. Praise lifts some things above others. When you praise your child's drawing, you are lifting it above other drawings in your evaluation. When you praise God, you are establishing his worth in your life. Without worship, your priorities and values can fall into disarray. This month let these psalms teach you how to worship God.

March 5-11
Psalm 148: Join the Universe in Praising God

March 5

Praise the Lord.
Praise the Lord from the heavens,
praise him in the heights above
(Psalm 148:1).

Many of us think of worship as something that only occurs within the walls of a church building on Sunday morning. Psalm 148 stretches our understanding of worship by revealing its cosmic scope. The entire universe—everything that has been created—is called to praise the Creator. This psalm invites the worshipper to join the universe in exalting the one true God. There are two parts to Psalm 148. In verses 1-6 all the heavens are called to praise God. In verses 7-14 the entire earth is called to praise God.

The last five psalms (Pss. 148-150) all begin and end with the phrase "Praise the Lord." The Hebrew is *hallelujah— hallelu* (the plural imperative of "praise") plus *jah* (the short form of the name of God, Yahweh or Jehovah). Would you pause right now to offer a prayer or song in praise to God? As you do, you will be joining the universe in worshipping him!

March 6

Praise him, all his angels,
praise him all his heavenly hosts.
Praise him, sun and moon,
praise him, all you shining stars.
Praise him, you highest heavens
and you waters above the skies
(Psalm 148:2-4).

The first section of Psalm 148 calls the heavens to praise the Lord. The call goes out in three sections. First, the call goes out to the very dwelling of God (v. 2). The angels are called to praise God. "Hosts" refers to the vast armies of angels in heavens. Second, the call to worship God moves to the galaxies of the universe (v. 3). Stars, planets, and moons are called to praise God. Third, the call moves down to our atmosphere (v. 4). The skies and clouds are called to praise God.

The worship of God is not limited to planet earth. The purpose of the entire universe is to bring glory to God. The occupants of heaven are eager to praise of God. The apostle John was given a glimpse into heaven, and he recorded his vision:

> Then I looked and heard the voice of many angels, numbering thousands upon thousands, and ten thousand times ten thousand. They encircled the throne and the living creatures and the elders. In a loud voice they sang: "Worthy is the Lamb, who was slain, to receive power and wealth and wisdom and strength and honor and glory and praise!" (Rev. 5:11-12).

When you offer praise to God, your life is in harmony with the purposes of the universe and of heaven.

March 7

Let them praise the name of the LORD,
for he commanded and they were created.
He set them in place for ever and ever;
he gave a decree that will never pass away
(Psalm 148:5-6).

These verses express the rationale and motivation for the heavens to praise God: he created them by his command and set them in place. The angels and the stars and the clouds owe their existence to God. He spoke them all into existence. "Lift up your eyes and look to the heavens: Who created all these? He who brings out the starry host one by one, and calls them each by name. Because of his great power and mighty strength, not one of them is missing" (Isaiah 40:26).

The fact that God is creator is also a big part of our rationale for worshipping him. We owe everything we have to God. He has created everything we call our own. He gives us every breath we draw and every bite of food we eat. He is the designer of the good world we enjoy.

March 8

Praise the LORD from the earth,
you great sea creatures and all ocean depths,
lightning and hail, snow and clouds,
stormy winds that do his bidding,
you mountains and all hills,
fruit trees and all cedars,
wild animals and all cattle,
small creatures and flying birds
(Psalm 148:7-10).

The second half of the psalm calls all the earth to praise the Lord. Earth is called to join heaven in praise. The progression in these verses roughly follows the order of creation. We can understand how angels could praise God. They have voices as we do. What does this psalm mean when it calls stars and clouds and mountains and trees and animals to praise God? I think there are two possible ways to understand these verses. First, this may be figurative language. These elements of creation praise him by their existence. They reflect the beauty and design and creativity of God. They bring honor and glory to him by the very splendor of their being. I think this is certainly true, but there is a second possible explanation to this psalm. This call to praise God could be fulfilled literally by elements of creation. As Jesus entered Jerusalem on Palm Sunday, the Pharisees tried to stop the disciples from praising him. Jesus replied, "If they keep quiet, the stones will cry out" (Luke 19:40). Why did Jesus say this? Jesus must be praised. If tongues refuse, rocks will cry out. Why does Scripture say the mountains and hills will burst into song and the trees and rivers will clap their hands (Isa. 55:12; Ps. 98:8)? Could it be the God who gave voice to Balaam's donkey will one day enable all his creation to shout and clap and dance and sing? In Revelation 5:13, John heard *every* creature in heaven and earth and sea praising God. When we praise God we anticipate the new age and bring some of it to earth.

March 9

Kings of the earth and all nations,
you princes and all rulers on earth,
young men and maidens,
old men and children.
Let them praise the name of the LORD
(Psalm 148:11–13a).

All humans are called to join the other residents of the earth in praise to God. Young and old, powerful and powerless, rich and poor, are to worship God. This psalm gives us a proper perspective on the whole world. Praise is a corrective to two dangers.

First, praising God keeps us from worshipping anything in creation. It keeps us from elevating angels or trees or pets or politicians to too high a place of honor or esteem. Only God is to be exalted. All else is to praise him with us. Nothing else in life is to be given ultimate place. In Acts 12:23, the Bible tells us King Herod was struck dead because he accepted the worship of the crowds and did not praise God.

Second, praising God keeps us from having too low a view of anything in creation. It reminds us not to abuse the earth or animals or children. They are all created by God and join us in praising him. We cannot devalue them. Praise gives our lives the proper order.

March 10

Let them praise the name of the LORD,
for his name alone is exalted;
his splendor is above the earth and the heavens.
He has raised up for his people a horn,
the praise of all his saints,
of Israel, the people close to his heart.
Praise the Lord
(Psalm 148:13–14).

Throughout Psalm 148 the writer has asserted that the Lord is to be praised as Creator. The psalm ends by reminding us he is also to be praised as Redeemer. God has uniquely revealed himself to humankind through one group of people, the nation of Israel. Through Israel he has raised up a "horn." The NIV footnote says the word "symbolizes strong one, that is, king." Jesus Christ is the ultimate king of Israel, the strong horn of salvation God has given us. Greater than God's splendor in creation is the splendor of his work in giving us a redeemer, King Jesus. The greatest reason to praise God is because of Jesus. There is no greater blessing in your life than the redemption that Jesus brings. Every prayer of praise we offer should center in his redemption.

March 11

Praise the Lord
(Psalm 148:14).

God is to be praised comprehensively—everywhere by everything. One day he will be. Currently God is not praised in every sector of his creation. There are spiritual powers that are in rebellion against him. Many of his human children do not acknowledge and praise him. When we praise the Lord here and now, we witness to the universe the proper order of things. We demonstrate to the universe how it supposed to be, and we testify how it one day will be. When we praise the Lord, we become an outpost of heaven, an embassy of his coming kingdom. Our praise and worship will be richer and more meaningful in our lives when we realize its cosmic scope and function in the universe. Praise the Lord!

March 12–18
Psalm 47: Express Your Praise

March 12

Clap your hands, all you nations;
shout to God with cries of joy
(Psalm 47:1).

Worship is an action, not a feeling. Worship must be expressed. That is why worship does not usually work on the couch in your living room or in a fishing boat on the lake. Is it possible to worship God in these places? Certainly. All of life is to be an act of worship presented to God. Yet, when we say, "I can worship God in my fishing boat on Sunday," what we usually mean by that statement is "I can feel a sense of awe and gratitude to God" in my fishing boat. We do not really intend to do anything to express our worship in that boat. The Psalms make it clear that worship must be more than a sentiment. Authentic worship is always expressed, usually in a corporate setting with other believers.

Psalm 47 tells us how to express our worship. Verse 1 urges us to worship God with clapping and shouting. Worship can be enthusiastic and exuberant. Worship can also be contemplative and silent. In the previous psalm, God says, "Be still and know that I am God" (Ps. 46:10). There is a place for reflective worship and celebratory worship. Many of us have no problem expressing our enthusiasm at a football game. Let us be more excited about our God than our alma mater. If we would do justice to the Psalms, we would encourage worship that is both reverent and rollicking, both silent and loud. With whatever worship styles we are comfortable, worship must be expressed!

March 13

How awesome is the LORD Most High,
the great King over all the earth!
(Psalm 47:2).

The object of worship is an encounter with God. Sometimes we become so enamored with a worship leader, a musician, or a worship experience that we lose sight of the object of our worship. The form of worship can become more important to us than the one who is being worshipped. Many churches have experienced tension over changing styles of worship.

The focus of Psalm 47 is not on the clapping or the shouting. The focus is on the Lord Most High. It is in worship that the writer comes to realize and celebrate that he is awesome! He is the great King over all the earth!

As you worship this Sunday, check your focus. If you find yourself thinking about the shortcomings of the accompanist or the new hairstyle of the soloist or the grammar of the person leading a prayer, you have become sidetracked. Allow the talents and efforts of your worship leaders—whether polished or woeful—to draw you toward the Living God, the King of the earth, who is indeed awesome!

March 14

God has ascended amid shouts of joy,
the LORD amid the sounding of trumpets
(Psalm 47:5).

Bible scholars debate the background and meaning of this verse. The wording is very similar to 2 Samuel 6:15, when David first brought the ark of the covenant to Jerusalem "with shouts and the sound of trumpets." Some scholars think Psalm 47:5 reflects an annual reenactment of this event in Jerusalem, celebrating the enthronement of God.[13]

Whether this is the background of Psalm 47 or not, we know that reenactments can be powerful acts of worship. The Lord's Supper is a periodic reenactment of the breaking of Christ's body on the cross and the pouring out of his blood. Baptism is a reenactment of the burial and resurrection of our Lord. It is also a reenactment of the spiritual death and resurrection of the new Christian who has repented and put his faith in Christ.

Psalm 47 reminds us that these special times of worship are to be times of great celebration. I heard of a church where the congregation exclaims "yes!" every time a new believer emerges from the waters of baptism. Our congregation applauds whenever someone is baptized. While some may think this should be a solemn ceremony, it seems to me this should be a time of exuberant celebration. How can you express your joy in Christ today?

---

13 Derek Kidner, *Psalms 1-72*, vol. 14a of *The Tyndale Old Testament Commentaries*, D. J. Wiseman, ed. (Downer's Grove, Ill: Intervarsity, 1973), 177-178.

March 15

Sing praises to God, sing praises;
sing praises to our King, sing praises
(Psalm 47:6).

Singing is the language of praise to God. Throughout Christian history, no matter the style of music or the setting of the assembly, singing has been integral to Christian worship. Four times this verse encourages and commands us to sing to God. Some of us are reluctant to sing to God because we feel we are not good singers. I have benefited from reading the thoughts of a seventeenth-century pastor, Thomas Fuller, on this subject:

> Lord, my voice by nature is harsh and out of tune, and it is hopeless to lavish any art on it to make it better. Can my singing of psalms be pleasing to your ears when it is so unpleasant to my own? Yet though I cannot sing with the nightingale, or chirp with the blackbird, I would rather chatter with the swallow—even croak with the raven—than be altogether silent. Had you given me a better voice, I would have praised you with a better voice. Now what my music lacks in sweetness, let it have in sense, singing praises with understanding. Create in me a new heart in which to make melody, and I will be contented with my old voice, until in due time, being admitted into the choir of heaven, I have another more harmonious voice given to me.[14]

This Sunday, lift up the voice God has given you in praise to him. Sing praises to God; sing praises!

---

14 Thomas Fuller, *Good Thoughts in Bad Times*, quoted by Sherwood Eliot Wirt, ed. *Spiritual Disciplines* (Westchester, Ill: Crossway, 1983), 27-28.

March 16

For God is the King of all the earth;
sing to him a psalm of praise
(Psalm 47:7).

The expression of praise is not to be limited to the place of worship on the Lord's Day. God is King of all the earth, and the singing of praises can be appropriate in almost any setting.

Orel Herschiser pitched for the Los Angeles Dodgers in their championship season in 1988. His performances near the end of the regular season were amazing. He pitched fifty-nine consecutive innings without allowing an earned run. He won the Cy Young Award and other honors. In the National League playoffs he continued his dominance, pitching a shutout in the championship game. In the World Series against Oakland, his complete game victory in game five clinched the championship. Throughout the playoffs, television cameras focused on Herschiser as he sat in the dugout between innings. The announcers noticed that he was softly singing to himself, and they speculated on what song he might be singing. After the Series was over, he appeared as a guest on *The Tonight Show*. Johnny Carson asked what song he had been singing and if he would sing it again. Herschiser was reluctant, but the audience cheered him on. Finally he agreed, and millions listened as Herschiser sang,

> Praise God from whom all blessings flow.
> Praise Him all creatures here below.
> Praise Him above, ye heavenly host.
> Praise Father, Son, and Holy Ghost. Amen.

Singing praises to God can bring strength and peace to the heart of a Christian in pressure-packed situations. Today as you drive to work or wash the dishes, why not softly lift your voice in praise to God?

March 17

God reigns over the nations;
God is seated on his holy throne
(Psalm 47:8).

In his book, *In the Presence of Mine Enemies,* Howard Rutledge tells of the years he spent in a prison camp in North Vietnam. The American prisoners were subjected to a steady stream of communist propaganda. They struggled to rediscover faith and to reconstruct workable value systems. Many of them turned to parts of the Bible they had memorized and to other Christian experiences to sustain them. As an adult, Rutledge had felt he was too busy to attend church with his wife. To survive confinement, he fell back on his experience earlier in life:

> I tried desperately to recall snatches of Scripture, sermons, the gospel choruses from childhood, and the hymns we sang in church. The first three dozen songs were relatively easy. Every day I'd try to recall another verse or a new song. One night there was a huge thunderstorm—it was the season of the monsoon rains—and a bolt of lightning knocked out the lights and plunged the entire prison into darkness. I had been going over hymn tunes in my mind and stopped to lie down and sleep when the rains began to fall. The darkened prison echoed with wave after wave of water. Suddenly, I was humming my thirty-seventh song, one I had entirely forgotten since childhood: "Showers of blessing, showers of blessing we need! Mercy drops round us are falling, but for the showers we plead." I no sooner had recalled those words than another song popped into my mind, the theme song of a radio program my mother listened to when I was just a kid: "Heavenly sunshine, heavenly sunshine, Flooding my soul with glory divine. Heavenly sunshine, heavenly sunshine. Hallelujah! Jesus is mine!"[15]

Rutledge survived his ordeal in large part because of worship. No matter where life takes you, you can praise him there. He reigns over the nations. He is seated on his throne. Do you have spiritual resources in your heart that could sustain you in difficult times?

15 Howard and Phyllis Rutledge, *In the Presence of Mine Enemies* (Old Tappan, NJ: Fleming H. Revell, 1973), 35.

March 18

The nobles of the nations assemble
as the people of the God of Abraham,
for the kings of the earth belong to God;
he is greatly exalted
(Psalm 47:9).

This verse is a prophecy of a time when the Gentile nations will assemble as the people of the God of Abraham. This verse has its fulfillment through the gospel of Jesus Christ, which broke down the dividing wall between Jew and Gentile (Eph. 2:14). Through faith in Christ, Gentiles become children of Abraham. Paul wrote, "Understand, then, that those who believe are children of Abraham" (Gal. 3:7).

This verse predicts a day when the nobles of the nations will assemble before God. This will happen when Christ returns and "at the name of Jesus every knee should bow, in heaven and on earth, and under the earth, and every tongue confess that Jesus Christ is Lord to the glory of God the Father" (Phil. 2:10-11).

God is deserving of praise. Some deny him that praise now, but he will not be denied forever. One day he will receive the glory due him. Every created being will exalt God and his Son Jesus. We who belong to him herald that day whenever we express our praise to God. Will you exalt him with your voice and your life today?

March 19–25
Psalm 138: Focus on His Name and His
Word

March 19

I will praise you, O LORD, with all my heart;
before the "gods" I will sing your praise.
I will bow down toward your holy temple
and will praise your name
for your love and your faithfulness,
for you have exalted above all things
your name and your word
(Psalm 138:1-2).

This psalm of praise focuses on the name and word of God. While the Hebrew of verse 2b is difficult to translate,[16] most translations render it to mean that God has exalted his name and his word above everything else. If God has done that, we should too! We should focus on the name of God and the word of God in our worship.

The name of God refers to his nature and character reflected in the revealed name "Lord." Biblical worship will not be generic; it will lift up the specific God of the Bible, the God of Israel and the father of Jesus Christ. It will celebrate his unique character.

The word of God refers to his declarations, commands, and promises recorded in the Bible.[17] If God exalts his word above all else, then our worship must focus on his word. Reading and preaching the Bible must be central to corporate worship. Reading and meditating on the Bible must be central to individual worship. Biblical worship must not be about us. It must be about God. This week we will study Psalm 138 to learn what it means to exalt the name and the word of God.

---

16 Kidner, *Psalms 1-72*, 462.

17 In this week's study, I have not capitalized "word" because it is not capitalized in Psalm 138 (NIV). Elsewhere in this book, I have followed the custom of capitalizing "Word" when it refers to the Bible.

March 20

I will praise you, O LORD, with all my heart;
before the "gods" I will sing your praise.
I will bow down toward your holy temple
and will praise your name
for your love and your faithfulness,
for you have exalted above all things
your name and your word
(Psalm 138:1-2).

God has exalted his name above all things. There are many names and titles given to God in the Bible, but God said the name by which he was to be known was the name he revealed to Moses when he was called to go to the Israelites in Egypt:

> Moses said to God, "Suppose I go to the Israelites and say to them, 'The God of your fathers has sent me to you,' and they ask me, 'What is his name?' Then what shall I tell them?" God said to Moses, "I AM WHO I AM. This is what you are to say to the Israelites: 'I AM' has sent me to you." God also said to Moses, "Say to the Israelites, 'The LORD, the God of your fathers—the God of Abraham, the God of Isaac and the God of Jacob—has sent me to you.' This is my name forever, the name by which I am to be remembered from generation to generation" (Ex. 3:13-15).

The Hebrew for this divine name is *Yahweh* (often previously transliterated as *Jehovah*). Jewish scholars reverently refused to speak the name and substituted the title *Adonai*, meaning "master, lord." Thus, both these Hebrew words are translated "Lord" in most modern translations of the Bible. *Adonai* is represented in the NIV by "Lord," and *Yahweh* is distinguished by printing the word in all capitals: "LORD." This is the name of God that appears in Psalm 138:1. (To view both names in one verse, check out Ps. 8:1 or 110:1). The name of God refers to his self-revelation as "I AM." His name indicates he is eternal, unchanging, and dependable, the one who has life in himself.

March 21

I will praise you, O LORD, with all my heart;
before the "gods" I will sing your praise.
I will bow down toward your holy temple
and will praise your name
for your love and your faithfulness,
for you have exalted above all things
your name and your word
(Psalm 138:1-2).

As the Old Testament exalts the name of the Lord, the New Testament exalts the name of Jesus. One day Peter healed a crippled man in the name of Jesus. He said, "By faith in the name of Jesus, this man whom you see and know was made strong. It is Jesus' name and the faith that comes through him that has given this complete healing to him" (Acts 3:16). The next day the religious leaders warned Peter and John to speak no longer to anyone in his name (Acts 4:17). Later they were beaten and ordered again not to speak in the name of Jesus (Acts 5:40). "The apostles left the Sanhedrin rejoicing because they had been counted worthy of suffering disgrace for the Name" (Acts 5:41). All authentic worship exalts the name of Jesus.

The early confession of Christians was "Jesus is Lord" (Rom. 10:9; 1 Cor. 12:3). This confession indicated a relationship to Jesus as one's master, but it also identified Jesus with the "LORD," the one true God of the Old Testament. When we praise the name of Jesus or pray in his name, we are exalting the name of the "LORD."

March 22

I will praise you, O LORD, with all my heart;
before the "gods" I will sing your praise.
I will bow down toward your holy temple
and will praise your name
for your love and your faithfulness,
for you have exalted above all things
your name and your word
(Psalm 138:1-2).

The Lord is the only true living God. However, there are other "gods" who compete for our worship.

First, there are the gods of other religions. We must sing the praise of the Lord before these gods. This does not mean that we are to be arrogant or unkind toward people of other religions. Paul wrote, "Be wise in the way you act toward outsiders; make the most of every opportunity. Let you conversation be always full of grace, seasoned with salt, so that you may know how to answer everyone" (Col. 4:5-6). To exalt the name of the "LORD" before other gods means that we graciously but unapologetically give credit for our blessings to the God of the Bible. It means we are not ashamed to declare his uniqueness and his superiority to the gods of the world.

Second, there are the gods of our culture. Materialism and hedonism are two of the greatest threats to Christian worship in America. We are tempted to worship the things money can buy or to worship the experience of pleasure. These gods rob us of time to worship and resources to give to the kingdom. We spend our days acquiring and managing stuff, chasing our favorite team, getting away to the hot new destination, or honing our bodies to attract someone new. To exalt the name of the "LORD" in our culture is to honor him above ourselves.

March 23

May all the kings of the earth praise you, O LORD,
when they hear the words of your mouth.
May they sing of the ways of the LORD,
for the glory of the LORD is great
(Psalm 138:4-5).

In addition to his name, God has exalted his word above all things. "The grass withers and the flowers fall, but the word of our God stands forever" (Isa. 40:8). This means whatever God has said is completely true and always dependable. If God exalts his word, we should too. How can we exalt the word of God in worship? We exalt the word by reading and proclaiming it in public worship. In 1970, James D. Smart wrote a book entitled *The Strange Silence of the Bible in the Church.* He contended, "The voice of Scriptures is falling silent in the preaching and teaching of the church and in the consciousness of Christian people, a silence that is perceptible even among those who are most insistent upon their devotion to the Scriptures."[18] Decades later, his thesis still seems to hold true. Even conservative, Bible-believing churches often spend little time in worship actually reading or explaining large sections of Scripture. We talk a lot about the Bible, but we actually share very little of it. In our worship, our small groups, and in our families, let us recommit ourselves to reading and exalting the word of God.

---

18 James D. Smart, *The Strange Silence of the Bible in the Church* (Philadelphia: Westminster Press, 1970), 15-16.

March 24

May all the kings of the earth praise you, O LORD,
when they hear the words of your mouth.
May they sing of the ways of the LORD,
for the glory of the LORD is great
(Psalm 138:4-5).

When the word of God is shared in worship, it is our responsibility to hear it. It is possible to hear the word without really *hearing* it. That is, we hear or read the words, but they make no impact on us. Jesus told a story about four different kinds of listeners. He compared them to four different types of soil where seed, or the word, is sown. Some of us are like hard soil. We are not very receptive to the word. We have our own agenda for our lives. Some of us are like rocky soil. Our hearts are shallow. Perhaps we have heard some Bible stories so often that they make little impact. Familiarity breeds contempt. The Bible is boring to us. We are much more excited by the latest novel. Some of us are like thorny soil. We like the Bible. We intend to consider its message, but all the other stuff in our lives crowds out its message. We have no time to contemplate what we have heard. Some of us are like good soil. We listen to the word as if God is talking to us. We are receptive, expectant, and engaged. After telling this parable Jesus urged, "He who has ears, let him hear" (Matt. 13:9). If you would grow in worship, learn to really listen to the word of God.

March 25

May all the kings of the earth praise you, O LORD,
when they hear the words of your mouth.
May they sing of the ways of the LORD,
for the glory of the LORD is great
(Psalm 138:4-5).

These verses tell us that we are not only to hear the words of the Lord but we are to sing them as well. Music is a powerful medium for communicating the word of God. Martin Luther is quoted as saying, "You can write the theology books and I will write the hymnal." He knew that much of our belief system is derived from what we sing. If you are a worship leader, choose songs that are biblical in wording or content. If you are a participant in worship, pay attention to the words you sing in worship. Think about the truth communicated in song. Download Scripture songs and sing them to the Lord in your personal worship or as you drive. Scripture songs are a great way to memorize the word of God. God has exalted his word above all things. He calls us to sing of his ways, for his glory is great!

March 26—April 1
Psalm 150: Praise Him with Everything
You Have

March 26

Praise the LORD.
Praise God in his sanctuary;
praise him in his mighty heavens
(Psalm 150:1).

With Psalm 150, the book of Psalms ends with a crescendo of praise to God. Some think this psalm may have been composed specifically to close the book. The theme of this psalm is that God deserves worship that is extravagant, lavish, exuberant, and comprehensive. I think a New Testament parallel to this psalm is the act of Mary in John 12:1-3. While Jesus was reclining at the dinner table with Lazarus, Mary took a pint of expensive perfume and poured it all on Jesus' feet. Then she wiped his feet with her hair. The whole house was filled with the fragrance of the perfume. Judas criticized Mary for her extravagance, but Jesus defended her. That which is given in worship to God is not wasted. God is worthy of our best. He is worthy of extravagant praise!

The first verse tells where God is to be praised. The two parallel lines could be repetitive, calling for God to be worshipped in his sanctuary in heaven. I think instead they are a contrast: God is to be worshipped both in his sanctuary on earth and in the heavens where he resides. God is to be worshipped everywhere. May he be worshipped every day of our lives, in all our activities, everywhere we go.

March 27

Praise him for his acts of power;
praise him for his surpassing greatness
(Psalm 150:2).

Verse 2 tells why God is to be praised. First, God is to be praised for his acts of power. This includes the revelation of God's acts in the Bible. It also includes his acts of provision, protection, redemption, and answered prayer in your life. Among the world religions, our God is unique in that he acts in our world. He is a God who guides world events and individual lives. He intervenes in our world with acts of power. Praise him for what he is doing in your life.

Second, God is to be praised for his attributes, specifically his surpassing greatness. We are to praise God not only for what he does in our lives but for who he is. We applaud greatness whether we see it in an Olympic athlete or in an accomplished musician. How much more should we applaud the surpassing greatness of our God. When Jesus healed a deaf man, the people of the Decapolis said, "He has done everything well" (Mark 7:37). We join them in saying of God, "He has done everything well."

March 28

Praise him with the sounding of the trumpet,
praise him with the harp and lyre
(Psalm 150:3).

Verses 3-5 tell how God is to be praised. Eight musical instruments are listed, encompassing wind, string, and percussion instruments. The whole orchestra is to be enlisted in praising God. Musically, this psalm suggests that any instrument can be used to praise God. There is no division between "sacred" musical instruments and "secular" ones.

In broader application, this psalm indicates that every ability, talent, and gift can be used in worship to God. The intent seems to be: "Praise him with everything you have!" Use whatever skill God has given you in worship to him. God can be honored in every creative activity. Whether you have skills as an artist or a carpenter, use them to bring glory and honor to the giver of those gifts. Perhaps you need to broaden your view of worship and began to use your abilities to worship God. Such worship is not simply using your talents to do "religious" things. It is using every avenue of life to bring glory to God. Christian volunteers have streamed to the Gulf Coast to build houses destroyed by hurricanes. These acts of kindness in Jesus' name—whether installing plumbing or hanging drywall—are also acts of worship that magnify the Savior. You may not be able to play the trumpet, lyre, or harp, but what gift has God given you that you could use to worship him?

March 29

*Praise him with tambourine and dancing,
praise him with the strings and flute
(Psalm 150:4).*

Halfway through the list of eight musical instruments to be utilized in praising God, the psalmist inserts a call to praise God with dancing. I admit I am not a dancer. The only times in my life I have danced were at the two high school proms I attended. These were slow dances. All I had to do was shift my weight from one foot to the other, sort of like an elephant at the zoo rocking back and forth. I come from a denomination that used to frown on all dancing as a tool of the devil. The fear seemed to be that any dancing might turn into the kind displayed by the daughter of Herodias (Mark 6:22). Our church wedding policy still bans dancing in our fellowship hall. Yet, here it is in the Bible. We are urged to praise him with dancing. Our church does include some mild dancing in our worship. Just to be safe, we call it "interpretive movement."

It is doubtful I will be dancing in our worship services any time soon (unless the elephant rock comes in vogue). What then does this verse say to me about worship? It reminds me that worship should be joyful. I don't think there are many sad dances. It reminds me that actions which can be abused can also be sanctified and lifted in worship to God. It reminds me to respect other people's styles of worship even when they differ from my own. It reminds me that all activities of life can be vehicles for honoring the mighty God. Even dancing!

March 30

Praise him with the clash of cymbals,
praise him with resounding cymbals
(Psalm 150:5).

I have always liked percussion instruments. When I was a child, I lined up an assortment of old bottles and pans near our barn and beat a wild variety of sounds with a pair of sticks in improvised sets. I joined the school band in the sixth grade as a drummer, but after one year it was suggested my gifts might lie in areas other than music. Undeterred, I still enjoy percussion instruments. The words in verse 5 probably refer to two different kinds of cymbals, although we are not certain of their exact meaning. Cymbals, it seems to me, are the exclamation points in the poetry of praise. They remind us that praise is to be dramatic and exciting. Whether or not cymbals are used in your worship experiences, is there exuberance in your worship? Do you sing with enthusiasm? Do you pray with fervor? Do you listen to the Word with eagerness? Is your worship a "resounding cymbal" type of worship?

March 31

Let everything that has breath praise the LORD
(Psalm 150:6).

Every breath is a gift of God. God included life-giving oxygen in the atmosphere he created around our planet. God gives you the ability to lower your diaphragm and pull air into your lungs. When you exhale, the air passes through your larynx and gives you the capacity to utter sounds. You can use God's gift of air to form words of cursing, complaint, or gossip. That seems a terrible use of God's gift of breath. It seems far more appropriate to use the breath God has given us to speak or sing words of gratitude, encouragement, and praise. Become aware of the air you are exhaling this very moment. How have you used the breath God has given you today? Why not breathe words of praise to your Creator right now?

April 1

Praise the LORD
(Psalm 150:6).

These are the last words of the book of Psalms. The book ends with one more call to worship God. If we are honest, many of us probably view worship as a superfluous activity. Worship is nice, but we do not think it really accomplishes anything. We think it is not as practical as feeding the hungry or writing a letter to our congressman or organizing a fundraiser.

Instead, worship may be our most practical activity. Worship focuses our lives on God, puts our world in perspective, and orders our priorities. What could be more practical than that? I believe there will be many activities throughout eternity in heaven. However, the book of Revelation seems to suggest that the greatest priority of heaven is worship. That activity seems to occupy the attention and enthusiasm of heavenly beings like no other.

The book of Psalms begins with the words "Blessed is the man..." and ends with the words "Praise the Lord." The path of happiness culminates in praise to God. We will find ourselves most blessed when we organize our lives around consistent, enthusiastic worship of the one true God. Praise the Lord.

April

The Passion of the Christ

On the first Easter Sunday, two disciples were walking from Jerusalem to Emmaus. They were discussing the arrest and crucifixion of their Lord Jesus and the report of some women that Jesus' tomb was empty. Jesus came along and walked with them, but they were kept from recognizing him. Jesus explained to them that the rejection, death, and resurrection of the Messiah had been predicted in the Old Testament. He went through all the Scriptures and explained the prophecies to them (Luke 24:13-27).

Later that evening Jesus appeared to the apostles. They were overcome with joy and amazement that he was alive. Jesus told them, "This is what I told you while I was still with you: Everything must be fulfilled that is written about me in the Law of Moses, the Prophets, and the Psalms" (Luke 24:44).

What psalms tell about Jesus? The four psalms we will study this month contain prophecies of his rejection, death, and resurrection. I believe these are among the passages Jesus explained to the two disciples as they walked along on that first Easter Sunday. Jesus wanted us to understand these predictions about him. Fulfilled prophecy is one of the most powerful pieces of evidence of the truth of the Bible and the deity of Jesus Christ.

April 2-8
Psalm 118: The Stone the Builders Rejected

April 2

O LORD, save us;
O LORD, grant us success.
Blessed is he who comes in the name of the LORD.
From the house of the LORD we bless you
(Psalm 118:25-26).

Psalms 113-118 are called the Egyptian hallel, or "praise." They were sung at the Passover to thank God for his salvation during the exodus. Verses 5-21 are a testimony of deliverance. Verses 22-29 make it clear the one being delivered is not just the nation of Israel or some Israelite who asked God for help. This psalm is about Jesus.

Let's start with verses 25-26. The phrase "save us" in verse 25 is the Hebrew word *hosanna*. When Jesus entered Jerusalem on a donkey the Sunday before Passover, the crowds shouted these two verses to Jesus (Matt. 21:9). They were proclaiming him Messiah and asking him to save them as God had saved Israel from the Egyptians. But Jesus knew the crowds did not want the salvation he came to bring. He knew they would soon reject him.

Two days later, on Tuesday of that week, Jesus himself quoted verse 26. He said to the city of Jerusalem: "You will not see me again until you say, 'Blessed is he who comes in the name of the Lord'" (Matthew 23:39). Jesus was referring to his second coming. Just as these words were spoken of Jesus at his first coming, they will be spoken again one day when he returns to earth, but it will be too late then for those who rejected him.

April 3

The stone the builders rejected
has become the capstone;
The LORD has done this,
and it is marvelous in our eyes.
(Psalm 118:22-23).

The word "capstone" is literally "the head of the corner." It can refer to a cornerstone, the first stone laid by a builder, which anchors a wall and keeps it plumb. It can also refer to a capstone, like the keystone in an arch or the final stone on a corner that solidifies a wall. Either way, it refers to a strategic stone that anchors all other parts of the structure.

On the Tuesday before he died, Jesus also quoted these verses about himself. He told the Pharisees the parable of the tenants. It was the story of a landowner who planted a vineyard and rented it to some tenants. At harvest time he sent servants to collect his fruit, but the tenants killed every representative he sent. Finally, the landowner sent his own son, thinking surely the tenants would respect his son. They killed him as well. Jesus ended the parable by quoting Psalm 118:22-23 (Matt. 21:42). He indicated these verses predicted his rejection by the religious leaders (or "builders") and his exaltation by God.

Jesus Christ is rejected by many people. The followers of Jesus will be rejected by many people as well. These are facts for which Christians must be prepared. Yet, God is able to turn even rejection into a part of his plan. He did that in the cross. He can do that in our lives as well.

April 4

The stone the builders rejected
has become the capstone;
The LORD has done this,
and it is marvelous in our eyes.
(Psalm 118:22-23).

In 1464 in Florence, Italy, officials commissioned a series of twelve large sculptures of Old Testament figures. Agostino di Duccio was contracted to create a statue of David from a huge block of marble seventeen feet high. He got only as far as roughing out the legs and then quit the project. Some speculated the marble was flawed or the stone was ruined by the sculptor. For twenty-five years the huge block of granite was neglected. It lay exposed to the elements in the yard of the cathedral workshop. In 1501 officials determined to find an artist who could salvage the project. The stone, which they called *The Giant*, was raised to its feet. A young artist named Michelangelo, only twenty-six years old, was given the daunting task of reclaiming the project. He worked for three years on the carving. His finished statue, *David*, is proclaimed as one of the greatest works of the Renaissance. What the builders had rejected became a masterpiece.

Jesus is also ignored and devalued by many people. Perhaps you have been ignoring Jesus while seeking stability for your life in prosperity or power. God has made Jesus the capstone of his plan. He can be the keystone of life for those who recognize his potential.

117

April 5

The stone the builders rejected
has become the capstone;
The LORD has done this,
and it is marvelous in our eyes.
This is the day the LORD has made;
let us rejoice and be glad in it
(Psalm 118:22-24).

Jesus celebrated the Passover with his disciples in the upper room on Thursday evening. As they reclined at the table, Jesus washed his disciples' feet. During the meal Jesus predicted his betrayal by one of the Twelve. Then he instituted what we call the Lord's Supper. After the meal Jesus and his disciples sang a hymn and went out to the Mount of Olives (Matt. 26:30). What did they sing? The tradition was to sing Psalms 113-114 before the Passover meal and Psalms 115-118 after the meal. Their final hymn would have been Psalm 118. Amazingly, these verses were among the final words on the lips of Jesus and his disciples before he went to the Garden of Gethsemane where he was arrested. The disciples would not realize until much later the significance of these words. Only later would they be able to understand, "The Lord has done this, and it is marvelous in our eyes."

It is often only much later that we see the rejections of our lives are part of God's good plan. Sometimes we can look back and sing, "The Lord has done this, and it is marvelous in our eyes."

April 6

The stone the builders rejected
has become the capstone;
The LORD has done this,
and it is marvelous in our eyes.
This is the day the LORD has made;
let us rejoice and be glad in it
(Psalm 118:22-24).

This psalm, and Jesus' quotation of it, especially stuck in Peter's mind. After the ascension of Jesus, he understood it. One day as Peter and John were going to the temple, a crippled beggar asked them for help. In the name of Jesus, Peter healed him. Many people came to believe in Jesus. The Sanhedrin was disturbed, and they arrested Peter and John. They wanted to know by what authority Peter had healed the crippled man. In his response Peter quoted Psalm 118:22 to them:

> It is by the name of Jesus Christ of Nazareth, whom you crucified but whom God raised from the dead, that this man stands before you healed. He is "the stone you builders rejected, which has become the capstone." Salvation is found in no one else, for there is no other name under heaven given to men by which we must be saved (Acts 4:10-12).

Notice that Peter changed one word in the quotation. He changed "the builders" to "you builders." Peter boldly confronted those who had rejected Jesus. When the Sanhedrin saw the courage of Peter and John, they were astonished.

Are you convinced Jesus is the capstone? Do you courageously hold to that conviction even when people around you reject him?

April 7

The stone the builders rejected
has become the capstone;
The LORD has done this,
and it is marvelous in our eyes.
This is the day the LORD has made;
let us rejoice and be glad in it
(Psalm 118:22-24).

Years later, when Peter was an old man, he still had not forgotten this verse. As he wrote to believers scattered throughout Asia who were suffering for their faith, he quoted Psalm 118:22 to encourage them: "Now to you who believe, this stone is precious. But to those who do not believe, 'The stone the builders rejected has become the capstone'" (1 Pet. 2:7). Peter linked this verse with another prophecy about Jesus from Isaiah 28:16: "A stone that causes men to stumble and a rock that makes them fall" (1 Pet. 2:8).

Jesus will be one of two kinds of stones in your life. He will be either a stumbling stone or a building stone. If you reject Jesus, he will be like a stone that trips you up and causes you to fall. If you trust in Jesus, he will be like a foundation stone that anchors and stabilizes your life. If you make Jesus your cornerstone, you will never be put to shame.

April 8

The stone the builders rejected
has become the capstone;
The LORD has done this,
and it is marvelous in our eyes.
This is the day the LORD has made;
let us rejoice and be glad in it
(Psalm 118:22-24).

I have read that the cornerstone of the Capitol building in Washington, D.C., has been lost. Through many remodelings, the cornerstone has been removed and misplaced. Perhaps that is a symbol of our nation's problems. Many in our nation have lost the foundation for their lives.

A house without a foundation may look good until a storm comes. A mudslide or a tornado or an earthquake reveals the lack of a proper footing. A life without a strong foundation may look good until a storm comes. In calm times, people admire your achievement and advancement. Then a storm comes and your life collapses. Perhaps your life is teetering on the brink of collapse. You can't hold it together much longer. Why don't you start over, and rebuild your life on faith in Jesus Christ and obedience to his plan? Jesus said, "Everyone who hears these words and puts them into practice is like a wise man who built his house on a rock. The rains came down, and the streams rose, and the winds blew and beat against that house; yet it did not fall because it had its foundation on the rock" (Matt. 7:24-25).

April 9–15
*Psalm 22: They Have Pierced My Hands
and My Feet*

April 9

My God, my God, why have you forsaken me?
Why are you so far from saving me,
so far from the words of my groaning?
O my God, I cry out by day, but you do not answer,
by night, and am not silent
(Psalm 22:1-2).

Psalm 22 is an amazing description of the crucifixion of Jesus. David wrote this psalm, but it is difficult to connect it with the life of David. It is the description of an execution. David never experienced anything like this. It can only be understood as a prophecy of the Messiah.

Jesus quoted this psalm while he was dying. Jesus hung on the cross from 9 a.m. to 3 p.m. During the first three hours his thoughts were of others. He forgave those who crucified him, pardoned a thief crucified next to him, and provided for his mother's care. Then, at noon, darkness covered the earth, lasting for three hours. Darkness seemed to cover the soul of Jesus as well. Doubtless his pain intensified. Jesus turned to this psalm for assurance that this experience was God's plan. About 3:00 p.m. Jesus quoted verse 1. He said, "My God, my God, why have you forsaken me?" (Matt. 27:46). Jesus must have felt abandoned by God as he bore the sin of the world in his body.

The Christian can only sit in awe and silence before these verses. The Son of God loved us so much that he took upon himself the curse of our sin and experienced isolation from the Father on our behalf.

April 10

All who see me mock me;
they hurl insults, shaking their heads:
"He trusts in the LORD;
let the LORD rescue him.
Let him deliver him,
since he delights in him"
(Psalm 22:7–8).

If Jesus continued to quote Psalm 22 to himself as he hung on the cross, he doubtless drew strength from verses 3-5, remembering saints who had gone before him who cried out to God for help and put their trust in him.

Verses 7-8 express the rejection and contempt Jesus felt as he hung upon the cross. Almost this exact wording is used in Matthew 27:39-43 of those who mocked Jesus:

> Those who passed by hurled insults at him, shaking their heads and saying, "You who are going to destroy the temple and build it in three days, save yourself! Come down from the cross if you are the Son of God!" In the same way the chief priests, the teachers of the law and the elders mocked him. "He saved others," they said, "but he can't save himself! He's the King of Israel! Let him come down from the cross, and we will believe in him. He trusts in God. Let God rescue him now if he wants him, for he said, "I am the Son of God." In the same way the robbers who were crucified with him also heaped insults on him.

The irony of their insults is inescapable. If Jesus had saved himself, he could not have saved us. By refusing to save himself, he made possible the salvation of those who watched him die and of those who would be born for generations to come. Thank Jesus today for his self-sacrifice. Determine to give your life as a living sacrifice in gratitude to him.

April 11

I am poured out like water,
and all my bones are out of joint.
My heart has turned to wax;
it has melted away within me.
My strength is dried up like a potsherd,
and my tongue sticks to the roof of my mouth;
you lay me in the dust of death
(Psalm 22:14–15).

These verses describe accurately the physical suffering Jesus must have felt upon the cross. The psalmist says his bones are out of joint. A victim of crucifixion might experience his bones being pulled from their sockets. The psalmist describes himself being poured out like water. Indeed, when a spear was thrust in Jesus' side, blood and water came out (John 19:34). The psalmist says his tongue sticks to the roof of his mouth. Jesus expressed his thirst on the cross: "Later, knowing that all was now completed, and so that Scripture would be fulfilled, Jesus said, 'I am thirsty.' A jar of wine vinegar was there, so they soaked a sponge in it, put the sponge on a stalk of the hyssop plant, and lifted it to Jesus' lips" (John 19:28-29). The soldiers who gave him vinegar did not know they were fulfilling another messianic prophecy in Psalm 69:21: "They put gall in my food and gave me vinegar for my thirst."

The gospel accounts of the crucifixion are restrained in their descriptions of the physical pain of crucifixion. Perhaps the first century readers knew it all too well. These prophecies in Psalm 22 provide an amazing account of how much Jesus suffered for us.

April 12

Dogs have surrounded me;
a band of evil men has encircled me,
they have pierced my hands and my feet.
(Psalm 22:16).

These words were written hundreds of years before the Roman practice of crucifixion was instituted, yet they describe it precisely. Jesus' hands were stretched out on the horizontal piece of the cross. Nails or spikes were driven through the palms of his hands, or perhaps through the wrists to support the weight of his body. The legs of the crucified person were bent and twisted to one side, and another spike was driven through both feet or both ankles. After being raised on the cross, breathing would become very difficult for the victim. To get his breath he would have to lift his body by pulling with his arms and pushing with his feet. Within a few hours the victim would be unable to pull himself up, and death would ensue. To lengthen the torture, Roman executioners added two supports. The first was a *sedile*, a small seat attached to the front of the cross. This enabled the victim to breathe longer, but the Romans made the seat pointed, thus inflicting even more pain. The second support was a *suppedaneum*, or foot support, which further prolonged the victim's agony. Historians record cases where victims survived for two or three days when these devices were used.[19]

---

19 "Remains of a Jewish Victim of Crucifixion Found in Jerusalem," *Biblical Archaeology Review*, January/February 1985, 49.

April 13

I can count all my bones;
people stare and gloat over me.
They divide my garments among them
and cast lots for my clothing
(Psalm 22:17-18).

This amazing detail was fulfilled precisely at the death of Christ. All four Gospels describe how the soldiers guarding Jesus cast lots for his clothes while he was hanging on the cross:

> When the soldiers crucified Jesus, they took his clothes, dividing them into four shares, one for each of them, with the undergarment remaining. This garment was seamless, woven in one piece from top to bottom. "Let's not tear it," they said to one another. "Let's decide by lot who will get it." This happened that the scripture might be fulfilled which said, "They divided my garments among them and cast lots for my clothing." So this is what the soldiers did (John 19:23-24).

Taken alone, this detail could seem coincidental. Taken with the other details of Psalm 22, it is powerful evidence that this psalm was intended to foreshadow the suffering of the Messiah. God had David write this psalm to give the first disciples and seekers today good evidence to believe in Jesus and follow him.

April 14

I will declare your name to my brothers;
in the congregation I will praise you
(Psalm 22:22).

This psalm reaches a low ebb in verse 18, but verses 19-21 mark a turning point. These verses are a prayer for deliverance: "O my Strength, come quickly to help me…. Rescue me from the mouth of the lions."

The prayer for deliverance is answered, and the tone of verses 22-31 is dramatically different. These verses exude confidence and victory. Someone has said that verses 1-18 describe the sob of the victim, but verses 22-31 describe the song of the victor. As Jesus hung on the cross, the Father heard his prayer and answered him. The Father gave him strength for his dying, and then delivered him by raising him from the dead.

Verse 22 says, "I will declare your name to the brothers." Jesus referred to this verse on Easter Sunday morning when he told the women at the tomb, "Go and tell my brothers to go to Galilee; there they will see me" (Matt. 28:10). The writer of Hebrews says that Jesus is not ashamed to call us his brothers. Then he quotes Psalm 22:22 to prove his point (Heb. 2:11-12). On Easter Sunday night Jesus appeared to his disciples as they gathered in a room. He fulfilled the last line of Psalm 22:22: "In the congregation I will praise you." This was all part of God's plan a thousand years before it happened!

April 15

Posterity will serve him;
future generations will be told about the Lord.
They will proclaim his righteousness
to a people yet unborn—
for he has done it
(Psalm 22:30-31).

The closing verses of this psalm encompass a worldwide scope: "All the ends of the earth will remember and turn to the Lord" (v. 27). These verses are full of hope and victory. Can you imagine Jesus quoting these promises as he hung on the cross? In verse 30 he says, "Future generations will be told about the Lord." That refers to us! You were on Jesus' mind and on his lips as he hung on the cross. He died thinking of you! As you read the words of this book, this prophecy is being fulfilled again as it has many times before.

The last phrase of this psalm corresponds to some of Jesus' last words from the cross. "He has done it" (Ps. 22:31) corresponds closely to Jesus' last words, "It is finished" (John 19:30). The other three gospels do not record these words of Jesus; they only note that he cried out in a loud voice before he died (Matt. 27:50; Mark 15:37; Luke 23:46). The great shout and the words "It is finished" must be one and the same. William Barclay notes that this phrase (the Greek word *tetelestai*) was not a cry of resignation or weary defeat, but a shout of victory at the conclusion of battle.[20] The work of atonement was finished. He accomplished the work God gave him to do. The psalm that began in desolation ends in triumph.

---

20 William Barclay, *The Gospel of John*, vol. 2, *The Daily Study Bible Series* (Philadelphia: Westminster Press, 1956), 301.

April 16–22
Psalm 16: You Will Not Abandon Me to the Grave

April 16

I have set the LORD always before me.
Because he is at my right hand,
I will not be shaken.
Therefore my heart is glad and my tongue rejoices;
my body also will rest secure,
because you will not abandon me to the grave,
nor will you let your Holy One see decay
(Psalm 16:8-10).

Dan Brown's novel, *The Da Vinci Code,* claims that the works of Leonardo da Vinci contain secrets about Jesus and Christianity written in code. I do not believe in the Da Vinci code, but I do believe in another code about Jesus. One of the reasons I believe the New Testament account of the death and resurrection of Jesus is what I call "The Jesus Code in the Old Testament." God wanted to help you believe in Jesus, so he put hints or prophecies of Jesus in the writings of the Old Testament hundreds of years before Jesus was born. On the first Easter Sunday Jesus went through the Old Testament and revealed the code to his disciples. Psalm 118 predicts the rejection of Jesus. Psalm 22 describes his crucifixion. This week we study Psalm 16, which provides code about his resurrection.

April 17

I have set the LORD always before me.
Because he is at my right hand,
I will not be shaken.
Therefore my heart is glad and my tongue rejoices;
my body also will rest secure,
because you will not abandon me to the grave,
nor will you let your Holy One see decay
(Psalm 16:8-10).

David wrote Psalm 16, apparently at a time when he was near death. It is a prayer for safety: "Keep me safe, O God, for in you I take refuge" (v.1). David comes to a great statement of faith in vv. 8-9. David has a sense of peace because he knows even if he dies God will not abandon him. In v. 10a, David is expressing a belief in resurrection: "You will not leave me in the grave." But verse 10b seems a little odd: "Nor will you let your Holy One see decay." Is David still talking about himself? Would David call himself "your Holy One"? Would David say about himself: "You will not let me see decay"? The resurrection of the dead is at the last day. Our bodies do decay before God brings their molecules back together again in resurrection. Who then could David be talking about? This is the Jesus code in the Old Testament! David, whether he knew it or not, was writing under the inspiration of the Holy Spirit about the Messiah to come. This was fulfilled by Jesus. He is the Holy One. His body did not see decay, because he was buried on Friday afternoon but arose from the dead before dawn on Sunday morning.

April 18

I have set the LORD always before me.
Because he is at my right hand,
I will not be shaken.
Therefore my heart is glad and my tongue rejoices;
my body also will rest secure,
because you will not abandon me to the grave,
nor will you let your Holy One see decay
(Psalm 16:8-10).

Jesus explained the Jesus code to his disciples on Easter Sunday. He went through the Psalms and explained how they spoke of him. Suddenly it all made sense to them. The rejection and death and resurrection of Jesus had been God's plan all along. Why am I so sure Jesus explained Psalm 16 on Easter Sunday? After Easter Jesus appeared to his disciples for forty days. Before he ascended into heaven, he told them to wait in Jerusalem until the Spirit came. A few days later, on Pentecost, the Spirit of God fell on the disciples. A crowd gathered. Peter stood up and preached. Do you know the text of his sermon? It was Psalm 16! Peter quoted Psalm 16:8-11 and then said,

> Brothers, I can tell you confidently that the patriarch David died and was buried, and his tomb is here to this day. But he was a prophet and knew that God had promised him on oath that he would place one of his descendants on his throne. Seeing what was ahead, he spoke of the resurrection of the Christ, that he was not abandoned to the grave, nor did his body see decay. God has raised Jesus to life, and we are all witnesses of the fact (Acts 2:29-32).

Peter correctly concluded that this psalm was part of the Jesus code!

April 19

I have set the LORD always before me.
Because he is at my right hand,
I will not be shaken.
Therefore my heart is glad and my tongue rejoices;
my body also will rest secure,
because you will not abandon me to the grave,
nor will you let your Holy One see decay
(Psalm 16:8-10).

Later in Acts, Paul became the missionary to the Gentiles. His first recorded sermon is found in Acts 13. Do you know what Paul preached? He explained the Jesus code in Psalm 16:

> Brothers, children of Abraham, and you God-fearing Gentiles, it is to us that this message of salvation has been sent. The people of Jerusalem and their rulers did not recognize Jesus, yet in condemning him they fulfilled the words of the prophets that are read every Sabbath. Though they found no proper ground for a death sentence, they asked Pilate to have him executed. When they had carried out all that was written about him, they took him down from the tree and laid him in a tomb. But God raised him from the dead, and for many days he was seen by those who had traveled with him from Galilee to Jerusalem. They are now his witnesses to our people…. The fact that God raised him from the dead, never to decay, is stated in these words: "I will give you the holy and sure blessings promised to David." So it is stated elsewhere: "You will not let your Holy One see decay." For when David had served God's purpose in his own generation, he fell asleep; he was buried with his fathers and his body decayed. But the one whom God raised from the dead did not see decay (Acts 13:26-31, 34-37).

Both Peter and Paul understood Psalm 16 as referring to the Messiah, the descendant of David. They viewed this passage as powerful evidence that God had planned all along to allow Jesus to die and then raise him from the dead.

April 20

I have set the LORD always before me.
Because he is at my right hand,
I will not be shaken.
Therefore my heart is glad and my tongue rejoices;
my body also will rest secure,
because you will not abandon me to the grave,
nor will you let your Holy One see decay.
(Psalm 16:8-10).

What does this Jesus code mean for you? It means you can face death—your death or the death of a loved one—with confidence and hope. Look again at verse 10. Because the second line of verse 10 ("you will not let your Holy One see decay") is true, the first line of verse10 ("you will not abandon me to the grave") is also true. This is the basis of our hope of heaven.

This is what separates the hope of Christianity from all other religions. Buddha died in 485 BC. His body was burned, but some of his followers saved one of his fingers. The finger was sealed under a temple in China until 1981. Heavy rains caused the pagoda to collapse and it had to be moved. So Buddha's finger has been on tour in Buddhist areas: in Korea, in Taiwan, and in Hong Kong in 2004. It was encased in a gold chest displayed behind bulletproof glass. Hundreds of thousands lined up to see it. One newspaper account displayed a picture of the finger and a quote from Margaret Luk, who said, "I think the finger will protect me through the pains of life." Buddhists have no doubt their leader died and decayed. He cannot be the Holy One. But Jesus is different. His tomb is empty. Mohammed died in 632 AD. He is buried in Medina, Saudi Arabia. His tomb is a holy site to Muslims. He cannot be the Holy One. His body saw decay. Jesus is different. His tomb is empty. The one who did not let his Holy One see decay will not abandon me to the grave.

April 21

You have made known to me the path of life;
you will fill me with joy in your presence,
with eternal pleasures at your right hand
(Psalm 16:11).

The Holy One has made known to us the path of life. The path of life is to follow Jesus Christ in a personal faith relationship. When you believe in Jesus, you are promised that after you die you will be filled with joy in his presence and that you will enjoy eternal pleasures at his right hand. Suffering in this life is always temporary, but the pleasure awaiting you in heaven will be eternal. The certainty of future joy should motivate you to endure present suffering: "Let us fix our eyes on Jesus, the author and perfecter of our faith, *who for the joy set before him endured the cross, scorning its shame,* and sat down at the right hand of the throne of God" (Heb. 12:2, emphasis mine).

April 22

I have set the LORD always before me.
Because he is at my right hand,
I will not be shaken
(Psalm 16:8).

Hans Christian Andersen, author of *The Ugly Duckling*, *The Little Mermaid*, and other children's books, lived in fear of death. He was afraid of fire, so he traveled with a rope in his suitcase so he could escape through a window if the hotel caught on fire. He was afraid of being buried alive, so at night he put a notice next to his bed that said, "I am not really dead."

Perhaps you live with fear of death or the unknown. Perhaps you are constantly worried. You do not have to live that way. If you set the Lord before you, you will not be shaken. That means to accept Jesus as your Savior and to make him the focus of your life. Because he rose from the dead, he is alive today. You can know him and experience his presence in your life. His companionship dispels fear and worry.

This is the Jesus code. It is what Jesus taught his disciples the first Easter Sunday. It is what Peter preached and what Paul proclaimed. It is the path of life.

April 23–29
Psalm 2: I Have Installed My King on Zion

April 23

Why do the nations conspire
and the peoples plot in vain?
The kings of the earth take their stand
and the rulers gather together
against the LORD
and against his Anointed One.
"Let us break their chains," they say,
"and throw off their fetters"
(Psalm 2:1-3).

Psalm 2 deals with the question of power. Have you ever witnessed a power struggle? You see them every day. Have you watched a political debate? Have you ever been in a meeting and watched two coworkers each trying to one-up the other? Have you ever witnessed two family members battling over the remote? Have you ever told a toddler not to touch the buttons on your electronics and watched his defiance? Those are power struggles! The ultimate power struggle is the struggle against the authority of Jesus in our world. There is a power struggle going in our world and in your life about who will be in control. That is what Psalm 2 is about.

Psalm 2 has four sections, each three verses long. There is a different speaker in each section. All four comment on the authority of God's Messiah, the Anointed One. This week I invite you to consider the authority of Jesus Christ over your life.

April 24

Why do the nations conspire
and the peoples plot in vain?
The kings of the earth take their stand
and the rulers gather together
against the LORD
and against his Anointed One.
"Let us break their chains," they say,
"and throw off their fetters"
(Psalm 2:1-3).

The speakers in the first section are the authorities of the earth. They resist the authority of Jesus and say, "Let us break his chains." They feel threatened by him. Peter quoted this section in Acts 4:25-26 in reference to Jesus' crucifixion. He said it referred to Herod (kings) and to Pilate (rulers). Jesus threatened the self-interest of these leaders. Peter also saw this as an explanation of the persecution of Christians. It was why he and John had been arrested for preaching about Jesus. Godless authority sees Jesus as a threat.

If you submit to the authority of Jesus and follow him, you will experience some kind of opposition, just as Jesus and his disciples did. Why? Your life of obedience bothers those who want to break the chains of Jesus. A life submitted to Jesus is a threat to a godless, immoral, greedy lifestyle. This explains irrational criticism of Christians in our culture.

This section also explains our own rebellion against Jesus. We are part of the world. We resist Jesus' authority. Our sin nature does not want to yield the throne of our lives to Jesus. You and I are right there with Herod and Pilate. What we rage about may be an indication of where we feel threatened. It may reveal areas where we are in rebellion against Jesus.

April 25

The One enthroned in heaven laughs;
the Lord scoffs at them.
Then he rebukes them in his anger
and terrifies them in his wrath, saying,
"I have installed my King
on Zion, my holy hill"
(Psalm 2:4-6).

In the second section of this psalm, God the Father is the speaker. God laughs in derision at human rebellion. He is not threatened by the plots of human authority. He scoffs at them. Then he rebukes them in his anger.

God affirms that the Messiah, Jesus, is his King. He has installed him on Zion. Zion refers to Jerusalem, and especially to the mountain where the temple stood. There Jesus was condemned by Pilate and crowned with thorns. There he died on a cross. The world powers viewed the death of Jesus as the execution of a criminal. The Father viewed it as the coronation of his Son. This was God's plan. A thousand years before it happened God had already planned this installation of his King.

April 26

I will proclaim the decree of the LORD:
He said to me, "You are my Son;
today I have become your Father.
Ask of me,
and I will make the nations your inheritance,
the ends of the earth your possession.
You will rule them with an iron scepter;
you will dash them to pieces like pottery"
(Psalm 2:7-9).

The speaker in the third section is the Son of God. He is quoting what God the Father has said to him. Here is what Jesus himself says about his authority: "I am God's Son, and he will give me the whole world as my inheritance."

Verse 7 is repeated by God at Jesus' baptism (Matt. 3:17). It is repeated again by God at Jesus' transfiguration (Matt. 17:5). It is quoted by Paul in Acts 13:32-33 and applied to Jesus' resurrection. It is quoted twice in Hebrews to show Jesus is greater than the angels (Heb. 1:5) and greater than any earthly priest (Heb. 5:5). Jesus has authority because he is the Son of God.

Because the King is God's Son, he will receive God's inheritance. God will give him the nations who have been rebellious. Jesus will possess the earth. The world is in rebellion now, but stay tuned. One day Jesus will rule the whole world. Verse 9 is referenced three times in the book of Revelation. Twice it refers to Jesus (Rev. 12:5; 19:15), and once it refers to Christians (Rev. 2:27). When Jesus returns to earth, he will judge the nations of the world. If we yield to Jesus' rule in our lives, we will reign with him.

April 27

Therefore, you kings, be wise;
be warned, you rulers of the earth.
Serve the LORD with fear
and rejoice with trembling.
Kiss the Son, lest he be angry
and you be destroyed in your way,
for his wrath can flare up in a moment.
Blessed are all who take refuge in him
(Psalm 2:10-12).

The psalmist, inspired by the Holy Spirit, speaks to us in the fourth section of this psalm. He urges us to surrender to Jesus. There is evidence in the Old Testament that idolaters kissed their idols as an act of submission (1 Kings 19:18; Hosea 13:2). The Holy Spirit urges us to "kiss the Son" in true worship and surrender to his rightful authority in our lives. He is our rightful king, the Son of God.

Perhaps you have never confessed "Jesus is Lord" in public baptism. Stop resisting the authority of Jesus in your life and surrender to him. You will find victory in surrender. Addison Leitch said, "When the will of God crosses the will of man, somebody has to die."[21]

---

21 Quoted by Elisabeth Elliot , *Passion and Purity* (Old Tappan, NJ: Fleming H. Revell, 1984), 72.

April 28

Therefore, you kings, be wise;
be warned, you rulers of the earth.
Serve the LORD with fear
and rejoice with trembling.
Kiss the Son, lest he be angry
and you be destroyed in your way,
for his wrath can flare up in a moment.
Blessed are all who take refuge in him
(Psalm 2:10-12).

Perhaps you are a Christian, but you have not surrendered every area of your life to Christ. Perhaps you have not surrendered your relationships to him. Perhaps you have not surrendered your time or finances.

Bob Carlisle, who wrote the song *Butterfly Kisses*, tells of his experience of surrender to Christ. Early in his career, he did background music and vocals for Barry Manilow, REO Speedwagon, and Juice Newton. Because he had a wife and a young daughter to support, he became a self-confessed "musical gun for hire." "I was playing at bars and clubs, and as a Christian I found myself hating it. Finally at a big club in California, I bottomed out." In the middle of the first set, a distraught Carlisle laid down his guitar, headed out into the alley, and vomited. "I prayed that night, 'God, I don't care where we go or what we do, just get me outta here! I'll do anything. I just can't do this anymore.'" Looking back, Carlisle noted, "Whenever I have come to a place of complete surrender is when God moves in my life."[22]

---

22 Audrey T. Hingley, *Christian Reader* (September/October 1997).

April 29

Kiss the Son, lest he be angry
And you be destroyed in your way,
For his wrath can flare up in a moment.
Blessed are all who take refuge in him
(Psalm 2:12).

Psalm 2 presents to you the authority of Jesus. The world says, "Let us break his chains." The Father says, "Jesus is my king. I have installed him on Zion." Jesus says, "I am God's Son, and He will give me the whole world as my inheritance." The Spirit says, "Kiss the Son lest he be angry. Blessed are all who take refuge in him."

Let's review the other incredible prophecies of Jesus in the Psalms we have studied this month:

- Psalm 118 predicted the rejection of Jesus as the Messiah. The psalm indicated this rejection would be part of God's ultimate plan. "The Lord has done this."
- Psalm 22 described the death of Jesus in amazing detail. The psalm described his hands and feet being pierced and his enemies hurling insults at him and casting lots for his clothing.
- Psalm 16 prophesied the resurrection of Jesus from the dead.

No one can prove that Jesus is the Messiah, the Son of God. That confession must be made by faith. However, it is not blind faith. God has lovingly provided credible evidence for faith in Jesus. He carefully placed prophecies—"the Jesus code"—in the Old Testament to help us understand the death and resurrection of Jesus was his plan all along.

May

Help, Lord!

This month we will read psalms that are known as personal laments. This is the single largest type of psalms. At least one third of the psalms fall into this grouping. They are complaints to God, in which the psalmist pours out his heart and cries for help during time of pain or anguish. I have entitled this group, "Help, Lord!" You can identify with these psalms and find comfort in them. Read them when you are going through a similar situation and let them speak for you.

April 30–May 6
Psalms 42–43: Help, Lord, I'm Depressed

April 30

Why are you downcast, O my soul?
Why so disturbed within me?
Put your hope in God,
for I will yet praise him,
my Savior and my God
(Psalm 42:5).

Psalms 42-43 express the complaint, "Help, Lord! I'm depressed." I place Psalms 42 and 43 together for two reasons. First, many Hebrew manuscripts present them as one psalm (see the NIV footnote). There is no title to Psalm 43, which suggests it may go with the previous psalm. Second, the two psalms share a common refrain. These psalms are like a hymn with three verses and a common chorus after each verse: first verse (42:1-4), chorus (42:5), second verse (42:6-10), chorus (42:11), third verse (43:1-4), and chorus (43:5).

The chorus describes the theme or problem in this psalm: "Why are you downcast, O my soul?" This is a psalm for times of depression. Read these psalms when you are "discouraged" (NLT), "in despair" (NASB), "sad" (TEV), or "down in the dumps, crying the blues" (THE MESSAGE). You need to talk to God at such times in your life. These psalms will give you a voice.

May I

As the deer pants for streams of water,
so my soul pants for you, O God.
My soul thirsts for God, for the living God.
When can I go and meet with God?
My tears have been my food
day and night,
while men say to me all day long,
"Where is your God?"
These things I remember
as I pour out my soul:
how I used to go with the multitude,
leading the procession to the house of God,
with shouts of joy and thanksgiving
among the festive throng
(Psalm 42:1-4).

The first stanza expresses the psalmist's complaint. He explains some of the causes of his depression. You may identify with some of these circumstances. First, he is away from home, and he is homesick. He may have been taken captive by a foreign army. This is a good psalm to read when you are separated from family, serving in the military, or in prison. Second, he is not able to go to worship (42:2). This psalm is applicable to the homebound and others cut off from corporate worship. Third, he is ridiculed by unbelievers (42:3, 43:10). Fourth, he is stuck in the past (42:4). He remembers when he used to lead the procession to the house of God with joy among the festive throng. This psalm applies to anyone who is going through a life change and is having a hard time moving on. Fifth, and most importantly, these circumstances have contributed to a feeling of distance from God (42:1). He longs for God as a deer pants for water in the desert. Even among the greatest of Christians, there are times of inexplicable spiritual depression and a sense of distance from God. Often this comes after times of great joy or triumph. Elijah experienced such a time just after he defeated the prophets of Baal on Mount Carmel (1 Kings 19:1-3).

May 2

My soul is downcast within me;
therefore I will remember you
from the land of the Jordan,
the heights of Hermon—from Mount Mizar.
Deep calls to deep
in the roar of your waterfalls;
all your waves and breakers
have swept over me.
By day the LORD directs his love,
at night his song is with me—
a prayer to the God of my life
(Psalm 42:6-8).

The second stanza (42:6-10) continues the complaint, but it contains a slightly more hopeful tone. Verse 6 is unclear. Mount Hermon was near the northern border of the land of Israel. Was this the psalmist's homeland which he was remembering fondly? Or is this where he is in exile, far from Jerusalem? Some have suggested that if he were being taken captive along the northern route, Mount Hermon would be the last visible landmark of his homeland. The roar of the mountain waterfalls seems to remind him of the troubles breaking over him. Yet in the midst of despair, there is a more hopeful note in verse 8. The psalmist is conscious that God is with him both during the day and at night—when depression is usually at its worst.

May 3

Vindicate me, O God,
and plead my cause against an ungodly nation;
rescue me from deceitful and wicked men.
You are God my stronghold.
Why have you rejected me?
Why must I go about mourning,
oppressed by the enemy?
Send forth your light and your truth,
let them guide me;
let them bring me to your holy mountain,
to the place where you dwell.
Then I will go to the altar of God,
to God my joy and my delight.
I will praise you with harp,
O God, my God
(Psalm 43:1–4).

The third stanza (43:1-4) is even more positive. It is a prayer to God for deliverance (43:1). It asks God to send light and truth (43:3). These are the two things a depressed person needs most. If you are depressed, you need physical light. Do not sit in a dark room; open the curtains. Take a walk in the sunshine. You also need spiritual light. God can lift the darkness of the soul as you gather with his people and worship him. You also need truth. Truth is the antidote to lies and half-truths that pull you into despair. Read the Bible, the Word of truth. Listen to the proclamation of the truth in church. Listen to a friend who is willing to risk telling you the truth.

The psalmist focuses now on the future rather than on the past (43:4). The depressed person needs to realize it will not always be this way. Depression is temporary. The final chorus is the same, but it somehow seems to have a more positive tone in the context of chapter 43.

May 4

Why are you downcast, O my soul?
Why so disturbed within me?
Put your hope in God,
for I will yet praise him,
my Savior and my God
(Psalm 43:5).

What then does this psalm teach about how to deal with spiritual depression? The chorus suggests three things you need to do in time of depression. *First, you must talk to yourself.* "Why are you downcast, O my soul?" Martyn Lloyd-Jones wrote *Spiritual Depression: Its Causes and Cure.* He said the mind must speak to the emotions rather than the emotions dictating to the mind.

You have to take yourself in hand, you have to address yourself, preach to yourself, question yourself. You must say to your soul, "Why are you downcast? What business have you to be disquieted?" You must turn on yourself, upbraid yourself, condemn yourself, exhort yourself, and say to yourself, "Hope thou in God."[23]

---

23 D. Martin Lloyd-Jones, *Spiritual Depression: Its Causes and Cure* (Grand Rapids: Eerdmans, 1965), 21.

May 5

Why are you downcast, O my soul?
Why so disturbed within me?
Put your hope in God,
for I will yet praise him,
my Savior and my God
(Psalm 43:5).

The chorus of these two psalms suggests a second thing to do in time of depression: *you must focus on what has not changed in your life rather than on what has changed.* "Put your hope in God." His character and his purposes for you have not changed. Choose to focus on these positive truths rather than the changes you have experienced. Once when Martin Luther was depressed, his wife met him at the door dressed in black. "Who died?" he asked. "God," she replied. "This is foolishness," Luther responded. "He must have," she said, "or you would not be so sorrowful."

When your life is in flux, you can choose to focus on the things in your life that are unchanging—the promises of God and his ultimate plan for your life.

May 6

Why are you downcast, O my soul?
Why so disturbed within me?
Put your hope in God,
for I will yet praise him,
my Savior and my God
(Psalm 43:5).

The chorus shares a third piece of advice for times of depression: *you must look to the future.* "I will yet praise him, my Savior and my God." Counselors say that 85 percent of the cases of major depression resolve themselves within one year.[24] You may feel you are in a hole so deep you can never escape. Depression seems permanent while you are in it. Do not judge what your future will be by what your present is. Repeat this phrase over and over: "I will yet praise him, my Savior and my God." You have a future. Even if your circumstances are lifelong, you have an eternity in heaven. You must find a future hope for your focal point if you are to emerge from spiritual depression.

---

24 www.mental-health-matters.com.

May 7–13
Psalm 141: Help, Lord, I'm Struggling with Temptation

May 7

O LORD, I call to you; come quickly to me.
Hear my voice when I call to you.
May my prayer be set before you like incense;
may the lifting up of my hands be like the evening sacrifice
(Psalm 141:1-2).

Psalm 141 is a prayer to turn to in times of temptation. Perhaps you are struggling with a specific weakness in your life: gossip, lust, greed, drugs, or other addictions. This is a prayer for deliverance from evil. This is a great psalm to pray for your kids or grandkids. Every parent or grandparent should have this psalm marked.

The introduction in verses 1-2 is a plea for help. There is a note of urgency in the prayer: "Come quickly to me." This psalm seems to have been an evening prayer. The evening hours are especially a time of temptation for many people. David asks that his prayer may rise to God as the smoke from the evening sacrifice.

There are five petitions in this prayer for protection from temptation. We will examine one petition each of the next five days.

May 8

Set a guard over my mouth, O LORD;
keep watch over the door of my lips
(Psalm 141:3).

The first prayer for times of temptation is to ask God to guard your mouth. Your words are the source of much of your sin. David speaks of his two lips as two swinging doors. He asks God to post a sentry at the doorway of his mouth to regulate what comes out. It is far better to control your words before they are spoken than to deal with the damage after words have left your lips.

This verse recognizes that God's help is needed to control the tongue. James describes the human tongue as a raging wildfire or an untamable beast (James 3:6-7). The wise person is not confident in his own ability to resist temptation but asks God for help. Pray this verse before you enter a meeting or break room or wherever you are tempted to sin with your mouth. Pause right now and ask God to set a guard over your mouth today.

May 9

Let not my heart be drawn to what is evil,
to take part in wicked deeds
with men who are evildoers;
let me not eat of their delicacies
(Psalm 141:4).

The second prayer for times of temptation is deeper than the first: Ask God to change your desires. "Let not my heart be drawn to what is evil." The Bible always goes to the source of the problem. Jesus said, "Out of the overflow of the heart, the mouth speaks" (Luke 6:45). Your heart is naturally pulled toward evil (the Hebrew word means to be stretched). Ask God to change your desires. "Keep me from wanting to do wrong" (TEV). "Take away my lust for evil things" (LB). Some people do not want their desires changed. They only want to manage the consequences of their lusts. They really like their evil desires and want to keep them as pets. Change comes when you can really pray for new desires.

159

May 10

Let a righteous man strike me—it is a kindness;
let him rebuke me—it is oil on my head.
My head will not refuse it
(Psalm 141:5).

The third petition for times of temptation is to pray for willingness to accept correction. Usually when you are wrestling with temptation, there is someone—a spouse or friend or pastor—telling you what is right. The problem is that you do not listen. People entrapped in sin often get in a "zone" where they refuse to listen to wisdom. They seem oblivious to wise counsel.

To avoid temptation, you must pray to be receptive to wisdom. Would you pray right now, "Let a righteous man strike me"? View the loving rebuke of a friend as a mark of friendship, like oil to your head. Proverbs says, "Wounds from a friend can be trusted, but an enemy multiplies kisses" (Prov. 27:6). Parents often jump to defend their children against any rebuke. Instead, you should pray for people in your kids' lives who will rebuke them in kindness.

May 11

Yet my prayer is ever against the deeds of evildoers;
their rulers will be thrown down from the cliffs,
and the wicked will learn that my words were well spoken.

Keep me from the snares they have laid for me,
from the traps set by evildoers.
Let the wicked fall into their own nets,
while I pass by in safety
(Psalm 141:5b-6, 9-10).

The fourth prayer for time of temptation is to pray against the influence of evil men. This theme is scattered throughout the verses of this psalm. The wicked want to involve others. They are not straightforward in their methods; they use deception. As a trapper camouflages his snare, so they cover up the consequences of sinful behavior. David prays for the downfall of those who influence others to sin.

There are people who set traps for you and your children. Pray that God will protect you. Pray that he will give you discernment to see through the camouflage of their snares. Pray that your children will see the ultimate end of the wicked.

May 12

But my eyes are fixed on you, O Sovereign LORD;
in you I take refuge—do not give me over to death
(Psalm 141:8).

The fifth petition for time of temptation is the most positive of all: pray for a preoccupation with God and the things of his kingdom. A key to resisting temptation is to find an alternative vision and passion. If you focus on a lust or desire and try to avoid it, you may instead be drawn to it as a moth to a flame. However, if you find another focus, you may forget all about that lust. "My eyes are fixed on you." To avoid temptation, become involved in active service to others through your church and community. Expend your energy in that which is positive. Focus on positive role models. Hebrews 12:2 says, "Let us fix our eyes on Jesus, the author and perfecter of our faith."

May 13

I invite you to pray through these five petitions right now. Pray this psalm for yourself, for a Christian friend, for your children, or for your grandchildren. Personalize the prayer by placing your name or the name of that person in each verse. Add phrases that relate to specific temptations. Here is a guide for praying this psalm:

O Lord, I call to you; come quickly to me.
Hear my voice when I call to you.

Set a guard over my mouth, O Lord.
Keep watch over the door of my lips as I _____ today.

Let not the heart of _____ be drawn to what is evil,
To take part in wicked deeds at _____.

Let a righteous man strike me—it is a kindness;
Let him rebuke me—it is oil to my head.
My head will not refuse it.

Yet my prayer is ever against evildoers
Keep _____ from the snares they have laid for him/her.
From the traps set by evildoers.
Let the wicked fall into their own nets,
While _____ passes by in safety.

My eyes are fixed on you, O Sovereign Lord.
In the area of _____, I take refuge in you.

May 14-20
Psalm 142: Help, Lord, I Feel No One Cares

May 14

*Look to my right and see;
no one is concerned for me.
I have no refuge;
no one cares for my life
(Psalm 142:4).*

This verse states the theme of Psalm 142. Have you ever felt this way? Perhaps you have been rejected or you are lonely. Perhaps you feel abandoned because of the death of a spouse or divorce. Perhaps you have moved to a new city and have no friends. The title says that David wrote this psalm "when he was in the cave." There were two such times in his life: in the cave at Adullam (1 Sam. 22:1) and in the cave at En Gedi (1 Sam. 24:1). The setting is probably the former. David had become a national hero when he killed Goliath, the Philistine warrior. However, King Saul became jealous and tried to kill David. David had to flee for his life. He went to Nob, where a priest, Ahimelech, gave him food and supplies. Saul found out and killed everyone in Nob including eighty-five priests. In his desperation David fled to Gath, a city of the Philistines. Someone recognized David there, and he escaped only by pretending to be insane. He fled to the cave at Adullam. You can see why he felt alone and that no one cared. If you can identify with David's feelings, this psalm is God's word to you.

May 15

I cry aloud to the LORD;
I lift up my voice to the LORD for mercy.
I pour out my complaint before him;
before him I tell my trouble.
When my spirit grows faint within me,
it is you who know my way.
In the path where I walk
men have hidden a snare for me.
Look to my right hand and see;
no one is concerned for me.
I have no refuge;
no one cares for my life
(Psalm 142:1-4).

David cried aloud to the Lord. Do you ever pray aloud? It helps to make the conversation real and forces you to express your thoughts. David poured out his complaint to God. While it is wrong to curse or blame God, you can be honest with God and tell him how you feel. "Before him I tell my trouble."

David described his feelings to God. His spirit grew faint. He was ready to give up. He invited God to see for himself that there was no one at his right hand. That was the place of one's legal advocate or helper—"a right hand man." It was probably not true that no one cared for David. Jonathan had pledged his loyalty. Still, that is how David felt while alone in the cave. He had to deal with his feelings. So do you.

May 16

I cry to you, O LORD;
I say, "You are my refuge,
my portion in the land of the living"
(Psalm 142:5).

This verse is a statement of faith. It is the answer David comes to and the therapy you need when you feel no one cares. David says, "God is my refuge." The word "refuge" is also translated "shelter." He wrote these words in a cave. He could not find adequate shelter, but God would be his shelter.

God told the Israelites when they settled the promised land to set aside six towns as cities of refuge (Num. 35). These were places of protection from retaliation. If a person murdered someone, his kin would kill that person. That was "an eye for an eye." However, if a person accidentally killed someone, he could flee to one of these cities of refuge and be safe until a trial could be held. The word "refuge" is not the same here, but the concept is similar. David could not flee to a city of refuge, but God would be his refuge. God will be your refuge when you feel no one cares. When you feel vulnerable and alone, flee to his presence for shelter and safety.

May 17

I cry to you, O LORD;
I say, "You are my refuge,
my portion in the land of the living"
(Psalm 142:5).

David says, "God is my portion." When the Israelites came into the promised land, each of the tribes was given a portion, or share, or allotment of the land. However, God said the Levites who ministered to him would not receive a portion. God said he would be their portion (Num. 18:20). David had no possessions or property. Like the Levites, he claimed God as his portion.

God can be your portion. God can satisfy you when you are needy. God can fill the void in your life when you are alone. He is real. I have heard widows, singles, and people going through divorce testify to the reality of God as a refuge and portion. Talk to him. Ask him to fill your heart.

I do not have a lot of family. I have gone through times in my life when I did not have a close friend. God can be a real friend. When I was a child, I learned a song entitled *My Best Friend Is Jesus*. Throughout my life, Jesus has indeed been my very best friend. He never disappoints. He always understands. I can talk to him any time. The Lord is my portion.

May 18

Listen to my cry,
for I am in desperate need;
rescue me from those who pursue me,
for they are too strong for me
(Psalm 142:6).

Often we do not ask for help until we experience desperate need. Pride hinders us from seeking the assistance we need. Sometimes we had rather suffer than ask for help. We begin to make progress when we let go of our stubborn self-sufficiency and admit our desperate need. This is what Jesus meant when he said: "Blessed are you who are poor, for yours is the kingdom of God. Blessed are you who are hungry now, for you will be satisfied. Blessed are you who weep now, for you will laugh" (Luke 6:20-21).

Admit your need to God. Ask God to help you. Ask him to rescue you from the problems that pursue you, the enemies who are too strong for you.

May 19

Set me free from my prison,
that I may praise your name.
Then the righteous will gather about me
because of your goodness to me
(Psalm 142:7).

This psalm ends with another statement of faith: "The righteous will gather about me." Here is another resource for your life when you feel no one cares: find companionship in the people of God. 1 Samuel 22:1-2 tells how people came to David in the cave and gathered around him: "When his brothers and his father's household heard about it, they went down to him there. All those who were in distress or in debt or discontented gathered around him, and he became their leader."

Find companionship in the people of God. Join a Sunday School class, a prayer group, a small group Bible study, or other group in your church. Force yourself to connect with people. You may say, "I have tried to find companionship in groups, but I don't fit in. No one reached out to me." Some people may not be sensitive to your needs, but others are feeling the same need for companionship you do. Notice it was the discontented who connected with David. Think of someone who seems to feel the same as you do. Contact that person and tell him or her how you are feeling. There are people who will gather around you if you give them a chance.

May 20

It is you who know my way
(Psalm 142:3).

When you feel no one cares, it helps simply to realize that someone knows what you are experiencing. God knows you. He knows your name (John 10:3). He knows your deepest thoughts (Ps. 139:2). He knows every move you make (Ps. 139:3). He even knows your future: "'I know the plans I have for you,' declares the Lord, 'plans to prosper you and not to harm you, plans to give you hope and a future'" (Jer. 29:11). God knows the way you have been, the way you are now, and the way he plans for you to go. He really does care.

Let's review what we have learned this week. What do you do when you feel no one cares for you? First, express your feelings honestly to God. Your feelings are important, and you need to voice them in prayer. It may help you to express them out loud. Second, confess what you believe. Beliefs trump feelings. Confess that God is your refuge and your portion. Visualize the protection of God like a wall around you. His presence is real. Regard him as your best friend. Third, reach out to other people. Get over your pride and fear and step outside your comfort zone. If you will be transparent, you will find in the family of God people who care.

May 21–27
Psalm 55: Help, Lord, I've Been Betrayed

May 21

Listen to my prayer, O God,
do not ignore my plea;
hear me and answer me.
My thoughts trouble me and I am distraught
at the voice of the enemy,
at the stares of the wicked;
for they bring down suffering upon me
and revile me in their anger
(Psalm 55:1-3).

Many of the Psalms deal with relationships to one's enemies. The word "enemy" (or "enemies") is mentioned ninety-three times in fifty-three different psalms. Psalm 55 is somewhat unique in that it describes a situation where a close friend has become an enemy. Psalm 55 is about betrayal. This is a psalm to turn to if you or someone you care about has been betrayed by an extramarital affair. A person whose spouse has unexpectedly divorced him may identify with the emotion in this psalm. It speaks to someone who has been slandered or has become the subject of gossip. This is the psalm to read when someone close to you has broken a promise or lied to you.

May 22

Listen to my prayer, O God,
do not ignore my plea;
hear me and answer me.
My thoughts trouble me and I am distraught
at the voice of the enemy,
at the stares of the wicked;
for they bring down suffering upon me
and revile me in their anger
(Psalm 55:1-3).

The title tells us that David wrote this psalm, but we do not know its particular setting. Bible students have speculated that David could be writing about Ahithophel. He was David's counselor, his chief of staff, and his closest advisor. His advice was trusted as the word of God (2 Sam. 16:23). When David's son Absalom revolted against his father, Ahithophel joined the rebellion. David must have been crushed. He prayed that God would turn Ahithophel's counsel to foolishness (2 Sam. 15:31). Absalom rejected Ahithophel's advice to attack David immediately, and Ahithophel hanged himself. Something like that is the setting of this psalm.

May 23

If an enemy were insulting me,
I could endure it;
if a foe were raising himself against me,
I could hide from him.
But it is you, a man like myself,
my companion, my close friend,
with whom I once enjoyed sweet fellowship
as we walked with the throng at the house of God.

My companion attacks his friends;
he violates his covenant.
His speech is smooth as butter,
yet war is in his heart;
his words are more soothing than oil,
yet they are drawn swords
(Psalm 55:12-14, 20-21).

In these two sections, David describes the betrayal he has experienced. In verses 12-14, he says the betrayal hurts worse because the betrayer was such a close friend. David sounds as if he is in shock in these verses; he can hardly believe it. The closer the connection, the more painful it will be when someone betrays you.

In verses 20-21 David indicates the betrayal was at least partly verbal, involving lies and slander. Words have great power. They can encourage and heal or they can wound and destroy. The words we speak are very important. Jesus said our words will be revealed in the time of judgment: "What you have said in the dark will be heard in the daylight, and what you have whispered in the ear in the inner rooms will be proclaimed from the roofs" (Luke 12:3).

May 24

My heart is in anguish within me;
the terrors of death assail me.
Fear and trembling have beset me;
horror has overwhelmed me.
I said, "Oh, that I had the wings of a dove!
I would fly away and be at rest—
I would flee far away
and stay in the desert;
I would hurry to my place of shelter,
far from the tempest and storm"
(Psalm 55:4-8).

This is a psalm of raw emotion. It captures the depth of hurt that betrayal brings. Betrayal produces fear and anguish. David wishes he could run away. Many people who have been betrayed simply want to escape. Perhaps you can identify with these feelings.

One way to apply this psalm is to turn it around. Are you a betrayer? Make sure that you keep your vows and promises. Make sure you do not betray a confidence. If you are tempted to spread gossip, you need to read this psalm and hear the pain it causes. If you are tempted to have an affair, read this psalm and be reminded of the hurt you could cause. Our culture takes these offenses too lightly.

May 25

Confuse the wicked, O Lord, confound their speech,
for I see violence and strife in the city.

Let death take my enemies by surprise;
let them go down to the grave,
for evil finds lodging among them
(Psalm 55:9, 15).

This psalm does not come to a neat resolution. You may notice we are not reading this psalm in order. David alternates between three things: describing the betrayal, praying judgment on the one who has betrayed him, and trusting his situation to God. Dealing with betrayal is a process that is ongoing.

In today's verses, David prays with vehemence against the people who have betrayed him. David wants them to go alive into hell. That may sound harsh to you. That may be because you have not experienced the raw pain of betrayal.

Note that David prays for vindication, but he does not take judgment or vengeance into his own hands. It is important that you do not retaliate against those who gossip or slander or cheat you. Leave their fate to a just God.

May 26

Let death take my enemies by surprise;
let them go down to the grave,
for evil finds lodging among them
(Psalm 55:15).

The New Testament has more to say about how to pray for enemies. Jesus teaches us to love our enemies (Matt. 5:43-47). Jesus was also betrayed by a best friend. Judas kissed him the very moment he turned him in. Jesus prayed, "Father, forgive them." Does that not contradict this psalm? No, this psalm gives voice to honest human emotion and prays for justice. The New Testament goes farther through the power of Christ and tells us to pray for mercy. Both are part of the nature of God.

The book *Peace Child* tells the story of missionary Don Richardson and his work with tribes of cannibals in Irian Jaya. These tribes valued betrayal. They loved to befriend a member of a neighboring tribe, gain his trust, then kill and eat him! Richardson sought to tell them the story of Jesus. When they heard the story of Judas' betrayal, they applauded. Judas was their hero! Richardson despaired of reaching these people. Then he witnessed a strange, new ceremony. Two tribes that had been in conflict faced off. The chief took his newborn son from his wailing mother. Each of his warriors laid his hands on the child. He gave the child to the opposing tribe, who turned with the child and disappeared into the jungle. Richardson asked what this meant. The chief explained that this was the peace child. As long as the child lived, the two tribes would be at peace. If the child died, they would be at war. Richardson had discovered the key to sharing the gospel with them. Jesus is our peace child. He is the atonement for any betrayal. He lives forever to give us peace.

May 27

But I call to God,
and the LORD saves me.
Evening, morning, and noon
I cry out in distress,
and he hears my voice.
He ransoms me unharmed
from the battle waged against me,
even though many oppose me.

Cast your cares on the LORD
and he will sustain you;
he will never let the righteous fall.

But as for me, I trust in you
(Psalm 55:16-18, 22, 23b).

There is another type prayer in this psalm. David not only prays about his betrayer. He also prays for himself and trusts his situation to God. He calls to God to save him, bringing his request to God three times a day. He advises us to cast our cares on God.

Verse 22 is repeated in 1 Peter 5:7. That book was written during time of Christian persecution. Friends may have been reporting Christians to the authorities. Peter reminded these Christians to cast their cares on God. The word "cast" means "throw" or "hurl." The idea is that you do not hang on to your burdens but transfer them to God.

David's final word is one of trust in God. Don't let betrayal make you jaded or bitter. Trust in God.

May 28—June 3
Psalm 77: Help, Lord, I Feel
Forgotten by You

May 28

Will the Lord reject forever?
Will he never show his favor again?
Has his unfailing love vanished forever?
Has his promise failed for all time?
Has God forgotten to be merciful?
Has he in anger withheld his compassion?
(Psalm 77:7-9).

This psalm is in a group (Pss. 73-83, also Ps. 50) written by Asaph, one of David's three choir leaders. He wrote very honest confessions. In this psalm Asaph expresses his feeling of abandonment by God.

This is a psalm to be read in times of unanswered prayer, in times of waiting, or when nothing seems to be happening in your life. This is the psalm for the times when you are in a hurry and God is not.

In verses 1-6 Asaph describes his distress and how he cried out to the Lord. In verses 7-9 Asaph confesses his doubts to God. He formulates his doubts into questions. These verses contain the theme of this psalm. Verse 9 sums it up: "Has God forgotten to be merciful?"

May 29

I remembered you, O God, and I groaned;
I mused, and my spirit grew faint.
You kept my eyes from closing;
I was too troubled to speak.
I thought about the former days,
the years of long ago;
I remembered my songs in the night
(Psalm 77:3-6).

Asaph's feelings of abandonment were spurred by his memories. He remembered better times, times when he sang songs, times when he felt close to God. Those memories made him sad. There was a sense of loss in his life. He groaned. Have you ever groaned in prayer? It is okay to groan to God. Even though he was a worship leader, Asaph came to a place in his life when he was too troubled to speak to God in prayer. The words did not come. You may come to a place in your life when you can't even pray, when words will not come. You can simply sit before the Lord. You can wait before God in silence. That too is a form of prayer.

One of the refreshing things about the psalms of petition is that they are very honest. The psalmists do no write pious platitudes. They pour out their feelings to God with raw honesty. It is good to know that you can be honest with God. He already knows your deepest feelings. You can express them to him or even groan before him.

May 30

Then I thought, "To this I will appeal:
the years of the right hand of the Most High."
I will remember the deeds of the LORD;
yes, I will remember your miracles of long ago.
I will meditate on all your works
and consider all your mighty deeds
(Psalm 77:10-12).

Memory may be the cause of feelings of abandonment, but it is also the cure for such feelings. The treatment for these kinds of doubts is to remember the deeds of the Lord. Memory is a powerful spiritual weapon. When it seems God is doing nothing in the present, you need to remember the deeds of God in the past. You need to take a broader view of reality than the slice of life that has caused you to feel forgotten. It is wrong at midnight to say it will never be daylight again simply because it is dark right now. It has been daylight before, remember? It will be daylight again.

Asaph had spoken of memory in the earlier part of this psalm in a negative sense. The difference is that those memories were self-centered, whereas these are God-centered. "I" and "me" occur eighteen times in verses 1-6, but God is mentioned only six times. In verses 13-20, God is mentioned twenty-one times but a personal pronoun only once. Memory can be very selective. When you feel forgotten by God, choose to focus on those memories that confirm the love and faithfulness of God in your experience.

May 31

Your ways, O God, are holy.
What god is so great as our God?
You are the God who performs miracles;
you display your power among the peoples.
With your mighty arm you redeemed your people,
the descendants of Jacob and Joseph
(Psalm 77:13–15).

Here Asaph recalls the miracles of God among his people Israel. The Bible does not record many miracles during the lifetime of Asaph. Contrary to what some people think, the story of the Bible is not one unbroken chain of miraculous events. There are clusters of miracles in the Bible: at the exodus from Egypt and the conquest of the land, at the time of Elijah and Elisha, at the time of Daniel, at the time of Jesus, and at the beginning of the church. God can do miracles at any time, but he seems especially to perform miracles when he is doing something new. At other times miracles seem scarce. The ministries of Jeremiah and Ezekiel, for example, were not marked by many miracles. During times when miracles seem scarce, it is important to remember the mighty works of God from other eras. Mature faith believes God can do a miracle at any time. Mature faith believes God has not changed even when there is no miracle. Mature faith obeys God even when no miracle is in sight.

June 1

The waters saw you, O God,
the waters saw you and writhed;
the very depths were convulsed.
The clouds poured down water,
the skies resounded with thunder;
your arrows flashed back and forth.
Your thunder was heard in the whirlwind,
your lightning lit up the world;
the earth trembled and quaked.
Your path led through the sea,
your way through the mighty waters,
though your footprints were not seen.
You led your people like a flock
by the hand of Moses and Aaron
(Psalm 77:16-20).

Verses 16-20 are a poetic retelling of the parting of the Red Sea during the exodus. Several psalms refer to this event. It was the defining miracle in Israel's history. Whenever they felt forgotten, they returned to what they knew of God's miraculous power at the Red Sea. They did not see his footprints, but they knew he was there.

You need an encounter with God that will sustain you through difficult times. You need to have personally experienced his love in such a way that there will be no doubt concerning its reality. Your conversion is your exodus from the bondage of sin. That experience needs to be the touchstone of your life. You need to be able to recount it with certainty, as Israel recounted the parting of the Red Sea.

June 2

You led your people like a flock
by the hand of Moses and Aaron
(Psalm 77:20).

You need a history with God to sustain you in times when you feel forgotten. You need two kinds of history. First, you need a sense of corporate history. That is, you need to know the story of God's activity among the people of God as recorded in the Bible. As the people of Israel often returned to the story of the parting of the Red Sea, you need to return to Bible narratives that confirm God's activity in our world. There is value in Bible stories.

You also need a sense of corporate history in your church. Do you know how your church was founded? Do you know the history of God's activity in your congregation? Do you know key events where God has been at work? You need this sense of corporate history.

When you feel forgotten by God, broaden your view of your life and world history. Recall the miraculous, sustaining work of a God who never changes.

June 3

*You led your people like a flock
by the hand of Moses and Aaron
(Psalm 77:20).*

You need a second type of history with God. You need a personal history of the activity of God in your life. You need to review and even record the activity of God in your life so that you can draw from it in times of seeming inactivity.

Write down your prayer requests to God. Then record God's answers to your prayers. Your prayer list becomes a history of the activity of God in your life. For more than twenty-five years I have made a prayer list each January of people who are not Christians. I have prayed for their salvation throughout the year. When one of those persons confesses Christ as Savior and Lord, I record that in my prayer notebook. I have kept those lists for over a quarter of a century. In times of unanswered prayer, they become an encouraging reminder of God's activity in my life.

Other Christians keep a daily journal of what happens in their lives. A journal can also function as an encouraging record of God's activity. Others keep a spiritual scrapbook or photo album, containing pictures of baptism, parent-child dedications, and other milestones. As Israel remembered the Red Sea, you need to regularly recall the key elements of God's work in your life.

June

Bulk Up Your Faith

Do you ever feel that you need a stronger faith in God? Do you tend to get discouraged at the smallest obstacle or crisis? Most of us need to grow in faith. This month we will study a group of psalms known as psalms of confidence. They are positive and encouraging. I have entitled this section "Bulk Up Your Faith."

There is a great emphasis in our culture on physical strength and fitness. Many homes contain some piece of exercise equipment. Physical exercise is good, but we must not neglect the health of our souls. While bulking up our bodies, we must not allow our faith to shrivel. The psalms of confidence, when applied consistently and repetitively to the muscles of our souls, will bulk up our faith.

June 4–10
Psalm 18: The Lord Is My Rock

June 4

I love you, O LORD, my strength.
The LORD is my rock, my fortress and my deliverer;
my God is my rock, in whom I take refuge.
He is my shield and the horn of my salvation, my stronghold.
I call to the LORD, who is worthy of praise,
and I am saved from my enemies
(Psalm 18:1-3).

Psalm 18 is a celebration of God's help in David's life. It is an exuberant, cartwheeling psalm. David may have written it near the end of his life, as he reflected back on God's deliverance from Saul and from the armies of his enemies. This psalm is duplicated in 2 Samuel 22. The theme of Psalm 18 is "The Lord is my Rock." This theme is introduced in verse 2, is repeated about halfway through the psalm (v. 31), and is stated again in the conclusion (v. 46). This phrase means God is my protection, my security, or my hiding place.

The two occurrences of the word "rock" in Psalm 18:2 translate two different Hebrew words. Both of these key words are found in 1 Samuel 23-24, when David was a fleeing from the deranged King Saul. The first word "rock" *(sela)* is found in 1 Samuel 23:25: "Saul and his men began the search, and when David was told about it, he went down to the rock and stayed in the Desert of Maon." The second word "rock" *(sur)* is translated "crags" in 1 Samuel 24:2: "Saul took three thousand chosen men from all Israel and set out to look for David and his men near the Crags of the Wild Goats." David is recalling real events in his life. He remembers the rocks, and he sees God in them. Rocks are very common in Israel. David saw the protection of God even in common things like rocks. If you would bulk up your faith, you must see God in the common things of your life.

June 5

In my distress I called to the LORD;
I cried to my God for help.
From his temple he heard my voice;
my cry came before him, into his ears.
The earth trembled and quaked,
and the foundations of the mountains shook;
they trembled because he was angry.
Smoke rose from his nostrils;
consuming fire came from his mouth,
burning coals blazed out of it.
He parted the heavens and came down;
dark clouds were under his feet.

He shot his arrows and scattered the enemies,
great bolts of lightning and routed them
(Psalm 18:6-9, 14).

David recalls a time in his life when he thought he was going to die. "The cords of the grave coiled around me; the snares of death confronted me" (v. 5). Suffering is the proving ground for faith. God uses trouble to bulk up your faith.

In his distress, David cried to God for help. God responded in dramatic fashion. God mounted the cherubim and rode them down from heaven. He was accompanied by thunder, lightning, and earthquake. He shot his arrows at David's enemies. There is no record of such a visible appearance of God to David. David is speaking of what happens behind the scenes when his people cry out to him. This is what happens when he responds to your prayers. To bulk up your faith, you need to look through the surface to God's dramatic activity behind the scenes.

June 6

He reached down from on high and took hold of me;
he drew me out of deep waters.
He rescued me from my powerful enemy,
from my foes, who were too strong for me.
They confronted me in the day of my disaster,
but the LORD was my support.
He brought me out into a spacious place;
he rescued me because he delighted in me
(Psalm 18:16–19).

God rescued David. God is a rescuing God. The whole theme of the Bible is rescue. David pictured himself drowning. Like a lifeguard, God saw David in trouble. He reached out to David, took hold of him, and pulled him to safety.

If you are in trouble, if this is "the day of your disaster," cry out to God right now. Ask him to reach down and take hold of you and pull you out of deep water. Ask him to support you and bring you into a spacious place.

God rescued David because he delighted in him. God loves you. You do not have to bargain with God to gain his assistance. God wants to help you not because of what you can offer him but because he delights in you.

June 7

To the faithful, you show yourself faithful,
to the blameless you show yourself blameless,
to the pure you show yourself pure,
but to the crooked you show yourself shrewd.
You save the humble
but bring low those whose eyes are haughty
(Psalm 18:25-27).

This passage says God acts in your life the same way you act. If you act tough and proud toward God, God will act tough and proud toward you. If you become tenderhearted and broken, God will deal tenderly with you. This principle is repeated in the New Testament: "God opposes the proud but gives grace to the humble" (James 4:6). Jesus said, "For if you forgive men when they sin against you, your heavenly Father will also forgive you. But if you do not forgive men their sins, your Father will not forgive your sins" (Matt. 6:14-15). This does mean you earn God's help. It means your attitude can be a roadblock or a conduit to God's help in your life.

June 8

You, O LORD, keep my lamp burning;
my God turns my darkness into light.
With your help I can advance against a troop;
with my God I can scale a wall
(Psalm 18:28-29).

David affirms the very real help of God in his life. These verses exude confidence and enthusiasm. With God's help we can conquer any enemy or overcome any obstacle. What is the darkness in your life? What walls are blocking your advance? Have you ever said, "I can't do this; I can't go on"? It is easy to say, "I can't." It becomes a self-fulfilling prophecy. Focus instead on what you can do with God's help.

Read these verses again, filling in the blanks with challenges from your own life: "With your help I can _____; with my God I can _____." If you are facing some tough situation, read these personalized verses every morning before you go to work or school. Memorize them and repeat them in times of stress. It will strengthen your faith to verbally affirm the positive power of God in overcoming challenges.

Paul did this same thing when he was in prison. He said, "I can do everything through him who gives me strength" (Phil. 4:13).

June 9

For who is God besides the LORD?
And who is the Rock except our God?
It is God who arms me with strength
and makes my way perfect.
He makes my feet like the feet of a deer;
he enables me to stand on the heights.
He trains my hands for battle;
my arms can bend a bow of bronze
(Psalm 18:31-34).

David returns to the theme that God alone is our Rock. God arms us with strength. Note that God does not fight our battles. God trains our hands for battle, and then we fight the battle. God does not scale our walls. We scale our walls with God's help. There is a combination of our best effort and God's infusion of power. "The horse is made ready for the day of battle, but victory rests with the Lord" (Prov. 21:31).

When you face challenges, you must prepare and act as best you can and then depend on the Lord. It is wrong to worry and think it all depends on you. It is also wrong to wimp out and do nothing. To bulk up your faith, do your very best and trust God to give you victory.

June 10

The LORD lives! Praise be to my Rock!
Exalted be God my Savior!
He is the God who avenges me,
who subdues nations under me,
who saves me from my enemies.
You exalted me above my foes;
from violent men you rescued me.
Therefore I will praise you among the nations, O LORD;
I will sing praises to your name
(Psalm 18:46–49).

The conclusion of this psalm returns to the overarching theme of God as our Rock. Do you have a rock in your life, a shelter, a hiding place? More and more homeowners are constructing safe rooms in their houses. Constructed of thick concrete or steel walls, these safe rooms are designed to provide protection from tornadoes, hurricanes, terrorist attacks, or home invasions. One manufacturer guarantees that its safe room will withstand 450 mph winds, over 100 mph above the highest ever recorded in a tornado. Some safe rooms are equipped with elaborate air filtration systems to protect against biological or chemical attack. Safe rooms in Hawaii have air purifiers to protect occupants from deadly gases and ash spewed by volcanoes on the islands.

It is wise to be prepared for disasters and to live as prudently as possible, but there is no place on earth that is completely safe. The believer finds his real security in the presence and protection of God. If David were writing today he might say, "The Lord lives! He is my safe room!"

June 11–17
Psalm 125: The Lord Surrounds Me

June 11

Those who trust in the LORD are like Mount Zion,
which cannot be shaken but endures forever
(Psalm 125:1).

Psalm 125 is another psalm of confidence. The theme of this psalm is the protection of God. This psalm provides another dose of truth that will bulk up your faith if you receive it and digest it.

Verse 1 says you can have an unshakeable faith if you put your trust in the Lord. Times of shaking are coming in your life. That is inevitable. You cannot wait until they come to bulk up your faith. You must make that preparation before the shaking comes. Earthquakes are coming in California, so they have building codes that require builders to prepare for an earthquake. Every new building must be prepared for a time of shaking. You cannot wait until crisis comes to shore up your faith. The time to bulk up your faith is now.

June 12

Those who trust in the LORD are like Mount Zion,
which cannot be shaken but endures forever
(Psalm 125:1).

The way to have an unshakable faith is to put your trust in the Lord. It is not so important how much faith you have initially as where you place it. For your faith to grow, you must place it in something. Money will not grow unless it is placed in some investment: a bank or the stock market or bonds. When you place it there, it has an opportunity to grow. How do you place your faith in God? It begins with an initial prayer of trust. It continues with daily affirmation of trust. It really grows when you act on that trust.

Those who trust in the Lord are compared to Mount Zion. That is the mountain on which Jerusalem is built. It is solid rock. Wars have destroyed the buildings but not the mountain itself. You can become like that if you will place your faith in the Lord.

June 13

As the mountains surround Jerusalem,
so the LORD surrounds his people
both now and forevermore
(Psalm 125:2).

Mount Zion is not the highest mountain in the area. A ring of higher hills surrounds it: the Mount of Olives to the east, Mount Scopus to the north, and other hills to the south and west. The Bible says if you put your trust in the Lord, you will be like Mount Zion; God will surround you as the hills surround Jerusalem. God is always around you in a ring of protection. Troubles may surround you. Psalm 40:12 says, "Troubles without number surround me." Yet, God surrounds your troubles. This is illustrated in the story of Elisha and his servant in 2 Kings 6. The Arameans surrounded them in the city of Dothan. The servant was afraid. Elisha prayed for his servant's eyes to be opened. Suddenly the servant saw chariots of fire encircling the enemy. Psalm 34:7 says, "The angel of the Lord encamps around those who fear him." Wherever you go today and whatever you do, God promises to surround you.

June 14

As the mountains surround Jerusalem,
so the LORD surrounds his people
both now and forevermore
(Psalm 125:2).

It is not just angels who surround you. Hebrews 12:1 says we are surrounded by a great cloud of witnesses. These are Christians who have died and gone to heaven and are cheering us on. The image is of a stadium. We are on the field. They are in the grandstands in heaven. I cannot be dogmatic, but I think those who have died are able to see us here on earth. I think they pray for us and root for us. That encourages me to run the race. More important than angels and saints, the very presence of God surrounds those who trust in him. "The Lord's unfailing love surrounds the man who trusts in him" (Ps. 32:10). The Lord himself is a watching my life, encouraging me, and cheering me on!

June 15

As the mountains surround Jerusalem,
so the LORD surrounds his people
both now and forevermore
(Psalm 125:2).

Thomas Cahill tells the story of how Saint Patrick brought Christianity to Ireland. When he was sixteen, Patrick was captured by Irish pirates and enslaved to an Irish chieftain. He escaped after six years and returned to his family, but God called him to return to Ireland as a missionary. The Roman Empire had collapsed into chaos, and the natives of Ireland were wild and fierce. Yet, in thirty years Ireland was transformed by the gospel. One of his prayers, known as *Saint Patrick's Breastplate*, describes the protection of God he experienced:

> I arise today through God's strength to pilot me: God's might to uphold me, God's wisdom to guide me, God's eye to look before me, God's ear to hear me, God's word to speak to me, God's hand to guard me, God's way to lie before me, God's shield to protect me, God's host to save me from the snares of devils, from temptations to vices, from everyone who shall wish me ill....

> Christ to shield me today against poison, against burning, against drowning, against wounding, so that there may come to be abundance of reward. Christ with me, Christ before me, Christ behind me, Christ in me, Christ beneath me, Christ above me, Christ on my right, Christ on my left, Christ when I lie down, Christ when I sit down, Christ when I arise.[25]

Patrick reflected the security that comes from knowing God surrounds his people.

---

25 Thomas Cahill, *How the Irish Saved Civilization: The Untold Story of Ireland's Heroic Role from the Fall of Rome to the Rise of Medieval Europe* (New York: Doubleday, 1995), 117-119, quoted in Boice, *Psalms*, vol. 3, 1107-1108.

June 16

The scepter of the wicked will not remain
over the land allotted to the righteous,
for then the righteous might use
their hands to do evil
(Psalm 125:3).

The Lord promises your problems will not last forever. This psalm may have been written during the exile or other time of foreign occupation by an evil power. God promised it would not be permanent "lest the righteous be forced to do wrong" (LB). The scepter of the wicked is temporary. Communism did not rule Russia forever, Saddam Hussein did not rule Iraq forever, and dictators will not rule Iran and North Korea forever. God will not allow it. Your problems will not last forever. When you are in your problems, they seem as if they will last forever. That is why you need to read and believe the Bible rather than heed your feelings.

June 17

Do good, O LORD, to those who are good,
to those who are upright in heart.
But those who turn to crooked ways
the LORD will banish with the evildoers.
Peace be upon Jerusalem.
(Psalm 125:4-5).

The Lord will do good to those who are upright in heart. Verses 4 and 5 reflect two very different outcomes for people. Every person is either in verse 4 or verse 5. It is like the continental divide—you are either on one side or the other. The key is the condition of your heart. If your heart is right with God, he will do good to you. If your heart is crooked, he will banish you with the evildoers. We know evildoers such as terrorists are going to hell unless they repent. Verse 5 says the crooked are going to hell with the evildoers. You and I share the same fate as terrorists.

You can cross the spiritual divide. You can move from verse 5 to verse 4 today. Put your trust in the Lord and you will be as unshakeable as Mount Zion. The Lord will surround you as the mountains surround Jerusalem. He will do good to you.

June 18–24
Psalm 121: The Lord Watches Over Me

June 18

I lift up my eyes to the hills—
where does my help come from?
(Psalm 121:1).

The theme of Psalm 121 is that God watches over the lives of those who are in a covenant relationship with him. The first verse is the most difficult to interpret. What does the reference to hills mean? There are three possible interpretations. First, it may refer to the hills positively as a source of help. The title tells us that Psalm 121 is a song of ascents. That means it was sung by pilgrims going up to Jerusalem for one of the times of worship. The pilgrim might catch his first glimpse of Mount Zion or the other hills around Jerusalem and be reminded of God. This is the interpretation of the King James Version: "I will lift up mine eyes unto the hills, from whence cometh my help."

Second, this verse may refer to the hills negatively as a source of anxiety. The pilgrim might see the hills and be fearful of the danger of ambush. Most modern translations render the second line as a question: "I will lift up my eyes to the hills—from whence comes my help?" (NKJV).

Third, this verse may refer to the hills as a source of idolatry or false help. The Canaanites worshipped Baal on "high places" (Num. 33:52). God told the Israelites to destroy them, but they did not (1 Kings 14:22-23). The Living Bible renders this verse as referring to this idolatry: "Shall I look to the mountain gods for help? No!"

June 19

My help comes from the LORD,
the Maker of heaven and earth
(Psalm 121:2).

Regardless of the meaning of verse 1, verse 2 is crystal clear. Real help comes only from the Lord who made heaven and earth. Would you like some help? God offers to help you with your life. Some people don't think they need any help. The first step in getting help is to admit need. The self-sufficient person who refuses to admit need is the farthest from God. Other people know they need help, but they seek it from sources that will not deliver—from creation rather than the creator. I love the mountains and I feel close to God there, but help comes from the one who made the mountains. In your search for help, don't stop short of the Creator. He wants to help you, not as a servant who fulfills your wishes but as a master who guides your life.

June 20

He will not let your foot slip—
he who watches over you will not slumber;
indeed, he who watches over Israel
will neither slumber nor sleep
(Psalm 121:3-4).

God promises to watch over his people. That is the theme of verses 3-8. The phrase "watches over" is found five times in these six verses, in every verse except one. God will look out for you when you belong to him.

Verses 3-4 emphasize that the Lord will guard you at night. These are great verses to read at night when you are worried or afraid. You can go to bed and sleep because God will sit up and watch over you. He never naps! You know from movies that in time of battle one guard is posted while everyone else sleeps. So, if God is going to stay awake, why don't you quit worrying, go to sleep tonight, and get some rest?

June 21

The LORD watches over you—
the LORD is your shade at your right hand;
the sun will not harm you by day,
nor the moon by night
(Psalm 121:5-6).

The Lord will be your shade. That image is probably not very meaningful to you unless you live in a desert climate. In the desert, shade is scarce. Shade is precious. Shade can mean the difference between life and death. Do you remember the story of Jonah? To teach Jonah a lesson, God sent a vine to grow and shade him. Jonah was very happy (Jonah 4:6). God sent a worm to chew the vine. It wilted, and the shade was gone. Jonah wanted to die (Jonah 4:8).

God shelters his people. In our culture, he might be compared to sunscreen that protects you from harmful rays. God is SPF 45!

We usually do not think of the moon as being potentially harmful. The idea is that God is on the job day and night. He watches over you 24/7!

June 22

The LORD will keep you from harm—
he will watch over your life;
the LORD will watch over your coming and going
both now and forevermore
(Psalm 121:7-8).

The Lord will watch over you as you travel. This has been called the traveler's psalm. It has been claimed by generations of Christian travelers. Travel is an increasing source of anxiety in a world of terrorism. Read these verses in the airport before you leave on a trip.

This might also be called the commuter's psalm. Many people spend a large amount of time each day traveling to and from work or school. God watches over you in traffic. Many times I have felt that angels were helping me as I drove, helping me see a car at the last second or dodge an obstacle. What a comfort to know God is watching over us as we make our way through our daily routine. If you will be driving today, why not recite this promise right now?

June 23

The LORD will keep you from harm—
he will watch over your life;
the LORD will watch over your coming and going
both now and forevermore
(Psalm 121:7-8).

The skeptic might question the truth of these verses. Verse 3 says, "He will not let your foot slip," yet Christians slip and break bones all the time. Verse 7 says, "The Lord will keep you from harm," yet Christians are injured and even killed in traffic accidents and plane crashes. Do these verses really have meaning, or are they just religious sentiment?

God does permit Christians to suffer injury or even death, but he does not permit us to be overwhelmed or destroyed. God must edit the script before any events can play out in our lives. God is with us in everything we face. God enables us to withstand anything life throws at us. If it is our time to die, God ushers us home. Our lives are never lost or destroyed. God will not permit that. He is watching over us.

June 24

The LORD will keep you from harm—
he will watch over your life;
the LORD will watch over your coming and going
both now and forevermore
(Psalm 121:7-8).

If this psalm is true, why do you worry? Why do you not live with confidence? Sometimes it does not seem he is watching over you. In those times you may choose to believe what seems to be so or you may choose to believe what the Bible says is so. Will you bulk up your faith by choosing to trust his Word rather than your feelings?

The Lord wants to help you with your life. Lift up your eyes, beyond the hills, to the one who made them. Ask him to be your help.

June 25—July 1
Psalm 91: The Lord Covers Me

June 25

He who dwells in the shelter of the Most High
will rest in the shadow of the Almighty.
I will say of the LORD, "He is my refuge and my fortress,
my God, in whom I trust"
(Psalm 91:1-2).

On the battlefield—at least in the battlefields depicted in movies—one might hear the expression, "Take cover!" When bullets fly or bombs explode, there is the need to find the protection of covering overhead.

The images in this psalm relate to shelter or covering. The psalmist uses four words that convey that image in these first two verses: "shelter," "shadow," "refuge," and "fortress." These words depict the covering of a rock overhang. The psalmist links four names of God to his four words for shelter. It is "the Most High," the Almighty," "the Lord," and "my God" who offers shelter. Derek Kidner writes, "'Most High' is a title which cuts every threat down to size."[26]

The psalmist says he dwells in the shelter of this God. Where do you live? You probably have a street address that locates your physical shelter. What is your spiritual address? Are you living under the shelter of the Most High? If you would live a life of faith, you need a sense of being "covered" by the Almighty himself.

---

26 Derek Kidner, *Psalms 73-150*, vol. 14b of *The Tyndale Old Testament Commentaries*, D. J. Wiseman, ed. (Downers Grove, Ill: Intervarsity, 1973), 332.

June 26

Surely he will save you from the fowler's snare
and from the deadly pestilence.
He will cover you with his feathers,
and under his wings you will find refuge;
his faithfulness will be your shield and rampart
(Psalm 91:3-4).

The image in these verses is of a mother bird covering her young with her wings to protect them from a predator. A mother hen foraging for food in a field will allow her chicks to roam some distance away from her. If she sees the shadow of a hawk, she will cluck to her chicks and spread her wings. The chicks, hearing the danger call, run to her and scoot under her wings.

Jesus will protect you in that same fashion if you will respond to his call. He said to the people of Jerusalem, "How often I have longed to gather your children together, as a hen gathers her chicks under her wings, but you were not willing" (Matt. 23:37). Are you seeking protection under the wings of Jesus?

June 27

You will not fear the terror of the night,
nor the arrow that flies by day,
nor the pestilence that stalks in the darkness,
nor the plague that destroys at midday
(Psalm 91:5-6).

When I was a kid, I slept in a bedroom by myself. My parents' bedroom at the other end of the hall seemed miles away. If our house creaked or a shadow from the window fell on the wall, I imagined all kinds of terror in the night. I would pull my covers over me. I always felt safer when I was under the covers. The simple covering of a blanket gave me the security I needed to go to sleep.

God covers his people. His covering is not the imaginary protection of a security blanket but a real presence that inspires confident living in any situation. The four time references in these verses (night, day, darkness, midday) indicate that God covers his people around the clock. If you are being attacked by coworkers or former friends (the arrow that flies by day), if you are battling physical problems (the pestilence that stalks in the darkness or the plague that destroys at midday), or if you cannot sleep because of worry (the terror of the night), would you ask God to cover you? Would you place your faith in his protection and relax? He's got you covered.

June 28

A thousand may fall at your side,
ten thousand at your right hand,
but it will not come near you.
You will only observe with your eyes
and see the punishment of the wicked
(Psalm 91:7-8).

Lord Craven lived in London during the plague. As the epidemic spread in his neighborhood, he decided to go to his country home until the danger was over. His coach and six horses were readied, and his baggage was packed. As he walked down the hall of his house with his hat, his cane, and his gloves, he overheard one of his servants say to another servant, "I suppose, by my Lord's quitting London to avoid the plague, that his God lives in the country, and not in town." Lord Craven stopped. "My God," he thought, "lives everywhere, and can preserve me in town as well as in the country. I will stay where I am. Lord, pardon this unbelief, and that distrust of thy providence, which made me think of running from thy hand." He immediately ordered his horses to be taken from the coach, and the baggage to be unloaded. He stayed in London, was a great help to his sick neighbors, and never caught the plague.[27]

There are times when we must stand our ground, refuse to run away from a tough situation, and trust the covering of God. These are times when our faith is made stronger.

---

27 C. H. Spurgeon, *Psalms 79-103*, vol.4 of *The Treasury of David* (Grand Rapids: Baker, 1977), 241-242.

June 29

If you make the Most High your dwelling—
even the LORD, who is my refuge—
then no harm will befall you,
no disaster will come near your tent.
For he will command his angels concerning you
to guard you in all your ways;
they will lift you up in their hands,
so that you will not strike your foot against a stone
(Psalm 91:9-12).

The promises of this psalm can be misapplied. The sweeping language of this psalm invites abuse. Satan misused these verses when he tempted Jesus in the desert (Luke 4:9-12). The devil took Jesus to a high point on the temple and tried to get him to jump off in order to prove he was the Son of God. Satan quoted these verses from Psalm 91 to Jesus as evidence no harm would come to him. Jesus responded by quoting Deuteronomy 6:16: "Do not put the Lord your God to the test."

It is not a mark of great faith to put ourselves in dangerous situations and demand that God care for us. Great faith does not demand that the armies of God show up according to our agenda. Great faith simply obeys God and trusts God's protection in the course of obedience.

Later in his ministry, God did send an angel to help Jesus. When Jesus submitted to the Father's will in the Garden of Gethsemane, an angel appeared from heaven to strengthen him (Luke 22:43). God sends angels according to his timetable, not ours.

June 30

You will tread upon the lion and the cobra;
you will trample the great lion and the serpent
(Psalm 91:13).

Both the lion and the serpent are used in Scripture to symbolize the danger of the devil. Peter says, "Your enemy the devil prowls around like a roaring lion, looking for someone to devour" (1 Pet. 5:8). John writes, "The great dragon was hurled down—that ancient serpent called the devil, or Satan, who leads the whole world astray" (Rev. 12:9). The Bible admonishes us to beware of the power of the devil and the danger of temptation in our lives. However, the Bible does not intend for us to fear the devil. Some Christians seem to worry about demons and other spiritual forces as if we are helpless before them. The Bible tells Christians instead to live with confidence. "You, dear children, are from God and have overcome them, because the one who is in you is greater than the one who is in the world" (1 John 4:4).

Because God covers me, I will tread on the lion and the cobra. I will be wary of evil, but I will not live in fear of evil. "The God of peace will soon crush Satan under your feet" (Rom. 16:20).

July 1

> *"Because he loves me," says the LORD, "I will rescue him;*
> *I will protect him, for he acknowledges my name.*
> *He will call upon me, and I will answer him;*
> *I will be with him in trouble,*
> *I will deliver him and honor him.*
> *With long life will I satisfy him*
> *and show him my salvation"*
> *(Psalm 91:14-16).*

How does one experience the promises of this psalm? The last three verses tell us our part and God's part.

Our part is to love God, to acknowledge his name, and to call to him. The promises of this psalm are for those who are in a love relationship with God, who acknowledge that he is Lord, and who call out to him in faith.

God's part is that he promises to rescue us, protect us, answer us, be with us in trouble, deliver us, honor us, satisfy us, and show us his salvation. Wow! That's a great deal for us! Would you reaffirm your covenant relationship with God and snuggle under the protection of his covering?

July

The Holiness God Desires

One of the greatest needs in the church in America today is for holiness—honesty, purity, righteousness, and integrity. There is a great deal of profession of religion in America, but there is a shortage of distinctive holiness. Three out of four adults in America identify themselves as Christians, but when questioned about matters of honesty or purity, many give answers no different from those who do not call themselves Christians. We seem to rationalize that salvation by grace lessens the need for holiness in our lives.

This month we will study a group of psalms that call us to holiness. These psalms remind us that God is holy and that those who belong to him must also be holy. They describe in practical terms what holiness means. Let's examine our lives this month as we discover the holiness God desires.

July 2–8
Psalm 101: I Will Be Careful to Lead a
Blameless Life

July 2

I will sing of your love and justice;
to you, O LORD I will sing praise.
I will be careful to lead a blameless life—
when will you come to me?
(Psalm 101:1-2).

The theme of this psalm is stated in the first line of verse 2: "I will be careful to lead a blameless life." The key word in the psalm is "blameless." It means "whole, complete, sound, without obvious defect." It does not mean perfection. The best commentary on this word is Job 1:1: "In the land of Uz there lived a man whose name was Job. This man was blameless and upright; he feared God and shunned evil." Job was not perfect. At the end of the book he had to repent of some things he had said. But Job was blameless. He was upright, he feared God, and he shunned evil. That is what it means to be blameless.

There are two applications of this psalm. First, apply it to yourself. In the first half of this psalm, David speaks primarily as a man of God. Second, pray this for our government leaders. In the second half of the psalm, David speaks as king. This psalm has been called "The King's Mirror." It has been loved by righteous kings and leaders throughout the centuries. The seventeenth century Duke of Saxon, Earnest the Pious, sent a copy of this psalm to an unfaithful official. It became a proverb when a leader did something wrong to say of him: "He'll be getting a copy of the prince's psalm to read."[28] As we celebrate our nation's birthday this week, it is a good time to pray for holiness among our nation's leaders.

---

28 Franz Delitzsch, *Psalms*, vol. 5 of *Commentary on the Old Testament*, C. F. Keil and F. Delitzsch, eds. (repr., Grand Rapids: William B. Eerdmans, 1984), 3:107.

July 3

I will sing of your love and justice;
to you, O LORD I will sing praise.
I will be careful to lead a blameless life—
when will you come to me?
(Psalm 101:1-2).

This psalm is a pledge, a commitment. I believe in the power of commitment. At least ten times in this psalm is the phrase "I will." The human will in its own power is weak, but the human will energized by the spirit of Jesus is strong. Paul wrote, "I can do everything through him who gives me strength" (Phil. 4:13). This week I challenge you to make five commitments, to make five "I will" statements.

First, I challenge you to say, "I will sing of God's love and justice." What does this statement have to do with integrity and righteousness? We become what we celebrate. If we celebrate the love and justice of God, we will become like God. If we celebrate love without justice, we become soft and compromising. If we celebrate justice without love, we become harsh and unforgiving. Thus, the foundation of integrity is worship. There is no morality without theology; there is no good without God. That is why we cannot sanitize faith from public life in America. We want kids to be righteous, but we will not let them mention God in a graduation speech. That will not work. We must not impose faith on anyone, but we must not deny our heritage. Before this psalm says, "I will lead a blameless life," it says, "I will sing of God's love and justice." I challenge you to deliberately choose to celebrate God's character. Will you say today, "I will sing of God's love and justice"?

July 4

I will walk in my house
with blameless heart
(Psalm 101:2).

Second, I challenge you to say, "I will walk in my house with a blameless heart."
What are you like at home? Are you nicer to the bank teller than to your
wife? Do you take your work frustrations out on your kids? It is easy to
walk at church with a blameless heart. What would your family say about
your walk at home? What is your reputation among those who know you
best? Perhaps you need to make some changes in the way you act at home.
Say today, "I will walk in my house with a blameless heart."

As we celebrate our nation's birthday today, pray this verse for the
leaders of our nation. Pray for their personal righteousness. Some people
say that the personal life of a public servant should not matter to us. They
say we should only be concerned with public policy and not with private
morality. The Bible will not allow that division between the private and the
public. It says what we are in public proceeds from what we are in private. A
leader who has no integrity in his home will have no integrity in his office.
Pray that our leaders may walk in their houses with blameless hearts.

July 5

*I will set before my eyes
no vile thing
(Psalm 101:3a).*

Third, I challenge you to say, "I will set before my eyes no vile thing." How relevant the Bible is to our video generation! Video is everywhere: in our cell phones, in our cars, and in our worship centers. The Internet gives us the opportunity to set almost anything in the universe before our eyes in the privacy of our homes. With opportunity comes temptation. What do you set before your eyes? Take control of what you view. Think about the websites you visit and the magazines you scan. Job made a covenant with his eyes not to look lustfully at a girl (Job 31:1). Say today, "I will set before my eyes no vile thing."

July 6

The deeds of faithless men I hate;
they will not cling to me.
Men of perverse heart shall be far from me;
I will have nothing to do with evil
(Psalm 101:3b–4).

Fourth, I challenge you to say, "I will have nothing to do with evil." David says he hates the deeds of evil men—not the people but their deeds. He recognizes that evil tends to cling to a person. If you see a tick crawling on your arm, do you leave it there? No, you remove it quickly because you recognize its nature is to cling to you. In the same way, evil must be quickly removed from your life.

David wants to keep evil far from him. Some people want to hang around the edge of evil and dabble in it just a little. However, it is hard to remain on the fringe of evil. It is like a whirlpool that pulls you into its vortex. Say today, "I will have nothing to do with evil."

July 7

Whoever slanders his neighbor in secret,
him will I put to silence;
whoever has haughty eyes and a proud heart,
him will I not endure.
My eyes will be on the faithful in the land,
that they may dwell with me;
he whose walk is blameless
will minister to me
(Psalm 101:5-6).

In the second half of this psalm David shifts to his role as king. The commitments in verses 5-8 are beyond our power to make, but we can pray them for our leaders. *Here is the fifth "I will" that I challenge you to state: I will pray that our government leaders will not tolerate evil in their administrations but will surround themselves with those who are blameless.*

A strong moral compass is the most important quality in a political leader. We often choose our elected officials based on economic policy or military experience or party affiliation. These are no substitute for personal righteousness. It is said that politics is the art of compromise. Yet, these verses reflect an unwavering commitment to truth and integrity. Some things must be non-negotiable in a leader's life. Pray for leaders with the backbone described in these verses. "By justice a king gives a country stability, but one who is greedy for bribes tears it down" (Prov. 29:4).

July 8

No one who practices deceit
will dwell in my house;
no one who speaks falsely
will stand in my presence.
Every morning I will put to silence
all the wicked of the land;
I will cut off every evildoer
from the city of the LORD
(Psalm 101:7-8).

THE MESSAGE translates verse 7: "No one who traffics in lies gets a job with me." The advisors and consultants that surround a leader have a powerful effect upon him and his policy. King David recognized the power of an advisor. When Absalom revolted against the king, David fled the capital city of Jerusalem. Hushai wanted to join David in exile. David sent Hushai back to Absalom to oppose the advice he would receive from Ahithophel. Absalom listened to the advice of Hushai rather than that of Ahithophel. Hushai's counsel gave David time to get away (2 Sam. 16-17).

We often pray for our president, Congress, and other elected leaders, but we should also pray for their staffs and advisors. These people have a huge impact upon the direction of our nation. Pray that our leaders will surround themselves with those who are blameless. "The wise king winnows out the wicked" (Prov. 20:26).

July 9–15
Psalm 15: What Does It Mean to Be Holy?

July 9

LORD, who may dwell in your sanctuary?
Who may live on your holy hill?
(Psalm 15:1).

Psalm 15 begins with a question. It is a question concerning who can approach God and live with him. God lives on a "holy hill." Where is God's holy hill? The phrase has two meanings.

First, it refers to Jerusalem, the hill where the temple was located, the place God made his presence known to Israel. Pilgrims may have sung this psalm as they traveled to Jerusalem for the annual feasts. This psalm helped them examine their hearts as they prepared to meet God in worship. This is an appropriate psalm for Christians to read as we examine our hearts in preparation for celebrating the Lord's Supper.

Second, the holy hill refers to heaven, the dwelling place of God. The person who lives with God in heaven must be holy. Holiness is not the means to salvation, but it is the result of salvation. This psalm is not about justification, but it is about sanctification. We get things backward. We sometimes think that we have to be holy to be saved, but that after conversion it does not matter how we live. Instead, God saves us when we recognize we are not holy. Then he begins to make us holy.

July 10

He whose walk is blameless
and who does what is righteous
(Psalm 15:2a).

What does God want you to be? Psalm 15 contains a checklist that is representative of the holiness God requires. The list includes six couplets, each beginning with "whose" or "who." Over the next six days we will consider one of these couplets each day. Our goal is to understand the holiness God expects. Let me ask you six questions based on these couplets.

The first question: Are you known as a person of character in your daily life? The person who may dwell with God is "he whose walk is blameless and who does what is righteous." This is a general statement about character. It is a summary of the other five couplets that follow. Your walk represents your daily routine. You walk into the kitchen, the office, the bank, the grocery store, or the classroom. Is your reputation in these places blameless? That does not indicate perfection. It refers to the general nature of your life. The Bible says, "Noah was a righteous man, blameless among the people of his time, and he walked with God" (Gen. 6:9). Is your walk blameless?

July 11

Who speaks the truth from his heart
and has no slander on his tongue
(Psalm 15:2b-3a).

With the second couplet, the psalmist begins to give more specific examples of the holiness God expects. Holiness or righteousness will be evident in the way you talk. *The second question is: Are the words you speak true and helpful?* What is your conversation like? The person who dwells with God speaks the truth from his heart. It is not enough just to speak the truth. Some things are true, but they do not need to be told. Some gossip is true, but it is destructive. The righteous person speaks words that are not only true but helpful and constructive as well. Alan Redpath writes of a fellowship group he formed in his church during a time of congregational conflict. The members subscribed to a simple formula before speaking of any person or subject:

> T—Is it true?
> H—Is it helpful?
> I—Is it inspiring?
> N—Is it necessary?
> K—Is it kind?

If what you are about to say does not pass those tests, you should keep your mouth shut![29] Marlo Schalesky has written that you enter every conversation with two hypothetical buckets. One is filled with gasoline, the other with water. When gossip is whispered, you choose which bucket you will empty.[30]

---

29 Alan Redpath, "The Making of a Man of God," in *A Passion For Preaching: Reflections on the Art of Preaching: Essays in Honor of Stephen F. Oldford*, compiled by David L. Oldford (Nashville: Thomas Nelson, 1989), 156-162.

30 Marlo Schalesky, "Gossip Extinguishers," *Discipleship Journal,* January/February 1996, 86.

July 12

Who does his neighbor no wrong
and casts no slur on his fellowman
(Psalm 15:3b).

Holiness exhibits itself in your relationships with those around you. *The third question: Do you treat your neighbors and work associates fairly?* In the 1980s Barry Minkow founded ZZZ Best Carpet Cleaning as a teenager. He built his business into an empire worth $250 million on Wall Street. He was called a "whiz kid" and a "wonder boy." In 1987 his empire crumbled. He was convicted of fraud and sentenced to twenty-five years in federal prison. After serving seven years, he was released. Minkow reflected on what he had learned:

> During the 87 months I was in federal custody, I met thousands of men, and we all shared on thing in common. None of us ever planned on being there. That's right. None of the doctors, lawyers, accountants and other professionals that I met ever started their careers with the premeditated plan of compromising their integrity. In every case they can pinpoint a specific time when they made a subtle departure from the legitimate....
>
> I was at a customer's house cleaning the carpeting. When I was finished I asked the lady if she wanted me to Scotchguard her carpets. The extra charge was $100 but when I went out to the truck to fill the sprayer, there was none left. Rather than telling the customer and going back to the shop to pick up another gallon, I took a shortcut: I sprayed water on her carpeting and said it was Scotchguard.[31]

Minkow traced a three-stage pattern in his life and in the lives of those he met in prison: compromise led to corruption, and corruption led to collapse.

---

31 Barry Minkow, "My Million-Dollar Lesson About Compromise," *New Man,* January/February 1996, 34, 36.

July 13

Who despises a vile man
but honors those who fear the LORD
(Psalm 15:4a).

The fourth question: Are you following good role models? Who are your heroes? A British poll conducted by Opinium Research asked adults who they would want their children to look up to. Family members topped the list, followed by multi-millionaire entrepreneur and daredevil, Richard Branson, in second. Jesus came in third. In fourth place were teachers, followed by South African leader Nelson Mandella in fifth, Princess Diana in sixth, and celebrity chef Jamie Oliver in seventh. Winston Churchill ranked eighth, Martin Luther King, Jr., ninth, and Microsoft founder Bill Gates, tenth. Jesus and King were the only two religious figures on the list.[32] One way to gauge American role models is to check the most popular celebrity searches on your Internet search engine.

Are you giving honor or approval or allegiance to those who have talent, beauty, or charisma but lack character? Your character is evidenced by the people you admire. More than that, you are likely to become like those you esteem. If you want to fear the Lord, focus on heroes who fear the Lord.

---

32 Ethan Cole, "U.K. Poll: Jesus Third Most Popular Role Model for Children," www. christianpost.com (posted February 29, 2008).

July 14

Who keeps his oath
even when it hurts
(Psalm 15:4b).

The fifth question: Are you keeping your commitments? Are you staying true to your word even when it brings you personal pain? The most solemn commitment in one's life, next to the commitment to follow Christ, is the marriage commitment. Many Christians are divorcing, not because of adultery, abuse, or abandonment, but because, "I am not happy anymore." More than one Christian has sat in my office and said to me, "I am divorcing my spouse. I have prayed about this. I am not happy, and I think God wants me to be happy." True holiness is keeping your commitments even when it hurts. There is something more important to God than your personal happiness. It is your personal faithfulness. This is why the Bible says to be very deliberate in making a commitment:

> Do not be quick with your mouth, do not be hasty in your heart to utter anything before God. God is in heaven and you are on earth, so let your words be few. As a dream comes when there are many cares, so the speech of a fool when there are many words. When you make a vow to God, do not delay in fulfilling it. He has no pleasure in fools; fulfill your vow. It is better not to make a vow than to make a vow and not fulfill it. Do not let your mouth lead you into sin. And do not protest to the temple messenger, "My vow was a mistake." Why should God be angry at what you say and destroy the work of your hands? (Ecc. 5:2-6).

July 15

Who lends his money without usury
and does not accept a bribe against the innocent.
He who does these things
will never be shaken
(Psalm 15:5).

The sixth question: Are you honest and fair in your business dealings? The Law required Jews to lend money without interest to fellow Jews. The timeless principle is that integrity and fairness in business dealings are essential components of biblical holiness. Some Christians seem to think there is a wall of separation between their personal lives and their actions in the marketplace. While they would espouse honesty in their personal lives, they think duplicity and deceit are just the way a person does business in the real world. Christ asserts his lordship over every area of your life. Your level of holiness is often more evident on Monday than on Sunday.

Some Christians think biblical principles are not practical in the business world. They feel they have to "play the game" to get ahead. Kickbacks and bribes are just a part of doing business in the real world. Psalm 15 ends with a promise that God's principles will work: "He who does these things will never be shaken."

July 16–22
Psalm 24: Clean Hands and a Pure Heart

July 16

Who may ascend the hill of the LORD?
Who may stand in his holy place?
He who has clean hands and a pure heart
(Psalm 24:3-4a).

Psalm 24 asks a question very similar to that of Psalm 15. It again implies that not just anyone can approach the holy God. Our culture has lost this sense of God's holiness. We treat God with a casual familiarity that neglects his holiness.

As Christians we know that we can approach God only through the intercession of Jesus Christ. He is the only mediator between God and man. He covers our sin with his righteousness and allows us to stand before God clothed in his holiness. He comes within us and begins to transform us into his image. As we approach God in prayer or in worship, we must be conscious of the need to confess and forsake our sin and ask Jesus to cleanse us.

What type cleansing needs to take place in our lives as we come into God's presence? "Who may stand in his holy place?" The psalmist answers his question in a memorable two-part phrase: "He who has clean hands and a pure heart." These two phrases indicate that our cleansing must be both outer and inner. If we would be holy, we must change our actions and change our hearts.

July 17

Who may ascend the hill of the LORD?
Who may stand in his holy place?
He who has clean hands and a pure heart
(Psalm 24:3–4a).

The person who desires fellowship with God must have clean hands and a pure heart. Let me ask you two questions based on this phrase. *The first question: Are your hands clean?* If you were standing before God right now, would you hide your hands behind your back? Is there dirt under your fingernails of which you are ashamed? Your hands refer to your actions. Are you doing anything wrong? Are you involved in activities that displease your Holy Father? Confess your sin and ask for God's cleansing.

Jesus said that salvation is like taking a bath (see John 13:10). He indicated that you only need one spiritual bath, but you need to "wash up" over and over. I will probably take only one shower today, but I will wash my hands several times. You are saved once, but repeatedly you need to be cleansed. Baptism symbolizes the bath of salvation, and the Lord's Supper symbolizes washing your hands. Do you need to wash your hands today?

"I want men everywhere to lift up holy hands in prayer, without anger or disputing" (2 Tim. 2:8). Look at your hands right now. Ask God to cleanse them. Then lift them up in a prayer of thanksgiving to God.

July 18

Who may ascend the hill of the LORD?
Who may stand in his holy place?
He who has clean hands and a pure heart
(Psalm 24:3-4).

The second question: Is your heart pure? God's righteousness goes far beyond outer action to inner desire and motive and thought. Your hands can be clean while your heart is impure. What are the motives behind your actions? What is your thought life like? What would you do if there were no consequences to your actions? If nothing was illegal, nothing was frowned upon, nothing would bring you personal pain, how would you act? Are your deepest secret desires driving you to please God or to satisfy your passions?

Changing your actions without changing your heart is like cutting a dandelion off at ground level. The root remains. It will soon grow back. The good news is that God's cleansing can remove the stain of your heart. God can even replace your old desires and passions with new and better ones. God can give you a heart that yearns for righteousness:

> I will sprinkle clean water on you, and you will be clean; I will cleanse you from all your impurities and from all your idols. I will give you a new heart and put a new spirit within you. I will remove from you your heart of stone and give you a heart of flesh. And I will put my Spirit in you and move you to follow my decrees" (Ezek. 36:25-27).

Will you ask God to give you a pure heart?

July 19

Who may ascend the hill of the LORD?
Who may stand in his holy place?
He who has clean hands and a pure heart
Who does not lift his soul to an idol
or swear by what is false
(Psalm 24:3-4).

Holiness involves not only your hands and your heart. It also involves your soul. The last couplet of verse 4 says the holiness God desires is not just ethical; it is also theological. It is not enough to be pure in your dealings with other people. Your worship of God must also be pure. The Bible asserts that God is a jealous God (Ex. 20:5). God even says that one of his names is "Jealous" (Ex. 34:14). Just as a wife does not want to share her husband's affection with other women, so God does not want to share your affection with other gods. He is not content to be one among many loyalties. The worship of the Lord must be exclusive worship. Are other loyalties in your life competing with your loyalty to God? Are other loyalties becoming idols in your life?

July 20

He will receive blessing from the LORD
and vindication from God his Savior.
Such is the generation of those who seek him,
who seek your face, O God of Jacob
(Psalm 24:5-6).

This psalm has spoken of holiness in terms of hands and hearts and souls. Now it relates holiness to the face of God. The holiness God desires is found in a person who seeks his face. To seek the face of God means to desire a relationship with God. Some people seek the hand of God; they want only what God will give them. Others seek the face of God; they want to know him. The face reveals one's emotions. A smile, a grin, a clenched jaw, and a furrowed brow communicate different emotions. To seek the face of God is to find what causes him to smile, what brings him pleasure. God loves you and seeks a love relationship with you. The person who seeks the face of God—who wants to learn what pleases and displeases God—will receive blessing and vindication from him.

July 21

Lift up your heads, O you gates;
be lifted up, you ancient doors,
that the King of glory may come in.
Who is the king of glory?
The LORD strong and mighty,
the LORD mighty in battle
(Psalm 24:7-8).

This psalm has related holiness to the hands and heart and soul and face. Now it relates holiness to the head. However, the "heads" refer not to the heads of people but to the gates of the city or the temple. The psalmist speaks directly to the gates and calls them to lift their "heads" (that is, to raise the gates), so the King of glory may come in. This is a dramatic and exciting announcement of the arrival of the Lord, the mighty warrior God.

These verses tell us that when we approach God properly in prayer or in worship, he comes to meet us. When we come with clean hands and pure hearts, when our worship is pure and we seek his face, God meets us in worship. We can experience his very real presence in our lives and in our churches.

July 22

Lift up your heads, O you gates;
lift them up, you ancient doors,
that the King of glory may come in.
Who is he, this King of glory?
The LORD Almighty—
he is the King of glory
(Psalm 24:9-10).

The call to the gates to lift their heads is repeated in the last two verses in this psalm. This time the King is identified in slightly different language. He is called "the Lord Almighty." "Almighty" translates the Hebrew word *Sabbaoth*. The King James Version translates this phrase "the Lord of Hosts." It means a commander or leader of divisions. It refers to the armies of angels under the Lord's command. The title emphasizes the majesty and might of our God.

There is a historical fulfillment of the invitation in these verses, a time when the King of glory did enter the gates of Jerusalem. On Palm Sunday, Jesus rode a donkey into the city and presented himself as the rightful king of Jerusalem. The people welcomed him that day, but they did not fully realize he was the King of glory, the Lord Almighty. Five days later they cried for his execution.

There will be yet another fulfillment of these verses. King Jesus will come to us again, riding on a white horse. On his head will be many crowns. He will wear a robe dipped in blood. The armies of heaven will follow him. On his robe will be written, "King of Kings and Lord of Lords" (Rev. 19:16). Those who have sought his face, who have lifted their souls to no other god, who have come before him with clean hands and pure hearts will rejoice as the gates are lifted up and the King of glory comes in.

July 23–29
Psalm 11: How to Live a Holy Life in an
Unholy World

July 23

In the LORD I take refuge.
How then can you say to me:
"Flee like a bird to your mountain.
For look, the wicked bend their bows;
they set their arrows against the strings
to shoot from the shadow
at the upright in heart"
(Psalm 11:1-2).

It is a challenge to live with righteousness and purity when culture is pulling in the opposite direction. Psalm 11 tells how to live a holy life in an unholy world. David wrote this psalm at a time when his values and lifestyle were under attack. What do you do in such a time? First, do not withdraw from the world. David was being counseled to run from his situation. He was encouraged to "flee like a bird to your mountain." Instead David chose to stand his ground with the Lord as his refuge.

Some Christians see no way to live for Christ in an unholy world. They want to get away from it. Some time ago a Christian came to me for counseling. He was tired of the lying, cheating, jealousy, bad language, and impurity in his workplace. He asked me if I knew of a Christian ministry that could use his skills. Certainly God calls some people to leave the marketplace and serve the kingdom vocationally, but he does not want everyone to do that. God wants his people to be engaged in the lost world. Jesus said, "You are the light of the world. A city on a hill cannot be hidden. Neither do men light a lamp and put it under a bowl. Instead they put it on its stand, and it gives light to everyone in the house. In the same way, let your light shine before men, that they may see your good deeds and praise your Father in heaven" (Matt. 5:14-16). God put you where you are for a reason. Do not run from that place unless he tells you to do so.

July 24

"When the foundations are being destroyed,
what can the righteous do?"
(Psalm 11:3).

Verse 3 continues the quotation of the counsel that David received from his advisors. The question reflects a sense of hopelessness, as if the population is so corrupt that the righteous can have no redeeming influence. It is easy for God's saints to feel that way. When the culture seems saturated with relativism, materialism, promiscuity, perversion, and an evolutionary worldview, it does seem that the moral and ethical foundations are being destroyed. Indeed, what can the righteous do?

Do not give up hope. Hopelessness and discouragement are tools of the devil. Elijah experienced this assault. He saw the ingrained idolatry of his culture and the corrupt leadership of the royal family and sank into despair. He told God: "The Israelites have rejected your covenant, broken down your altars, and put your prophets to death with the sword. I am the only one left, and now they are trying to kill me too" (1 Kings 19:14). God revealed to Elijah that all was not hopeless. He had already selected new leadership for Israel. He told Elijah there were seven thousand in Israel who had not bowed their knees to Baal. God always has a plan and a people, even in an unholy world.

David rejected the counsel of hopelessness. You can too. You are not alone in your pursuit of holiness. God is working his plan in your world.

July 25

The LORD is in his holy temple;
the LORD is on his heavenly throne
(Psalm 11:4a).

In order to live a holy life in an unholy world, we must not focus on the situation around us. Certainly we must be aware of our culture so that we can engage it, but that must not be our focus. Our focus must be on the ultimate reality of heaven. That is why Jesus taught us to pray: "Your kingdom come, your will be done, on earth as it is in heaven" (Matt. 6:10). No matter how unholy the world is around us, the Lord is in his holy temple. Even when our society seems to plunge toward new depths of degradation, the Lord is on his heavenly throne. That never changes. Do not be overwhelmed by what is wrong with our world. Focus your attention on what is right in heaven.

July 26

He observes the souls of men;
his eyes examine them
(Psalm 11:4b).

A child is less likely to hit his sister when his father is present. A student is less likely to copy another student's paper when the teacher is in the room. Prisoners are less likely to try to escape when a guard is watching them from the wall. The eyes of an authority figure are a deterrent to evil and a motivation to righteousness. God is watching you. He differs from a parent or teacher or prison guard in that he not only observes your actions but your soul as well. He examines your thoughts and intentions.

However, God's observation of your life is not only to be viewed negatively. It also means that your righteousness never goes unnoticed. In the context of this psalm, David is saying that faithfulness does not escape God's notice. He knows when you reject the pressure of your peers to compromise. God watches as you battle to keep your heart pure. He smiles. He cheers you on. He will remember.

July 27

The LORD examines the righteous,
but the wicked and those who love violence
his soul hates
(Psalm 11:5).

Does God really hate the wicked? Doesn't God love everybody? What does this verse mean? God loves everyone, even the worst sinners. "God demonstrated his love for us in this: While we were still sinners, Christ died for us" (Rom. 5:8). Christians have often explained verses such as Psalm 11:5 by saying God hates the sin but loves the sinner. That is true. However, it goes deeper than that. When we try to soften the wrath of God, we lose sight of its intensity. Verses like this one remind us of the depth of God's wrath and his abhorrence of sin. We add so many clauses explaining the wrath of God that we imply he will probably one day say, "Oh, that's all right. I love you so much I will just overlook your sin." Verses such as this one remind us that God's wrath will indeed remain forever on those who remain in their sin. Only the blood of Jesus can turn away the wrath of God.

July 28

On the wicked he will rain
fiery coals and burning sulfur;
a scorching wind will be their lot
(Psalm 11:6).

Not many devotional books focus on verses like this one! We prefer in our devotional time to meditate on warm statements about the love and mercy of God. When we ignore statements about God's judgment we forfeit a powerful source of motivation for holiness. There may be higher motives for serving God, but there is nothing wrong with shunning sin because of fear of judgment.

This verse reminds us of God's judgment on Sodom and Gomorrah. He rained down burning sulfur on those two cities because of their great wickedness (Genesis 19:24). It also anticipates God's eternal judgment in hell. It too is described in terms of burning sulfur (Rev. 14:10; 20:10). God does not want us to go to hell. That is why he puts clear warnings like this one in the Bible. The fear of God is a powerful motivation for holy living.

July 29

For the LORD is righteous,
he loves justice;
upright men will see his face
(Psalm 11:7).

This psalm concludes with the ultimate motivation for living a holy life. The Lord is righteous. He loves justice. Upright people will see the face of God. To "see the face" of a king was a phrase that indicated special access (Gen. 43:3). Old Testament saints longed to "see the face" of God. Moses asked for that privilege, but his request was denied (Ex. 33:20). Still, these saints clung to that hope of somehow knowing God intimately and seeing his face. That hope, and the prophecy contained in this psalm, is fulfilled in Jesus Christ. Those who are declared holy through his blood and are transformed by his power to live holy lives will see the face of God. "We know that when he appears, we shall be like him, for we shall see him as he is" (1 John 3:2). Of all the rewards of heaven, none will be greater than the privilege of seeing God. May that vision motivate you to live a holy life in an unholy world. Whenever you are tempted to sink to the attitudes and practices of those around you, remember this: the Lord loves justice; upright people will see his face.

August

Learn to Listen to God

Some people say that God seems very distant. They pray and get no answer. They do not hear from God. They conclude God is silent. The problem is not that God is not talking but that we are not listening. The Psalms tell us that God is continually speaking to us. We must learn to recognize how he communicates with us. This month we will study psalms that help us learn to listen to God.

July 30--August 5
Psalm 81: If My People Would Listen to Me!

July 30

If my people would but listen to me,
if Israel would follow my ways
(Psalm 81:13).

Have you ever wanted to tell someone something important but you could not get that person's attention? Perhaps the person was too busy talking to listen. Or perhaps he was so engrossed in the television or some other distraction that he did not hear what you were saying. Psalm 81 indicates that is the way God feels about his people. This psalm expresses the longing of God for his own people to listen to him. Asaph, the writer of the psalm, allows God to speak in the first person through much of this psalm. You can hear the frustration in God's voice. He wants to help his people. He can bless them and guide them, but they do not always listen.

The first thing you must do if you want to hear God is to develop a listening heart. Your lack of communication with God is not a problem with the transmitter; it is a problem with the receiver.

July 31

He says, "I removed the burden from their shoulders;
their hands were set free from the basket.
In your distress you called and I rescued you,
I answered you out of a thundercloud;
I tested you at the waters of Meribah"
(Psalm 81:6-7).

God reminds Israel that they called to him, and he listened and responded. This is a reference to the cries of the Israelites when they were in slavery in Egypt:

> During that long period, the king of Egypt died. The Israelites groaned in their slavery and cried out, and their cry for help went up to God. God heard their groaning and he remembered his covenant with Abraham, and with Isaac and with Jacob. So God looked on the Israelites and was concerned about them (Ex. 2:23).

God responded to their prayers by sending Moses to deliver them from Egypt. He sent a cloud to guide them by day and a pillar of fire to guide them by night. God is implying, "I listened to you. Why won't you listen to me?"

That is a fair question for you as well. God hears your prayers. Do you ever stop and ask, "What do you want to say to me?" Could it be that God is trying to get your attention today so that he can guide you? Would you pray the prayer Samuel prayed: "Speak, for your servant is listening" (1 Sam. 3:10)?

August 1

Hear, O my people, and I will warn you—
if you would but listen to me, O Israel!
You shall have no foreign god among you;
you shall not bow down to an alien god
(Psalm 81:8-9).

I have a combination smoke/carbon monoxide detector in my home. Rather than beeping, it actually talks to me. If it senses smoke or high temperatures, it says, "Warning! Fire! Fire!" If it senses the presence of carbon monoxide, a voice says, "Warning! Carbon monoxide!" It would be foolish for me to ignore that voice in the middle of the night. It would be even more foolish to disable the device because the warning is irritating.

God speaks to you to warn you of spiritual danger. He warns you not to worship other gods. He warns you of the danger of allowing anything other than the living God to receive your greatest allegiance or be your greatest priority. It would be foolish to ignore that warning. It would be even more foolish to stop reading the Bible or going to church so that you would not constantly hear that warning.

August 2

I am the LORD your God,
who brought you up out of Egypt.
Open wide your mouth and I will fill it
(Psalm 81:10).

A robin built her nest on my windowsill. I watched her lay her eggs and hatch them. I watched as she fed her babies. I noticed that the baby birds crouched low in the nest to hide from predators. When they heard a noise that they thought was their mother landing on the nest, they would stretch out their necks and open wide their mouths. They did not want to miss anything she had for them. If they heard me tap on the windowpane, they would immediately open their mouths, thinking the sound might be their mother returning with food.

God tells us to have that kind of attitude. We are to be listening for his voice, because his word is always good, always what we need. He is trying to feed us, if only we would be like the robins and open wide our mouths. God wanted to continue to help Israel as he had in the exodus. He could not feed them if they would not open wide their mouths.

God cannot help you if you are not in a position to receive his help. Faith is the channel through which you receive what God has for you.

August 3

But my people would not listen to me;
Israel would not submit to me.
So I gave them over to their stubborn hearts
to follow their own devices
(Psalm 81:11-12).

When we continually refuse to listen to God, he abandons us to the consequences of our choices. He lets us have our own way. He removes his restraints and allows us to experience the full impact of our rebellion. Even this abandonment is an act of love, for pain is sometimes the only stimulus that will cause us to listen. God "gives over" an individual or a nation as a last resort when they continually refuse to hear him. Paul describes this same process in Romans 1:

> For although they knew God, they neither glorified him as God nor gave thanks to him, but their thinking became futile and their foolish hearts were darkened....
>
> Therefore *God gave them over* in the sinful desires of their hearts to sexual impurity for the degrading of their bodies with one another. They exchanged the truth of God for a lie, and worshipped and served created things rather than the Creator— who is forever praised. Amen.
>
> Because of this, *God gave them over* to shameful lusts. Even their women exchanged natural relations for unnatural ones...
>
> Furthermore, since they did not think it worthwhile to retain the knowledge of God, *he gave them over* to a depraved mind, to do what ought not to be done (Rom. 1:21,24-26, 28, emphasis mine).

The depravity of our culture is evidence God has abandoned our society to the outcomes of its rebellion. You must not let this affect you. Keep your heart tender to the voice of God so that he will never have to "give you over" to get your attention.

August 4

If my people would but listen to me,
if Israel would follow my ways,
(Psalm 81:13).

How does one listen to God? In this verse listening to God is coupled with following his ways. If you want to hear God's voice, daily obey his commands. Perhaps you are praying for direction in your life. Perhaps you have a decision to make, and you want God's guidance. How do you hear from God? When you *don't know* God's plan for you, follow what you *do know* of God's ways. You do know from the Bible much of God's will for you:

- It is God's will that you live with integrity (Micah 5:8).
- It is God's will that you lead a holy life (1 Thess. 4:3).
- It is God's will that you be thankful in all circumstances (1Thess. 5:18).
- It is God's will that you be actively involved in a church family (Heb. 10:25).
- It is God's will that you submit to authority in your life (Rom. 13:1).
- It is God's will that you put his kingdom before personal comfort (Matt. 6:33).
- It is God's will that you be on mission for him (Acts 1:8).

It is in the context of following what you do know that you are able to hear God's voice concerning the things you don't know.

August 5

If my people would but listen to me,
if Israel would follow my ways,
how quickly would I subdue their enemies
and turn my hand against their foes!
Those who hate the LORD would cringe before him,
and their punishment would last forever.
But you would be fed with the finest of wheat;
with honey from the rock I would satisfy you
(Psalm 81:13-16).

God is eager to bless us. God wanted to give Israel victory. He only waited for them to listen to him and follow his ways. Many Christians seem to feel that the guidance of God is mysterious and hidden. They picture themselves eager to do God's will if they could only discover it. They look for signs and methods to discover God's elusive will. That's not the biblical picture. The Bible says the problem is exactly the opposite. The Bible says God longs to bless and guide us, but we keep putting ourselves in a position where it is impossible for him to do so. The key issue in hearing from God in our lives is to align ourselves with his purposes for us.

Imagine a thirsty traveler with an empty cup. Picture a cistern full of water with two pipes protruding from it. One pipe is dry. The other gushes water. The thirsty traveler holds his cup under the dry pipe and prays for God to give him water. How silly! Why does he not simply move to where the water is flowing freely? You may be praying for God's blessing and wondering why he does not send it. God says, "Why don't you move to where I am already pouring out blessing?"

August 6–12
Psalm 19: God Is Talking to You!

August 6

The heavens declare the glory of God;
the skies proclaim the work of his hands.
Day after day they pour forth speech;
night after night they display knowledge
(Psalm 19:1-2).

Psalm 19 describes the two ways God is talking to you—two books he has written to you, two channels he is broadcasting on. This psalm describes God's general and specific revelation of himself to humans.

The first half of this psalm says that God is talking to you through his creation (vv. 1-6). Creation points to a Creator and tells you something of what he is like. Particularly, the psalmist focuses on the revelation of God in the skies. The heavens are talking to you! They "declare" the glory of God. They "proclaim" the works of his hand. Both the daytime and nighttime skies "pour forth speech." The universe announces the majesty, order, and precision of God. Many people spend so much time indoors and so much time with artificial lights blinding them to the stars that they miss this conversation from God. The skies shout that there is a God of glory and creative power.

This is true on a scientific level as well as a personal and emotional level. Some think that astronomy and other sciences tend to lessen or even disprove the mystery or existence of God. This is not true today. In the past century astronomers have learned that the universe had a beginning. Somehow it started. Many astronomers today are open to belief in God.

August 7

There is no speech or language
where their voice is not heard.
Their voice goes out into all the earth,
their words to the ends of the world
(Psalm 19:3–4a).

This revelation of God in the skies is universal. There is no place on earth where God has not revealed himself through creation. Paul makes this point in Romans 1:20: "For since the creation of the world God's invisible qualities—his eternal power and divine nature—have been clearly seen, being understood from what has been made, so that men are without excuse." The Bible says that no one on earth can claim he has not heard communication from God. All people are without excuse for their sins because God has revealed himself worldwide through his creation.

Are you listening to God through his creation? Do you take time to marvel at his sense of beauty and design and rhythm and humor in nature? He designed the universe as a broadcast to humanity.

August 8

In the heavens he has pitched a tent for the sun,
which is like a bridegroom coming forth from his pavilion,
like a champion rejoicing to run his course.
It rises at one end of the heavens
and makes its circuit to the other;
nothing is hidden from its heat
(Psalm 19:4b–6).

These verses celebrate the glory of God in our star, the sun. The sun's course across the sky is compared to a bridegroom coming forth from his tent and to a runner running his race. It is easy to take the sun for granted. It comes up every day. We have all seen it hundreds of times. Yet, the sun is one of God's great gifts to us. It speaks of his careful and faithful provision for us. For example, our earth is tilted toward the sun at a twenty-three degree angle. Scientists tell us that if the angle were only three degrees less, our planet would receive too much heat from the sun and we would not be able to live. If the angle were only three degrees greater, the sun would melt the polar icecaps and throw off the balance of oxygen and carbon dioxide in our atmosphere. God has positioned our planet in the exact relationship to the sun that will allow human life to flourish.

This psalm calls you appreciate the activity of God and recognize the voice of God in the routine workings of creation. God is speaking to you of his majesty and dependability if you will only listen.

August 9

The law of the LORD is perfect,
reviving the soul.
The statutes of the LORD are trustworthy,
making wise the simple.
The precepts of the LORD are right,
giving joy to the heart.
The commands of the LORD are radiant,
giving light to the eyes.
The fear of the LORD is pure
enduring forever.
The ordinances of the LORD are sure
and altogether righteous
(Psalm 19:7-9).

The second half of this psalm reveals a second way God is speaking to you. God is talking to you through the Bible. The skies are an incomplete revelation of God. They cannot communicate the depth of his mercy and love. They do not tell us how to respond to God. God has a second book, a second channel, the Bible. It is his specific revelation to humankind through the nation of Israel. Creation testified to "God" (v. 1), his general name, but Scripture reveals "the Lord" (v. 7), his covenant name. The Bible is a much fuller revelation of God than creation.

Verses 7-9 describe six titles for the Bible: the law of the Lord, the statutes of the Lord, the precepts of the Lord, the commands of the Lord, the fear of the Lord, and the ordinances of the Lord. The fear of the Lord is an unusual title that seems to indicate the proper response to God's Word.

August 10

The law of the LORD is perfect,
reviving the soul.
The statutes of the LORD are trustworthy,
making wise the simple.
The precepts of the LORD are right,
giving joy to the heart.
The commands of the LORD are radiant,
giving light to the eyes.
The fear of the LORD is pure
enduring forever.
The ordinances of the LORD are sure
and altogether righteous
(Psalm 19:7-9).

The six couplets in these verses describe six characteristics of the Bible: The Bible is "perfect." It is without error. The Bible is "trustworthy." It will not lead you astray. The counsel it gives you is always dependable. The Bible is "right." The Bible is "radiant." The Bible is "pure." The Bible is "sure."

These six couplets describe six effects of the Bible. The Bible can revive the soul and can "make wise the simple." The Bible gives "joy to the heart" and "light to the eyes." The Bible "endures forever" and is "altogether righteous." You can experience these benefits in your life if you will learn to listen to God through his written Word, the Bible.

August 11

They are more precious than gold,
than much pure gold;
they are sweeter than honey,
than honey from the comb.
By them is your servant warned;
in keeping them there is great reward
(Psalm 19:10-11).

These verses describe the immense value of the Bible. *The Bible offers great profit: it is more precious than gold.* At one time, I thought about buying some gold as an investment. Advertisements touted gold as the ultimate secure investment. I spent some time researching the gold market, but ultimately my decision not to buy gold was more procrastination than anything else. As I write this, gold has lost a third of its value in the last year. The time I spent studying the Bible this past year has proven far more profitable than the time I spent researching the gold market. I should have spent even more.

The Bible offers great pleasure: it is sweeter than honey. When I was growing up, our family had several hives of bees. Each year we would "rob" honey from the hives. There is nothing quite like honey straight from a hive. Yet, the Bible yields greater sweetness and joy in life than any other pleasure.

The Bible offers great protection: by its words one is warned of disaster. Our nation has an Early Warning System to warn against nuclear attack. The Bible warns of dangers that will destroy our relationships and our souls. By reading and heeding the Bible we are protected from catastrophic danger.

August 12

Who can discern his errors?
Forgive my hidden faults.
Keep your servant also from willful sins;
may they not rule over me.
Then will I be blameless,
innocent of great transgression.
May the words of my mouth and the meditation of my heart
be pleasing in your sight,
O LORD, my Rock and my Redeemer
(Psalm 19:12-14).

Psalm 19 ends with a prayer for forgiveness and protection and guidance. The last verse is a great prayer to pray as you begin each day.

This prayer indicates the ultimate purpose of God's revelation. Why is God talking to you through creation and through the Bible? The ultimate purpose of his communication is to bring you into a relationship with him. The glory of creation reveals God's perfection. The righteousness of the law reveals your imperfection. When you become aware of this inconsistency, you may be moved to confess your failures and seek his mercy. It is then that you can know God as your Rock and your Redeemer.

August 13–19
Psalm 119: Learn to Value God's Word (Part 1)

August 13

Blessed are they whose ways are blameless,
who walk according to the law of the LORD
(Psalm 119:1).

While Psalm 19 tells us that God speaks through both creation and Scripture, Psalm 119 focuses exclusively on the clearer of God's method of revelation, his written Word.

Psalm 119 is a unique psalm in many ways. It is the longest psalm and the longest chapter in the Bible with 176 verses. George Wishart, a Bishop of Edinburg in the seventeenth century was saved from death by the length of this psalm. Wishart was sentenced to be hanged. There was a custom that permitted the condemned person to choose a psalm to be sung before his execution. He chose Psalm 119. Before two-thirds of the psalm was sung, a pardon arrived and his life was spared![33] Because of its length we will spend two weeks on this psalm.

Psalm 119 is a celebration of Scripture. Each verse is a prayer or affirmation about the Word of God. The psalmist uses seven different names for the Bible: law, commands, precepts, promises, decrees, word, and statutes. One of these titles is found in every verse except four (vv. 3, 84, 121, 122). God or a pronoun referring to him is contained in every verse but one (v. 121).

The psalmist expresses his high estimation of the Bible. He expresses his feelings toward Scripture. The one who emulates his responses to the Bible will be better able to hear God speak.

---

33 Boice, *Psalms,* vol. 3, 970.

August 14

Blessed are they who keep his statutes
and seek him with all their heart
(Psalm 119:2).

Psalm 119 is an alphabetical acrostic poem. That is, the verses in each section begin with a certain letter of the alphabet. There are other psalms that are acrostic poems, but none as extended as Psalm 119. This psalm has twenty-two sections, one for each of the twenty-two letters in the Hebrew alphabet. Each section contains eight verses, and each verse in that section begins with the same letter of the Hebrew alphabet. For example, you will see in your Bible the Hebrew letter and the word *aleph* before verse 1. That is the first letter in the Hebrew alphabet. Each of the first eight verses begins with a Hebrew word that starts with the letter *aleph*. You will see the Hebrew letter and the word *beth* before verse 9. That is the second letter in the Hebrew alphabet, and in Hebrew each of the next eight verses begins with a word starting with *beth*. I have never seen an English translation that attempts to duplicate this pattern. It would be an interesting exercise to try to paraphrase this psalm so that verses 1-8 each begin with "A," verses 9-16 each begin with "B," etc.

Because of its structure, we will not move through Psalm 119 in order. Instead, we will look at four categories of responses to the Bible expressed by the psalmist. In each case, ask yourself: "Is this my response to the Word of God? Would I be better able to hear God speak to me if I cultivated this attitude toward the Bible?"

August 15

Oh, how I love your law!
I meditate on it all day long
(Psalm 119:97).

I love the Bible!

Nine times the writer of Psalm 119 says he loves the Word of God (vv. 47, 48, 97, 113, 119, 159, 163, 167). His love for the Scriptures prompts him to meditate upon them: "I lift up my hands to your commands, which I love, and I meditate on your decrees" (v. 48). His love for God's commands motivates him to obey them: "I obey your precepts and your statutes, for I love them greatly" (v. 167).

What are your feelings toward the Bible? Your attitude toward the Bible will influence your level of interaction with the Bible. Do you view Bible reading only as an obligation? Is it something you check off your list so you won't feel guilty? Do you look for a short chapter or passage to read so you can get it over with? If so, you are a long way from the attitude of this psalmist. A key to your spiritual growth will be your effort to cultivate a love for the Bible. Ask God to give you a desire for his Word. As you discover truth from the Bible, as you experience its power in your life, and as you meet God through its pages, your love for the Bible will intensify.

August 16

I delight in your decrees;
I will not neglect your word
(Psalm 119:16).

I love the Bible!

Nine times the psalmist says he delights in the Scriptures (vv. 16, 24, 35, 47, 70, 77, 92, 143, 174). He delights especially in the fact that the Word of God has given him guidance in tough times: "Your statutes are my delight; they are my counselors" (v. 24). "If your law had not been my delight, I would have perished in my affliction" (v. 92). "Trouble and distress have come upon me, but your commands are my delight" (v. 143).

On December 26, 2004, a tsunami struck the Indian Ocean. One of those affected by the terrible tidal wave was Michael Mangal, a coconut farmer who had spent his entire life on the tiny island of Pillowpanja in the Andaman Sea. Michael had spent the previous day with other fellow believers celebrating the birth of Jesus. The next morning, as he was preparing for church, the tsunami hit. Waves tore across the island, destroying all that he had ever known. In an instant, everyone and everything on Pillowpanja was swept out to sea. Miraculously, the waves washed Michael back to shore. He was alone. There were no other survivors. His home was gone. He was dirty and dehydrated. The only thing he had was a ring on his right hand. Others might have given into hopelessness, but Michael rejoiced to find a Bible washed up on shore. For twenty-four days Michael read the Bible and drank the milk of coconuts. On January 19, he was rescued by a passing motorboat. The Bible sustained his life through those days.

August 17

The law from your mouth is more precious to me
than thousands of pieces of silver and gold
(Psalm 119:72).

I love the Bible!

You love what you regard as valuable. J. I. Packer writes that the British coronation service includes a time when the moderator of the Church of Scotland hands the new monarch a Bible and calls it "the most valuable thing that this world affords...the royal law...the lively oracles of God." Packer says that the point of his writings has been to confirm that estimate of the Bible. He goes on to recall a hymn by John Newton:

Precious Bible! What a treasure
Does the Word of God afford!
All I want for life or pleasure,
Food and medicine, shield and sword;
Let the world account me poor—
Christ and this, I need no more.[34]

You will delight in the Bible when you come to see its value in your life.

---

34 J. I. Packer, "Our Lifeline," *Christianity Today*, October 28, 1996, 25.

August 18

Your statutes are my heritage forever;
they are the joy of my heart
(Psalm 119:111).

I love the Bible!

Two times the psalmist refers to the joy that the Bible gives him (vv. 14, 111). Many American Christians have lost a sense of joy in the Bible because of overexposure. One can recapture that joy through the eyes of those who discover it for the first time. Marek Kaminski grew up in Communist Poland. His mother possessed no religious beliefs. His father was killed in an automobile accident when Marek was fourteen. Shortly afterward, he found a Bible and began to read it. He had heard that it was a fortune-telling book, but as he read he realized that was not the case. He took three years to read the Bible, two or three chapters a day. After he read the Bible the first time, he became a Christian. Yet, he felt he was missing something, and he wanted to know more. So, he began copying the Bible with his left hand, even though he was right-handed. He felt this process would force him to consider every word. He started copying it when he was nineteen and stopped when he was twenty-two:

> To me, the Word of God is like music. You can listen to the same piece several times and get the melody of it. But to hear the whole sound of it, every instrument, every line, you have to listen several times and pay a lot of attention.... The word of God is so beautiful, the more time you spend in it, the more you appreciate it.[35]

---

35 Marek Kaminski, "My Left-handed Bible," *Christianity Today*, October 23, 1995, 24.

August 19

I open my mouth and pant,
longing for your commands
(Psalm 119:131).

I love the Bible!

The psalmist longs for exposure to the Bible. He can't get enough of the Scriptures. "My soul is consumed with longing for your laws at all times" (v. 20). How does a person come to this kind of longing for the Bible? Mortimer J. Adler wrote a book entitled *How To Read A Book.*[36] He wrote that people read for all they are worth when they are in love and are reading a love letter. They read and reread. They read between the lines. They analyze phrases to discern shades of meaning and clues to the author's heart. They look for nuance and tone and subtleties of expression.

You will love the Bible when you fall in love with its Author. When you love God you will eagerly devour his communication to you. You will open wide your mouth and long for his commands.

---

36 Mortimer J. Adler, *How to Read a Book* (New York: Simon & Schuster, 1967).

August 20–26
Psalm 119: Learn to Value God's Word (Part 2)

August 20

You are good, and what you do is good;
teach me your decrees
(Psalm 119:68).

I want to know the Bible!

Because Psalm 119 is so long, we will devote a second week to the study of this psalm. Last week we examined verses that spoke of the psalmist's attitude toward the Bible. This week we consider his actions toward the Bible.

Ten times the psalmist asks God to teach him his decrees (vv. 12, 26, 33, 64, 66, 68, 108, 124, 135, 171). Have you ever prayed a prayer like that? Do you ask God to teach you his Word? There is a lack of basic Bible knowledge among Christians of our generation. In one of his *Jaywalking* segments, Jay Leno asked people basic Bible questions. In response to "Name one of the ten commandments," one person answered, "Freedom of speech." When asked, "Who was swallowed by a whale?" another person responded, "Pinocchio." A recent Barna poll asked Christians to rate their spiritual maturity in seven areas. Among the seven dimensions of faith maturity, Bible knowledge ranked dead last.[37]

Ask God to teach you his decrees. Then put feet to your prayers by beginning to read the Bible. The New Testament is only about 240 pages long. If you read only eight pages a day, you can read it in a month. Even better, get involved in a Bible study group so that you can discuss the Bible with other people.

---

37 The Barna Report, June 14, 2005, www.barna.org.

August 21

I am your servant; give me discernment
that I may understand your statutes
(Psalm 119:125).

I want to understand the Bible!

It is not enough to know the content of the Bible. The psalmist also asks God to give him understanding. He recognizes that God's wisdom is necessary for understanding and applying the Bible. There are many people who know the stories of the Bible and may even know a great deal about its history, literature, and cultural background, but they do not understand its central message. The New Testament makes clear that it is the Holy Spirit who enables us to understand biblical truth:

> The Spirit searches all things, even the deep things of God. For who among men knows the thoughts of a man except the man's spirit within him? In the same way, no one knows the thoughts of God except the Spirit of God.... The man without the Spirit does not accept the things that come from the Spirit of God, for they are foolishness to him, and he cannot understand them, because they are spiritually discerned (1 Cor. 2:10-11, 14).

Ask God's Spirit to give you discernment that you may understand the message of the wonderful book he has inspired.

August 22

*I meditate on your precepts
and consider your ways
(Psalm 119:15).*

I want to understand the Bible!

Eight times the writer of Psalm 119 speaks of meditation as one way to understand the Bible (vv. 15, 23, 27, 48, 78, 97, 99, 148). Christian meditation is different from meditation in Eastern religions in that Christian meditation is content-oriented. Other religions advise trying to empty the mind in meditation, but biblical meditation exhorts the believer to fill the mind with God's Word. The Bible recommends meditating on God's "wonders" (v. 27), his "precepts" (v. 78), and his "promises" (v. 148). Here's how to meditate on God's Word:

1. As you read the Bible, hear a sermon, or study a Bible lesson, pick out a verse or passage that sparks your interest or stirs your heart.
2. Study a good commentary about this verse to make sure that you understand the correct interpretation. This will keep you from getting off base in your meditation.
3. Pray and ask God to speak to you through this portion of his Word.
4. Read the verse or passage several times. Read it aloud. Read it with emphasis on various words. Read it in different situations throughout the day.
5. Consider your life, your relationships, and your church in light of this verse. What does it mean for your world? What would God have you believe or say or do differently in light of this verse?

August 23

*I have hidden your word in my heart
that I might not sin against you
(Psalm 119:11).*

I want to understand the Bible!

Another key to understanding Scripture is memorization. The psalmist says he has hidden God's word in his heart. Have you memorized any of the Bible? What is the purpose of memorizing scripture?

First, you are better able to meditate on a verse when you have memorized it. You are able to roll it over in your mind again and again until you have heard God speaking through it.

Second, you are able to call verses to mind when you need them in times of temptation or crisis. This is what Jesus did. When Satan tempted him in the desert, he was able to answer him with verses he had memorized from Deuteronomy and Psalms (Matt. 4:1-11). Have you memorized any verses from Deuteronomy or Psalms? If Jesus thought it was important, perhaps it should be important to you, too. The Bible is one of the primary weapons for spiritual warfare (Eph. 6:17). Perhaps you are carrying a weapon without any "bullets" in it, because you have not learned any of God's Word!

Why not start today memorizing Scripture? Select a verse that is meaningful to you. Read it several times. Read it aloud. Write it down. Review it until you can say it from memory. Say it to another person. Stick with that verse until you know it confidently, no matter how long it takes. Then move to another verse. Keep going back to review what you have learned previously.

August 24

I will always obey your law,
for ever and ever
(Psalm 119:44).

I am determined to obey the Bible!

Sixteen times the writer of Psalm 119 expresses his commitment to obey God's commands (vv. 8, 17, 34, 44, 56, 57, 60, 67, 88, 100, 101, 129, 134, 145, 167, 168). He is dismayed by those who do not obey God's law: "Streams of tears flow from my eyes, for your law is not obeyed" (v. 136). It is not enough to know and understand the Bible. One must do what it says. We have seen that there is a great gap in Bible knowledge in our culture. There is an even greater gap in Bible obedience. Our biggest problem is that we do not obey what we know the Bible plainly teaches. We spend more energy trying to determine the timing of the rapture or debating the doctrine of predestination than we do putting the plain truth of the Bible into practice. We are like the two men in Alabama engaged in a Bible-quoting contest. At the end of the heated exchange, the loser apparently shot the winner in the face, killing him. "The suspect retrieved his Bible and realized he was wrong. That made him mad," reported the local police chief.[38]

Are you missing the point of Bible study? "Do not merely listen to the word and so deceive yourselves. Do what it says" (James 1:22). Are you ignoring, rationalizing, or refusing to obey some clear teaching in the Bible?

---

38 "Loser in Bible-Quoting Contest Suspect in Death of Winner," *The Tennessean*, July 19, 1996, 6A.

August 25

I have taken an oath and confirmed it,
that I will follow your righteous laws
(Psalm 119:106).

I am determined to obey the Bible!

Four times the psalmist speaks of the importance of following the commands of the Bible (vv. 33, 63, 106, 166). He recognizes that obeying the Word is a lifelong journey that requires persistence and endurance. Many who confess faith in Christ start out obeying God's Word. They begin well, but somewhere along the way they get discouraged, distracted, or sidetracked. When John Bisagno was a young pastor, his father-in-law, Paul Beck, warned him that few pastors endure in ministry to the end of their careers. Beck noted that many fall victim to immorality or discouragement or liberalism. He said that for every ten people who start out in ministry at age twenty-one, only one is still engaged in ministry at age sixty-five. Bisagno was shocked. He wrote in his Bible the names of twenty-four young men committed to the Lord and his service. Thirty-three years later he reported that only three of the twenty-four were still in ministry.[39] "Teach me, O Lord, to follow your decrees; then I will keep them to the end" (v. 33).

---

39 Steve Farrar, *Finishing Strong* (Colorado Springs: Multnomah, 1995), 15-16.

August 26

My comfort in my suffering is this:
Your promise preserves my life
(Psalm 119:50).

I claim the promises of the Bible!

Six times the psalmist speaks of the promises of the Bible (vv. 41, 50, 76, 116, 140, 154). The writer finds the Bible to be completely true and trustworthy: "Your promises have been thoroughly tested, and your servant loves them" (v. 140). He clings to these promises and stakes his life on them: "Defend my cause and redeem me; preserve my life according to your promise" (v. 154).

Have you claimed the promises God has made to those who are in a covenant relationship with him? Why not take time today to claim those promises either verbally or in writing? I invite you to pray these words aloud right now: "I claim the promise of the Bible that I am right with God through faith alone" (Rom. 3:26). "I claim the promise of the Bible that Jesus is always with me" (Matt. 28:20). "I claim the promise that the Father will provide for my basic needs in life" (Matt. 7:30). "I claim the promise of the Bible that nothing in life can ever separate me from the love of God" (Rom. 8:38-39). "I claim the promise that the Lord is my helper and there is nothing any man can ever do to me" (Heb. 13:6). "I claim the promise that Jesus is coming back for me and will take me to heaven to be with him forever" (John 14:3). You will find spiritual strength by reciting and reaffirming the promises of God's Word. Through them you will hear him speak to you with power and love.

September

Overcome Your Fears

We live in a culture of fear. We have identified and categorized hundreds of kinds of phobias. Verminophobia is the fear of germs. Bathmophobia is the fear of stairs. Myctohylophobia is the fear of dark, wooded areas. Domatophobia is the fear of one's house being on fire. Pupaphobia is the fear of puppets. Triskaidekaphobia is the fear of the number thirteen. Gamophobia is the fear of marriage. Neophobia is the fear of anything new. (Many people in churches have this fear!) Arachibutyrophobia is the fear of peanut butter sticking to the roof of one's mouth. Oddly enough, sequipedalophobia is the fear of long words![40]

God does not want you to live a life paralyzed by fear. He wants you to fear only him. That is the only healthy fear. He does not want you to fear anything or anyone else. This month we will study a group of psalms that tell us how we can overcome our sinful fears and replace them with a healthy fear of God.

---

40 www.phobialist.com (accessed October 9, 2009).

August 27—September 2
Psalm 23: I Will Not Fear Poverty or Death

August 27

The LORD is my shepherd,
I shall not be in want
(Psalm 23:1).

Psalm 23 is the most familiar of the psalms, and one of the most familiar passages in the Bible. Other than the Lord's Prayer, this may be the most memorized passage in the Bible. It has been called the psalm of psalms.

One of the reasons it is so loved is that it addresses two of our most common and biggest fears. The first is the fear of want. One of our greatest fears concerns economic security. Will I be able to pay my bills? Will I get laid off? Can I meet my mortgage? Do I have enough insurance? How will I retire? The other fear is the fear of death. This is the ultimate fear of life. The theme of Psalm 23 is that you need not fear because God takes care of his people.

August 28

The LORD is my shepherd,
I shall not be in want
(Psalm 23:1).

David uses two metaphors to describe this personal, loving care of God for his people. The first metaphor is of a shepherd. God cares for you as a good shepherd cares for his sheep (vv. 1-4). Verse 1 summarizes this section. The first line says, "The Lord is my shepherd." Every word in this great line deserves emphasis.

The Lord is my *shepherd*. David was a shepherd in his youth and a shepherd-king of Israel as an adult (Ps. 78:70-72). He realized everything he had done for sheep, God had done for him. Sheep are foolish and need care. You are like that. God cares for you.

The *Lord* is my shepherd. Yahweh, the only true God, is my manager and caretaker. Jesus identified himself as the good shepherd (John 10:14). Jesus is God. This psalm is about what Jesus wants to be in your life.

The Lord is *my* shepherd. This psalm is true only if you belong to Jesus. If you are fearful, it could be because you are trying to be your own manager.

The implication of all this is stated in the second line of verse 1: "I shall not be in want." This is parallelism by extension in Hebrew poetry. What does it mean to have the Lord as your shepherd? The result is that you will lack nothing. "I have everything I need" (NLT). You need not fear financial loss, because God promises to care for you.

August 29

He makes me lie down in green pastures,
he leads me beside quiet waters,
he restores my soul
(Psalm 23:2-3a).

Verses 2-4 unfold the truth of verse 1, describing the shepherd's care in specific terms. The good shepherd supplies your basic needs. Sheep need food, water, and rest. The good shepherd makes sure the sheep have all three.

"He makes me lie down in green pastures." Green grass is rare in the desert. The good shepherd seeks out lush meadows and beds the sheep there.

"He leads me beside quiet waters." Water is essential to life, and it too is scarce in the land of David. The word "quiet" may be translated "dependable." Many water sources in the desert are not dependable in certain times of the year. The good shepherd takes his sheep to dependable waters.

"He restores my soul." The word soul also means "breath" or "wind." This might be translated, "He lets me get my second wind."

God promises to meet the basic needs of your life. He will provide you with food, water, and rest. You need not fear.

August 30

He guides me in paths of righteousness
for his name's sake
(Psalm 23:3b).

The good shepherd promises to guide you. "Paths of righteousness" means the right or best paths. Sheep are dumb. The shepherd keeps them from dangerous ledges and thorns. People are dumb. We wander, and we choose harmful paths. God guides us in the best paths because he cares for us.

Perhaps you have walked a dog on a leash. The dog may strain at the leash to go in a certain direction, but you, his owner, know what is best and guide him onto the best paths. It is easier for you and better for the dog when he learns to cooperate with you, obey you, and trust you. The same is true in your life. Learn to trust God's direction in your life. Cooperate with the Good Shepherd. He will guide you in the best paths for your life.

How do you know the Good Shepherd will choose the paths that are best for you? It reflects upon the shepherd if something happens to one of his sheep. He guides the sheep in paths of righteousness "for his name's sake." As caretaker of the sheep, the shepherd's reputation is on the line. You need not fear because your welfare is backed by the name of God!

August 31

Even though I walk
through the valley of the shadow of death,
I will fear no evil,
for you are with me;
your rod and your staff,
they comfort me
(Psalm 23:4).

The good shepherd protects you. In order to move the sheep from one oasis to another, the shepherd must take them through some narrow wadis, or ravines. These are places of danger from ambush. The shadows may conceal a crouching lion or bear. You may be going through some dark valley in your life. You may be wondering why God is taking you there. God may be taking you to greener pastures!

Christians go through the valley of the shadow of death. That shadow may be caused by the death of a loved one or your own impending death. You are not exempt from that valley, but you do not have to fear it, because your shepherd is with you. Note that here David turns from speaking about God to speaking to him. He moves from the third person (he) in verses 1-3 to the more personal second person (you) in verse 4. This emphasizes the presence of God. The Christian does not fear the shadows of death because he is never alone.

The shepherd has two pieces of equipment. His rod is a short club to beat off predators. His staff is a long pole with a crook on the end, used to lift a fallen sheep from a crevice. The shepherd protects and rescues. God will protect and rescue you.

September 1

You prepare a table before me
in the presence of my enemies.
(Psalm 23:5a).

Some Bible experts think the image of a shepherd continues throughout this psalm. However, the talk of a house and table and oil do not readily fit that image. I think David transitions here from the experience of his youth as a shepherd to the experience of his adult life as a shepherd-king. The remainder of this psalm suggests that God cares for you as a good host cares for his guests.

The good host prepares a feast and provides a safe haven. Hospitality was and is among the highest virtues in the Eastern world. The host provides protection from enemies. Lot was willing to do almost anything to protect the guests who were residing with him in Sodom. David knew what it was to be a good host. He wanted to show kindness to a descendant of Saul for the sake of his friend Jonathan. He learned Saul was survived by a crippled grandson, Mephibosheth. David invited him to Jerusalem, where he lived in safety, eating at David's table like one of the king's sons (2 Sam. 9). In the same way, God promises to protect you and provide for you at his table.

September 2

You anoint my head with oil;
my cup overflows.
Surely goodness and love will follow me
all the days of my life,
and I will dwell in the house of the LORD
forever
(Psalm 23:5b–6).

The good host shows affection and generosity to his guests. Anointing the head with oil was the common courtesy of the East. Jesus mentioned the failure of Simon to provide this courtesy when he was a guest in Simon's home (Luke 7:46). Perhaps it would be comparable in our society to offering to take someone's coat or offering someone a chair. The overflowing cup is still the mark of a good waiter or host. The amazing thing about these images is that God promises to serve us! Certainly we should be the servants serving him, but God loves us and treats us as honored guests in his home.

Verse 6 is the most amazing verse of all. The good host invites us to live with him forever! The promises of the good shepherd are fulfilled in this life. The promises of the good host are fulfilled in heaven.

Because God meets my every need so graciously and completely, because his care for me extends throughout this life, through the valley of the shadow of death and into eternity, I will fear neither poverty nor death.

September 3–9
Psalm 46: I Will Not Fear Natural Disasters

September 3

*Therefore we will not fear though the earth give way
and the mountains fall into the heart of the sea,
though its waters roar and foam
and the mountains quake with their surging
(Psalm 46:2-3).*

Every area of our country is threatened by some kind of natural disaster. On the west coast the threat is an earthquake, on the east and gulf coasts it is a hurricane, in the interior it is a tornado or flood or drought, and in the mountains it is an avalanche or a blizzard. Are you afraid of storms? When there is a tornado watch or a hurricane watch, how do you respond? Are you agitated and fearful? Sophisticated weather forecasting helps us be prepared for storms, but it also heightens our fears. We know about every storm cell and wind rotation within hundreds of miles. Many people live with a fear of natural disasters.

Psalm 46 helps us deal with this fear. This psalm is a song. It has three stanzas, each marked by the musical term *selah.* There is a chorus after stanzas two and three. Each stanza shares a reason why we do not have to fear natural disasters.

September 4

God is our refuge and strength,
an ever-present help in trouble.
Therefore we will not fear though the earth give way
and the mountains fall into the heart of the sea,
though its waters roar and foam
and the mountains quake with their surging
(Psalm 46:1-3).

The first stanza of this song declares that we will not fear because God is our refuge and our strength. "Refuge" refers to outer protection, and "strength" refers to inner assistance. God will help us in one of two ways. He will either protect us *from* the storms or give us strength *through* the storms. He is an ever-present help in trouble. "He is always ready to help us in time of trouble" (TEV).

On February 5, 2008, a tornado hit Union University in Jackson, Tennessee. Heather Martin was in her dorm room when the storm struck. Her roommate yelled, "Get into the tub, now!" and five girls piled into the bathtub just as the building collapsed. Heather did not get her legs completely in the tub, and they were pinned by the debris. Compressed beneath her, her friend Julie was having difficulty breathing. Heather later wrote about her experience:

> I cannot begin to describe the fear in my heart that this precious person was going to die underneath me. I prayed aloud. I quoted Scripture. At some point I found another friend's hand and she was praying as well. After realizing that this would likely be the night of my death, I was able to move on and focus on simply breathing. At one point I had to tell Julie that I was out of breath and couldn't pray out loud anymore, but that I was still praying in my heart and mind. This was not me being strong or brave or courageous. It was the power of Christ in me. He guided my thoughts. He helped me focus on breathing, praying, and helping encourage Julie to breathe. The whole experience was terrifying, but God was in the midst of us. I recall at times just crying out: "God, You are here. Give us strength."[41]

After forty-five minutes of digging through fifteen feet of rubble, rescue workers were able to reach the five girls. All five survived.

---

41 Heather Martin, "Union student's reflections: My experience in the tornado," www.bpnews.net, posted on February 14, 2008.

September 5

God is our refuge and strength,
an ever-present help in trouble.
Therefore we will not fear though the earth give way
and the mountains fall into the heart of the sea,
though its waters roar and foam
and the mountains quake with their surging
(Psalm 46:1-3).

We will not fear even though the earth gives way and the mountains quake. One of the worst earthquakes in North America occurred near New Madrid, Missouri, on December 16, 1811. Eyewitnesses reported that the ground rolled like waves and that huge cracks opened in the land and then closed. The Mississippi River ran backward. Every home within 250 miles was damaged. Church bells rang on their own a thousand miles away in Boston. In 1811 there were few people in the area. Today the cities of Memphis and Saint Louis sit on the fault line. The United States Geological Survey says there is a 90 percent probability of a significant earthquake by 2040.[42] Should the residents of Memphis and Saint Louis be gripped with fear? No. We will not fear though the earth gives way. However, we need a refuge and strength now before disaster comes. The time to buy a flashlight and bottled water is not after a natural disaster has hit. An emergency kit must be assembled before disaster strikes. Do you have a spiritual emergency kit? Do you have a relationship with God that will sustain you through any disaster?

---

42 www.usgs.gov/prepare/factsheets/NewMadrid.

September 6

There is a river whose streams make glad the city of God,
the holy place where the most high dwells.
God is within her, she will not fall;
God will help her at break of day.
Nations are in uproar, kingdoms fall;
he lifts his voice, the earth melts
(Psalm 46:4-6).

The second stanza of this song declares that we will not fear because our real home is secure. The peaceful tone of these verses contrasts dramatically with the turmoil of verses 2-3. The city of God will not fall. What is the city of God? Jerusalem is the city of God, but that does not fit here. There is no river in Jerusalem. Jerusalem has fallen repeatedly. This city of God is the heavenly Jerusalem (Rev. 21:2). The river is the river of life that flows from the throne of God (Ezek. 47:1-12; Zech. 14:8; Rev. 22:1-2). Even when nations are in uproar, this city will not fall. In 410 AD, the city of Rome fell to the Visigoths. Some were disillusioned. Augustine wrote *The City of God*. He said there are two cities, the city of man and the city of God. The city of God will not fall.

No matter what happens, God is on his throne in heaven. No matter what happens, we are going to heaven to drink from the river of life. If you are not a Christian, you have reason to fear natural disasters. Your fear is justified. You are one lightning bolt, one falling rafter from an eternity in hell. Your fear is intended to bring you to God, so that you will no longer fear.

September 7

Come and see the works of the LORD,
the desolations he has brought on the earth.
He makes wars cease to the ends of the earth;
he breaks the bow and shatters the spear,
he burns the shields with fire.
Be still and know that I am God;
I will be exalted among the nations,
I will be exalted in the earth
(Psalm 46:8-10).

The third stanza of this psalm declares that we will not fear because we can be still and know God. This stanza speaks of God's ultimate victory over all his foes. One day God will conquer his enemies in a great battle and will make all wars cease. The Bible indicates the last days will be a time of both battle and natural disasters. God will be victorious. The psalmist says we should surrender to God now. That is the meaning of the phrase, "Be still." Stop and know God, because he will be exalted among the nations.

Terri Blackstock's novel, *Last Light*, depicts a nominal Christian family in a suburb in Birmingham, Alabama, that experiences the trials of a natural disaster.[43] Suddenly, all devices with computer chips fail— computers quit, cars stop, planes fall, electricity fails, pumps halt. They think it may be a solar event. This church-going family has little strength to deal with this crisis. The only character who is not afraid is an elderly neighbor with cancer. She is unable to get to her chemotherapy, yet she remains calm. She has surrendered her life to God, and she has stilled her heart. When you still your heart, you will not fear.

---

43 Terri Blackstock, *Last Light* (Grand Rapids: Zondervan, 2005).

September 8

The LORD Almighty is with us;
the God of Jacob is our fortress
(Psalm 46:7, 11).

There is a two-line chorus after the second and third stanzas of this song. The first line of the chorus is: "The Lord Almighty is with us." This is the Hebrew name *Yahweh Sabaoth,* which means "The Lord of Hosts." Sometimes in the Bible the word "hosts" refers to the host of stars under God's control. Usually it refers to the divisions or armies of angels under his command. This mighty commander is with us in our daily lives!

The second line of the chorus is: "The God of Jacob is our fortress." Jacob was the least impressive of the patriarchs, a liar and a conniver. Why give God this title? Why not call him the God of Abraham? Because God claims sinners! He is faithful to his covenants! He is the God of us "Jacobs" as well as the Lord of angels!

September 9

The LORD Almighty is with us;
the God of Jacob is our fortress
(Psalm 46:7, 11).

Martin Luther wrote his hymn, *A Mighty Fortress is our God,* based on this psalm. It is one of the greatest hymns ever written. It is a fitting review and conclusion to our study of this psalm:

A mighty fortress is our God,
A bulwark never failing;
Our helper he, amid the flood
Of mortal ills prevailing.
For still our ancient foe
Doth seek to work us woe;
His craft and power are great;
And, armed with cruel hate,
On earth is not his equal.

Did we in our own strength
confide,
Our striving would be losing:
Were not the right man on our side,
The man of God's own choosing.
Dost ask who that may be?
Christ Jesus, it is he,

Lord Sabaoth his name,
From age to age the same,
And he must win the battle.

And though this world, with devils
filled,
Should threaten to undo us;
We will not fear, for God hath
willed
His truth to triumph through us.
The prince of darkness grim,
We tremble not for him;
His rage we can endure,
For lo! His doom is sure,
One little word shall fell him.

September 10–16
Psalm 27: I Will Not Fear the Attack of Terrorists

September 10

When evil men advance against me to devour my flesh,
when my enemies and my foes attack me,
they will stumble and fall.
Though an army besiege me,
my heart will not fear;
though war break out against me,
even then will I be confident
(Psalm 27:2-3).

The events of September 11, 2001, shattered our sense of national security. We now live with color-coded warnings about the extent of danger. Many people identify anxiety concerning terrorism as one of their greatest fears. God does not want us to live in fear of terrorism. Long before 9/11 he inspired David to write the words of Psalm 27.

David knew a lot about the attacks of an enemy. When he was about sixteen years old, the Philistines attacked his nation. Their champion was Goliath. He was nine feet tall, wore armor that weighed 125 pounds, and carried a spear with a fifteen-pound spearhead. The Bible says the Israelites were "terrified." That's terrorism. David was not afraid. He volunteered to face Goliath. The giant threatened to feed his flesh to the birds, but David killed Goliath.

David came into King Saul's service. Saul grew jealous of David and tried to kill him. For seven years Saul pursued David. After Saul died, David became king, but Saul's general, Ishbosheth, led eleven tribes against David. The civil war lasted seven more years.

Finally, David became king. Then the Philistines attacked again! David also battled the Ammonites, Moabites, Arameans, and Edomites. He knew about attacks and terrorism. Yet, he did not live in fear. How did he do it?

September 11

The LORD is my light and my salvation—
whom shall I fear?
The LORD is the stronghold of my life—
of whom shall I be afraid?
(Psalm 27:1).

David was not afraid of armies and wars because he focused on three roles that God played in his life. *First, David said, the Lord is my light.* Fear is associated with darkness. Haunted houses and scary movies are dark. Most crimes are committed at night. Many disasters affect power supplies and plunge their victims into darkness. Darkness is frightening because it cloaks the unknown. Light dispels darkness. Jesus said, "I am the light of the world" (John 8:12). Jesus reveals to us the truth about our lives. We have insight that dispels the darkness and reveals the unknown. We know we are not alone. We know there is a plan for our lives. We know good will eventually triumph over evil. We know where we are going. This insight enables us to live above our fears.

Nelson Price tells about his brief football career. One night during a big game he picked up a fumble and, with ninety-five yards of open field ahead of him, started running for the end zone. As he ran, he glanced over his left shoulder to see if anyone was coming after him. There was nothing there but his shadow. He glanced over his right shoulder, however, and saw another shadow looming behind him. He knew he was about to be tackled. He cut left, then right. Every time he glanced back, the shadow was still there. He zigzagged and dodged all the way down the field. Winded, he reached the end zone and looked around. No one was there. The fans in the stands were laughing. He slowly realized the stadium lights created criss-cross shadows. He had been running from his own shadow.[44]

---

44 Nelson Price, *Shadows We Run From* (Nashville: Broadman Press, 1975), 9-10.

September 12

The LORD is my light and my salvation—
whom shall I fear?
The LORD is the stronghold of my life—
of whom shall I be afraid?
(Psalm 27:1).

Second, the Lord is my salvation. Confidence in life comes from knowing we are saved. The root fear of our lives is punishment for our sins in hell. It is wise to fear hell if that is where we are headed. The fear of hell is designed to drive us to the love of God. God has heaped hell upon his only Son so that we do not have to experience it. The name "Jesus" is a form of this word "salvation" (Matt. 1:21). He is the only one who can save us from our sins and enable us to live a life without fear. "Since the children have flesh and blood, he too shared in their humanity so that by his death he might destroy him who holds the power of death—that is, the devil—and free those who all their lives were held in slavery by their fear of death" (Heb. 2:14-15). When the Lord is my salvation, I no longer need to fear death or hell.

September 13

The LORD is my light and my salvation—
whom shall I fear?
The LORD is the stronghold of my life—
of whom shall I be afraid?
(Psalm 27:1).

Third, the Lord is my stronghold. David had several fortresses. He conquered Jerusalem and made it his stronghold. Yet, David did not find his security in these defenses. The Lord was his real protection and defense. We might paraphrase this line to read, "The Lord is my homeland security."

Notice the personal pronoun "my" in each of these three phrases—my light, my salvation, and my stronghold. These benefits come from a personal relationship with God through Jesus Christ.

God does not want us to live with a fear of flying or paranoia about entering tall buildings. We can live with confidence. Lisa Beamer is the widow of 9/11 hero Todd Beamer. Todd was among those who attacked the terrorists on Flight 93 and prevented them from crashing another plane into Washington. You might expect that Lisa would live with fear and anxiety after all she experienced. Lisa said, "I am less afraid now than I was before September 11, because I have a greater sense of God's sovereignty. He's in control, and he has a plan for the world. Not only that, he has plans for me individually. And he loves me more than any human being ever could love me. So what's really to fear?"[45]

---

45 Lisa Beamer, "Looking Up," *Today's Christian Woman*, September/October 2002, 50.

September 14

One thing I ask of the LORD,
this is what I seek;
that I may dwell in the house of the LORD
all the days of my life,
to gaze upon the beauty of the LORD
and to seek him in his temple.
For in the day of trouble
he will keep me safe in his dwelling;
he will hide me in the shelter of his tabernacle
and set me high upon a rock.
Then my head will be exalted
above the enemies who surround me;
at his tabernacle will I sacrifice with shouts of joy;
I will sing and make music to the LORD
(Psalm 27:4-6).

We can overcome our fear by focusing on the presence of God with us. David says he "desires one thing." God's presence is his focus. David shares a powerful image of God's presence: God hides us in his temple. David uses four different terms in these verses to refer to God's meeting place: house, temple, dwelling, and tabernacle. David wanted to build the temple, but the dwelling of God was still a tent or tabernacle. This was the place where God's presence was manifested on earth. God was everywhere, but he made himself accessible there. David says God will hide us in his tabernacle. David is speaking figuratively of God's presence that dispels his fear. As Christians, our lives are hid with Christ in God (Col. 3:3). Everyday it is as if we are in God's temple, hidden from anything that can destroy us.

September 15

Hear my voice when I call, O LORD;
be merciful to me and answer me.
My heart says to you, "Seek his face!"
Your face, O LORD, I will seek.
Do not hide your face from me,
do not turn your servant away in anger;
you have been my helper.
Do not reject me or forsake me,
O God my Savior.
Though my father and mother forsake me,
the LORD will receive me
(Psalm 27:7–10).

The presence of God dispels fear. In this section David shares a second image of the presence of God: God turns his face toward us. In this section, David begins to talk directly to God in prayer. He seeks God's face. God is spirit, but the face of God represents his presence, his character, and his personality. Many Arab women veil their faces from everyone but their husbands. In heaven the church will be like a radiant bride, and we will see the face of God (Rev. 22:4). Those in hell will be shut out from the face of God (2 Thess. 1:9).

Even now we can experience something of the face of God through Jesus. "For God who said, 'Let light shine out of darkness,'" made his light shine in our hearts to give us the light of the knowledge of the glory of God in the face of Christ" (2 Cor. 4:6).

September 16

I am still confident of this:
I will see the goodness of the LORD
in the land of the living.
Wait for the LORD;
be strong and take heart
and wait for the LORD
(Psalm 27:13-14).

David ends this great psalm with a statement of confidence. If you belong to God, you can be confident that you will see the goodness of God in the land of the living. You can have this kind of confidence through a relationship with Christ.

On September 11, 2001, insurance executive Leslie Haskin was on the thirty-sixth floor of the World Trade Center's North Tower. At 8:46 a.m., a plane smashed into the building fifty floors above. "I was standing there in front of this window just watching the debris, the pieces of furniture and paper…that's when I started to notice the body parts and everything falling outside the window. It was almost immediate." Raised in a Christian home, Leslie had made professional achievement and wealth, not God, the focus of her life. After 9/11, post-traumatic stress syndrome took away her ability to work. She had recurring nightmares and was afraid to cross bridges, enter buildings, ride elevators, or even drive a car. Unable to work, she lost her savings and her home. Leslie's brother reached out to her, prayed with her, and used Scripture to restore her peace of mind. "I repented before the Lord and gave him my life," Leslie said. "I gave him my heart, my pain, my September 11, the monster that it is, and everything else. I gave him all of me, and that's when the healing and the recovery actually started."[46]

---

46 www.coralridge.org/impact/newsletter/September headlines 2006.

September 17–23
Psalm 56: I Will Not Fear What Other
People Say

September 17

Be merciful to me, O God, for men hotly pursue me;
all day long they press their attack.
My slanderers pursue me all day long;
many are attacking me in their pride.

All day long they twist my words;
they are always plotting to harm me.
They conspire, they lurk,
they watch my steps,
eager to take my life
(Psalm 56:1-2, 5-6).

The fear of what people say about you may seem a lot smaller than the fear of terrorists or hurricanes, but it can be a powerful force in your life. The title tells us that David wrote this psalm when the Philistines had seized him at Gath. David was a fugitive from King Saul. In desperation, he ran to Gath, the hometown of Goliath! On top of that, David was carrying Goliath's sword! The Philistines recognized David and imprisoned him. While being held by the Philistines he wrote this psalm. Amazingly, David seemed more concerned with what people were saying about him than with the possibility of his death. That is the power of this fear. David was affected by the lies of Saul about him. He even cared what the Philistines said! David bemoaned that "all day long they twist my words." Have you ever had someone do that?

September 18

Be merciful to me, O God, for men hotly pursue me;
all day long they press their attack.
My slanderers pursue me all day long;
many are attacking me in their pride.

All day long they twist my words;
they are always plotting to harm me.
They conspire, they lurk,
they watch my steps,
eager to take my life
(Psalm 56:1-2, 5-6).

This fear can cause you to mold your life to fit the expectations of others. In one of Aesop's fables, a miller and his son were driving a donkey to town to sell him. They met a group of girls. One of them cried, "Did you every see such fools, to be trudging along on foot when they ought to be riding!" So the man put the boy on the donkey, and they continued. They met a group of old men. One of them huffed, "No one pays any respect to old age in these days. Look at that idle young rogue riding, while his poor old father has to walk." So the son dismounted, and his father got on the donkey. They soon came to a group of women. "Shame on you, lazybones!" they cried. "How can you ride while that poor little lad can hardly keep up with you?" The miller took his son on the donkey with him. As they came to the edge of the village, a townsman called out, "I have a good mind to report you to the authorities for overloading that poor beast so shamelessly. You big fellows should be better able to carry that donkey than the other way around." So the miller and his son tied the donkey's legs together and, with a pole across their shoulders, carried it over the bridge that led to town. The crowd laughed at the sight. The donkey became frightened in the uproar, struggled to free himself, slipped over the bridge rail, and was drowned. Aesop's moral is: try to please all and you end by pleasing none.[47]

---

47 *Aesop's Fables* (New York: Lancer Books, 1968), 53-54.

September 19

On no account let them escape;
in your anger, O God, bring down the nations.
Record my lament;
list my tears on your scroll—
are they not in your record?
Then my enemies will turn back
when I call for help.
By this I will know that God is for me
(Psalm 56:7-9).

God is very aware of the pain this fear can cause in your life. These verses are a prayer by David asking God to help him and bring down his enemies. Verse 8 is a great verse of comfort. The New International Version strays from the consensus translation at two points. First, "lament" is usually translated "wanderings" or "tossings." "You've kept track of my every toss and turn through sleepless nights" (THE MESSAGE). Second, the New International Version says, "List my tears in your scroll," but most translations read, "Put my tears in your bottle" (NKJV, NRSV). In Israel, glass blowers make tiny tear bottles to sell. Whether the image is a scroll or a bottle, the point is the same: God keeps track of your tears. God knows every time you turn over in a worry-filled, sleepless night. God keeps a record of every single tear that runs down your cheek. If you are the victim of slander or gossip or unfounded criticism, God knows and cares about you.

September 20

When I am afraid,
I will trust in you.
In God, whose word I praise,
in God I trust; I will not be afraid.
What can mortal man do to me?
(Psalm 56:3-4).

This is the chorus of this psalm. These verses are repeated with slight variation in verses 10-11. Here David shares how he was able to overcome his fear of gossip, slander, and false accusation. You can overcome your fear of what others say if you with do three things.

First, choose to trust God. You have a choice when confronted with the whispers of your accusers. You can choose to worry or your can choose to trust God. Make a deliberate choice to trust God. Every time you are tempted to worry about what someone says about you, stop yourself and reaffirm your choice to trust God rather than to worry. You will have to do this repeatedly. You may have to do it several times a day or even several times an hour. Gradually, you can retrain your mind. You can develop new thought patterns, choosing to consciously replace worry with faith.

September 21

When I am afraid,
I will trust in you.
In God, whose word I praise,
in God I trust; I will not be afraid.
What can mortal man do to me?
(Psalm 56:3-4).

The second thing you can do to overcome this fear is to evaluate criticism by the Word of God. You must not totally ignore what other people say about you. The Bible says to seek counsel and accept correction. You can learn even from your enemies. A teachable spirit is the beginning of wisdom.

How do you know whether someone's opinion is valid and worthy of consideration or whether it should be ignored? David says, "In God, whose word I praise." David had the Torah, and he had the promise of God to him when he was sixteen that one day he would be king. He evaluated the words of Saul and the Philistines by the words of God.

You must evaluate criticism by the Word of God in the Bible and by his call on your life. If the words of others do not square with the message and spirit of the Bible, ignore them. If someone gives you advice that contradicts God's clear call on your life, do not listen to what they say.

September 22

When I am afraid,
I will trust in you.
In God, whose word I praise,
in God I trust; I will not be afraid.
What can mortal man do to me?
(Psalm 56:3-4).

There is a third thing you can do to overcome the fear of what others say about you. Ask yourself the question: "What can man do to me?" David asked that question. You might be thinking, "People can do a lot! People can kill me, abuse me, ruin my reputation, and make my life miserable." That is true, but in the long run, in light of eternity, people can do nothing to you. Your standing with God cannot be altered by the words of human beings. Your acceptance with the Father cannot be affected by rumor or criticism. The things that matter most in your life are secure.

"If God is for us, who can be against us? He who did not spare his own Son, but gave him up for us all—how will he not also, along with him, graciously give us all things? Who will bring any charge against those whom God has chosen? It is God who justifies. Who is he that condemns?" (Rom. 8:31-34).

September 23

I am under vows to you, O God;
I will present my thank offerings to you.
For you have delivered me from death
and my feet from stumbling,
that I may walk before God
in the light of life
(Psalm 56:12-13).

David ends this psalm with a renewed commitment. He promises to keep his vows to God no matter what. He focuses, not on the opinions of others or the pain they cause, but on the positive blessings of God for which he is grateful.

That needs to be your commitment and focus as well. Even when you are under attack, keep your commitments to God and focus on his blessings with a positive spirit. Do not let the attacks of others drag you into negativity.

I want to close our study of this psalm by sharing a personal testimony. God used this psalm mightily in my own life. My father died in an accident just before Christmas in 1979. He was driving a tractor when a tree fell on him and killed him. He was fifty-eight years old. I was in seminary in Texas. I flew home to Georgia for the funeral but then had to fly back immediately for final exams. I returned a week later for Christmas and then left again. I am an only child, and I hated to leave my mother alone. I had been studying through Psalms in my prayer time for a few months. One morning in early January 1980, I came to this psalm. God used these words to comfort me, and I wrote a hymn based on this text:

I Trust in God without a Fear

When life becomes a vicious throng,
I turn to God for He is strong.
He knows my tossings and my tears.
I trust in God without a fear.

When trouble lurks at every turn,
I cast on God all my concern.
His presence bottles up my tears.
I trust in God without a fear.

Though Satan toss and buffet me,
My refuge shall forever be,
In God whose word I hold so dear,
In God I trust without a fear.

My vows to him I must fulfill.
I fail, but he is faithful still.
He has no equal, has no peer.
I trust in God without a fear.

September 24–30
Psalm 112: I Will Fear the Lord

September 24

Praise the LORD.
Blessed is the man who fears the LORD,
who finds great delight in his commands
(Psalm 112:1).

The Bible tells us that we should not live in fear. We need not fear terrorists or disasters or criticism or peer pressure or poverty or death. However, there is one healthy fear. We are to fear the Lord. Many people are confused about what it means to fear God. Psalm 112 answers some of our questions.

Why fear God? To understand Psalm 112, you have to begin with Psalm 111. These two psalms go together. Each is an acrostic. Each has twenty-two lines, and each line begins with a successive letter of the Hebrew alphabet. Psalm 111 is a poem about the greatness of God. Psalm 112 is about the fear of God. The bridge is 111:9-10:

He provided redemption for his people;
he ordained his covenant forever—
holy and awesome is his name.
The fear of the Lord is the beginning of wisdom;
all who follow his precepts have good understanding.
To him belongs eternal praise.

You are to fear God because He is holy and awesome. You are to fear him because, in contrast to his holiness, you are a sinner. God's wrath is upon sin. One reason I became a Christian is because I did not want to go to hell. There is nothing wrong with that motivation. Teachers and parents know the value of a healthy fear of punishment. That healthy fear is the fountain of wisdom.

September 25

Praise the LORD.
Blessed is the man who fears the LORD,
who finds great delight in his commands
(Psalm 112:1).

Can you fear God and love him at the same time? Yes. The Bible says, "Love the Lord your God with all your heart and with all your soul and with all your strength" (Deut. 6:5). It also says, "Fear the Lord your God, serve him only and take your oaths in his name" (Deut. 6:13). The same passage that says to love God also says to fear him.

Isn't fear just an Old Testament response to God? No. Jesus said, ""I tell you, my friends, do not be afraid of those who kill the body and after that can do no more. But I will show you whom you should fear: Fear him who, after the killing of the body, has power to throw you into hell. Yes, I tell you, fear him" (Luke 12:4-5).

Why fear God after you are saved? You no longer fear going to hell, but you still fear his displeasure. "Then the church throughout Judea, Galilee, and Samaria enjoyed a time of peace. It was strengthened; and encouraged by the Holy Spirit, it grew in numbers, living in the fear of the Lord" (Acts 9:31). Love heightens this kind of fear. The more you love God, the more you fear him and desire to please him.

September 26

Praise the LORD.
Blessed is the man who fears the LORD,
who finds great delight in his commands
(Psalm 112:1).

How do you know if you fear God? There is a simple test in Psalm 112:1. Remember that Hebrew poetry features parallelism; the second line of a verse restates the first. When you fear God you delight in his commands. Psalm 128:1 states the same truth in a similar way: "Blessed are all who fear the Lord, who walk in his ways." Fear of God is evidenced by obedience to God. If you are cheating on your wife, lying to your boss, disrespecting your parents, stealing from your company, or worshipping something besides God, you do not fear the Lord. The conduct of our society is evidence that most people do not fear God.

Henry Blackaby was asked what it would take for a moral and spiritual turnaround in our country. He noted every great awakening rediscovered some lost truth about God. When asked what truth we had lost he replied, "The fear of the Lord."[48] Do you fear the Lord? Do you delight in his commands? Do you walk in his ways?

---

48 John Franklin, "The Root Cause of America's Moral Collapse," *Light*, September-October 1999, 4.

September 27

His children will be mighty in the land;
the generation of the upright will be blessed
(Psalm 112:2).

What are the benefits of fearing God? This is the main theme of this psalm. It lists three results of fearing God. *First, when you fear God, you provide a blessing to your children.* Children tend to absorb the fears of their parents. If you fear storms, you will likely transmit that anxiety to your children. If you are stressed over money, they will probably unconsciously adopt that same fear. Conversely, if you fear God you pass on a great heritage that will make them mighty in the land and bless them. Your children need to see you in awe of God and his holiness.

One of my favorite passages in C. S. Lewis's *The Lion, the Witch, and the Wardrobe* is the scene where Mr. Beaver describes the majesty of the lion Aslan to the children. Lucy asks, "Is—is he safe?" Replies Mr. Beaver: "Safe? Who said anything about safe? 'Course he isn't safe. But he's good. He's the King, I tell you."[49] Our God is not safe, but He is good. He's the King, I tell you.

---

49 C. S. Lewis, *The Lion, the Witch and the Wardrobe* (1950, New York: Collier Books, 1970), 75-76.

September 28

Wealth and riches are in his house,
and his righteousness endures forever.
Even in darkness light dawns for the upright,
for the gracious and compassionate and righteous man.
Good will comes to him who is generous and lends freely,
who conducts his affairs with justice.
Surely he will never be shaken;
a righteous man will be remembered forever
(Psalm 112:3-6).

What are the benefits of fearing God? Second, when you fear God, you give yourself the best opportunity for a prosperous and stable life. The right life is the best life. God had our well being in mind when he gave us his commandments. The fear of the Lord brings an order to our lives that conveys blessing. It produces a graciousness, compassion, fairness, and generosity that make for good relationships and good business.

My dad was a kind, Christian man. I loved him, but I also respected him. I feared his punishment if I did wrong. That healthy fear was a deterrent from evil when I was growing up. I stayed away from some things simply because I didn't want to get a spanking! That fear protected and blessed me. It saved me from some bad choices. The same is true with our Heavenly Father. We love him, but we also fear him. That fear channels us into a life of stability and blessing.

September 29

He will have no fear of bad news;
his heart is steadfast, trusting in the LORD.
His heart is secure, he will have no fear;
in the end he will look in triumph on his foes.
He has scattered abroad his gifts to the poor,
his righteousness endures forever;
his horn will be lifted high in honor
(Psalm 112:7-9).

What are the benefits of fearing God? Third, when you fear God you fear nothing else. There is a serenity in life when you rest in the sovereign plan of a holy and awesome God. Oswald Chambers said: "The remarkable thing about fearing God is that when you fear God, you fear nothing else, whereas if you don't fear God you fear everything else." [50]

In an interview with USA Weekend, actor Will Smith was asked about his belief in God. He responded, "I don't believe in God anthropomorphically. I don't believe God gets angry and zaps someone." Later in the interview he was asked what scares him. He answered, "I am afraid of everything.... I'm most afraid of being afraid."[51]

---

50 Oswald Chambers, *Run Today's Race* in *The Complete Works of Oswald Chambers* (Grand Rapids: Discovery House, 2000), 1147.
51 *USA Weekend*, November 22, 1998, 7.

September 30

The wicked man will see and be vexed,
he will gnash his teeth and waste away;
the longings of the wicked will come to nothing.
(Psalm 112:10).

What is it like for those who do not fear God? The psalm ends with a brief summary of the fate of those who do not fear God: in frustration and anger, they waste away. Without the proper foundation of a healthy fear of God, lives tend to self-destruct.

After the death of Christian philosopher Blaise Pascal in 1662, a servant found a piece of paper in the lining of his master's coat. It contained Pascal's handwriting. The date revealed he had carried it for eight years. He had written,

> In the Year of Grace, 1654,
> On Monday, 23rd of November, Feast of St. Clement,
> Pope and Martyr, and of others in the Martyrology,
> Vigil of Saint Chrysogonus, Martyr and others,
> From about half past ten in the evening
> until about half past twelve
> > FIRE
> God of Abraham, God of Isaac, God of Jacob
> not of the philosophers and scholars.
> Certitude. Certitude. Feeling. Joy. Peace.
> God of Jesus Christ.[52]

Apparently Pascal had encountered the holiness of the Living God, and that had made all the difference.

---

52 Donald W. McCullough, *The Trivialization of God* (Colorado Springs: NavPress, 1995), 77.

October

How to Live Wisely

The biblical books of Job, Psalms, Proverbs, Ecclesiastes, and Song of Songs are called wisdom literature. These books give practical advice about wise living. This month we will study a group of psalms that are especially designated as wisdom psalms. They help us know how to live wisely. The opposite of wisdom is folly. Some of these psalms describe what it means to be a fool. This month we will examine two psalms that expose folly and two that portray wisdom.

October 1–7
Psalm 14: How to Recognize a Fool

October 1

The fool says in his heart,
"There is no God."
They are corrupt, their deeds are vile;
there is no one who does good
(Psalm 14:1).

When the Bible says something once, you should pay attention. When the Bible says something twice, you should really take notice. Psalm 14 is repeated, with only minor variations, in Psalm 53. Psalms 14 and 53 describe folly. They tell us how to recognize a fool. I want to learn the characteristics of a fool, because I do not want to be a fool in God's eyes.

There are three Hebrew words translated "fool" in the wisdom literature of the Old Testament. *Kesil* refers to someone who is stubborn, hotheaded, and reckless. *Ewil* is a person who is even more hardened, impatient, and always thinks he is right. *Nabal* is the fool who is completely close-minded and insensitive.

Bible students may remember this third word from the name of a foolish man in 1 Samuel 25. David's men had protected Nabal's flocks, and David asked for provisions for his men. Nabal was completely insensitive to David's request. Nabal's wife, Abigail, sought to control the damage Nabal had done. She went to David and apologized, "May my lord pay no attention to that wicked man Nabal. He is just like his name—his name is Fool, and folly goes with him" (1 Sam. 25:25). This word, *nabal*, is the word translated "fool" in Psalm 14. Folly is by definition close-mindedness to wise counsel.

October 2

The fool says in his heart,
"There is no God."
They are corrupt, their deeds are vile;
there is no one who does good
(Psalm 14:1).

There are two characteristics of this kind of fool according to this verse. First, he denies or ignores God. "The fool says in his heart, 'There is no god.'" The Bible says the fear of the Lord is the beginning of wisdom, so the denial of God is the foundation of folly. You may be an educated, intellectual person, but if you deny the existence of God, the Bible says you are a fool. Why? Romans 1:19-22 is a commentary on this verse. Paul says the existence of God is plain to everyone through creation. Paul says humans who deny God in spite of the evidence become confused in their thinking: "For although they knew God, they neither glorified him as God nor gave thanks to him, but their thinking became futile and their foolish hearts were darkened. Although they claimed to be wise, they became fools" (Rom. 1:21-22).

A fool may say with his mouth that there is a God, but he says in his heart that there is not. In other words, this verse may reflect a kind of practical atheism. A person may say all the right things about the existence of God, but the inner rationale of his life is that God does not exist in the biblical sense. Psalm 10:4 says, "In his pride the wicked does not seek him; in all his thoughts there is no room for God." Practical atheism does not deny God. It simply ignores him.

October 3

The fool says in his heart,
"There is no God."
They are corrupt, their deeds are vile;
there is no one who does good
(Psalm 14:1).

The second half of this verse reveals a second characteristic of a fool. The deeds of a fool are vile, and he does no good. There is a moral component to wisdom. A person who ignores God's commands cannot claim to be wise no matter his education or experience or accolades from society. If there is an omnipotent Creator God who has instructed his human creation how to live, it is sheer folly to ignore his commands.

This verse asserts folly is both theological and moral. The Bible links the denial of God to the denial of good. There is a vital connection between what you believe and how you behave, between loving God and loving neighbor.

How do you recognize a fool? A fool is someone who denies or ignores God and turns aside from the way God has prescribed to live.

October 4

The LORD looks down from heaven
on the sons of men
to see if there are any who understand,
any who seek God.
All have turned aside,
they have together become corrupt;
there is no one who does good,
not even one
(Psalm 14:2-3).

As you read verse 1, you could probably think of someone you know at work or school who fits the definition of a fool. It is easy to find people in our culture who fit this profile. However, the psalm takes a disturbing turn in verses 2-3. It says all have turned aside. No one seeks God. No one does good, not even one. The language is surprisingly universal and inclusive. It says we are all fools, because we have all rebelled against God. Even the best of us has acted foolishly in choosing his or her own way over God's way. How then do you recognize a fool? Look in the mirror.

This realization is the first step in the plan of salvation. Paul quotes these verses in Romans 3:12 to show that we are all sinners. We are all completely and utterly lost with no hope of reforming ourselves. If you think you are basically a good person, you do not yet "get it." As long as you think you are better than someone else, you are far from the kingdom. When you come to see the complete folly of your life, your utter foolishness, then you are near the door to the kingdom of God.

October 5

The LORD looks down from heaven
on the sons of men
to see if there are any who understand,
any who seek God.
All have turned aside,
they have together become corrupt;
there is no one who does good,
not even one
(Psalm 14:2-3).

This psalm is a counterpoint to Psalm 8. Psalm 8 describes the inherent worth of each person, and Psalm 14 reveals the folly of every person. You need both of these psalms in your life.

You need the affirmation of Psalm 8. There will be times in your life when you feel small and insignificant. "When I consider your heavens, the work of your fingers, the moon and the stars, which you have set in place, what is man that you are mindful of him?" (Ps. 8:3-4). You need to know that God created you in his image and that you have intrinsic value and worth just as you are: "You made him a little lower than the heavenly beings and crowned him with glory and honor" (Ps. 8:5).

You also need the conviction of Psalm 14. There will be times in your life when you feel big and important and self-righteous. You need to be reminded that you have been a fool. You need to see that the best of your efforts have a measure of corrupt motives. "There is no one who does good." You are a sinner in need of God's grace.

These are the two basic truths the Bible teaches about people. All humans are valuable by virtue of their creation in the image of God. All humans are fools who have chosen their own way. You will get off course in life if you lose sight of either one of these truths.

October 6

Will evildoers never learn—
those who devour my people as men eat bread
and who do not call on the LORD?
There they are, overwhelmed with dread,
for God is present in the company of the righteous.
You evildoers frustrate the plans of the poor,
but the LORD is their refuge
(Psalm 14:4-6).

While verses 2-3 are words of conviction, verses 4-6 are words of encouragement. Those who recognize they are fools become wise. They receive God's grace and become teachable by him. They become righteous, because they receive by faith the righteousness of Christ and begin to follow his commands.

Those who recognize they are fools will be attacked by those who do not recognize their folly. Fools will devour God's people as men eat bread. You have seen slanted media attacks that ridiculed Christians and belittled their faith. Perhaps you have been subjected to attack at work or school because of your beliefs or values.

These verses offer encouragement to the people of God when they are devoured as bread. God says these fools will be overwhelmed with dread, because he is present in the company of the righteous. God's presence gives you the strength to withstand ridicule and the courage to answer your critics with truth and grace.

October 7

Oh, that salvation for Israel would come out of Zion!
When the LORD restores the fortunes of his people,
let Jacob rejoice and Israel be glad!
(Psalm 14:7).

This psalm ends with the plea that salvation would come from Zion. Zion is a name given to the hill on which the city of Jerusalem is built. This prayer was answered when Jesus died for our sins on Mount Zion.

> As you come to him, the living Stone—rejected by men but chosen by God and precious to him—you also, like living stones, are being built into a spiritual house to be a holy priesthood, offering spiritual sacrifices acceptable to God through Jesus Christ. For in Scripture it says: "See, I lay a stone in Zion, a chosen and precious cornerstone, and the one who trusts in him will never be put to shame" (1 Pet. 2:4-6).

Salvation has come from Zion for fools who will admit their folly.

At Christ's second coming, salvation will come from Zion to deliver God's people from the oppression of fools who have not believed in him: "Then I looked, and there before me was the Lamb, standing on Mount Zion, and with him 144,000 who had his name and his Father's name written on their foreheads" (Rev. 14:1).

Do you want to live wisely? The first step is to recognize that you are a fool. Admit you have acted foolishly in rejecting God's way. Become humble and teachable. That is the path to wisdom.

October 8–14
Psalm 73: Are You Thinking as a Fool?

October 8

Surely God is good to Israel,
to those who are pure in heart.
But as for me, my feet had almost slipped;
I had nearly lost my foothold.
For I envied the arrogant
when I saw the prosperity of the wicked
(Psalm 73:1-3).

Even the wise can sometimes think as fools think. Your perspective on life makes all the difference in your spiritual health. If you can maintain a positive, biblical perspective on life, you can live with faith and joy in any circumstance. However, the problems of life will distort your thinking if you let them.

Psalm 73 is a case study in the importance of perspective. The writer of this psalm experiences some problems in his life. Though he does not tell us specifically what those problems are, we can infer from his writing that they include health problems, financial problems, criticism, and injustice. This causes a crisis of faith in his life. This psalm was written by Asaph, who was a Levite. He was David's minister of music. Even a spiritual leader can lose faith if his perspective on life becomes distorted.

Asaph wrote verses 1-3 after he had come through the crisis. These verses are an introduction looking back on his experience, written after the rest of the psalm. Now he has the right perspective on life (v. 1). But he recalls how close he came to spiritual disaster (v. 2). He was "close to the edge of the cliff" (LB). "My faith was almost gone" (TEV). The root of his problem was that he compared his situation to that of others and thought everyone else was better off than he. He began to envy the wicked (v. 3). Have you ever thought that way?

October 9

They have no struggles;
their bodies are healthy and strong.
They are free from the burdens common to man;
they are not plagued by human ills.
Therefore pride is their necklace;
they clothe themselves with violence.

They say, "How can God know?
Does the Most High have knowledge?"
This is what the wicked are like—
always carefree, they increase in wealth.
Surely in vain have I kept my heart pure;
in vain have I washed my hands in innocence.
All day long I have been plagued;
I have been punished every morning
(Psalm 73:4-6, 11-14).

These verses are in the present tense, written while Asaph was in the middle of his crisis. They reflect his distorted thinking. In verses 4-12 he describes his view of the wicked. He sees them as healthy, arrogant, and prosperous. Do you ever feel that those who scoff at God seem to suffer no ill effects? That was Asaph's thinking.

By contrast, in verses13-14 he describes his condition. He feels he has kept himself pure in vain and that he is plagued with troubles every day. Do you ever feel that it does not pay to serve God?

Psychologists say that depression is sometimes caused by distorted thinking. David Burns describes the common elements of distorted thinking: (1) overgeneralization: seeing single events as a never-ending pattern (Note the words "always" in verse 12 and "never" in verse 14.); (2) mental filter: picking out a single negative detail and dwelling on it exclusively; (3) all or nothing thinking: perceiving issues entirely one way or the other.[53] These elements of negative thinking can produce a crisis in marriage or in one's relationship with God.

---

53 David Burns, *Feeling Good: The New Mood Therapy*, rev. ed. (New York: Avon Books, 1999), 32-34.

October 10

If I had said, "I will speak thus,"
I would have betrayed your children.
When I tried to understand all this,
it was oppressive to me
till I entered the sanctuary of God;
then I understood their final destiny
(Psalm 73:15-17).

How did Asaph get out of this pattern of thinking? How did he recover his perspective on life? These verses reveal the turning point in his battle with despair. There is a glimmer of hope in verse 15. Asaph recognizes he should not spread his attitude to others, especially children. He recognizes something is wrong in his thinking and for the first time thinks of someone other than himself. Still, he cannot reason his way out of his distorted thinking (v. 16). The key to his turnaround is worship (v. 17). His perspective is restored when he enters the sanctuary of God. Worship restores a right perspective in life. It takes our eyes off ourselves. It focuses our vision on the character of God. In worship we experience the greatness of God and the littleness of humankind. Worship does not answer all our questions, but it restores our perspective on life.

You will probably not reason your way out of discouragement. You will regain your proper perspective on life as you encounter God in worship. Some people do not go to church when they are depressed. That is the time you most need worship in your life! Sing songs to God even when you do not feel like it. Listen to his word. Greet his people. You will encounter him there.

October 11

Surely you place them on slippery ground;
you cast them down to ruin.
How suddenly are they destroyed,
completely swept away by terrors!
As a dream when one awakes,
so when you arise, O Lord,
you will despise them as fantasies
(Psalm 73:18-20).

The remainder of this psalm is dramatically different. Verses 4-14 display a distorted perspective, verses 15-17 mark a turning point, and verses 18-28 exhibit a return to right thinking. Asaph sees the wicked differently. He recognizes their position is precarious (v. 18), their judgment is inevitable (v. 19), and their seeming prosperity is a mere fantasy (v. 20).

The wise person must realize things are not always what they seem. Charles Allen told of a farmer who wrote the editor of a newspaper: "Dear Mr. Editor: My neighbor goes to church and observes Sunday. I ploughed my fields on Sunday. I sowed my fields on Sunday. I harvested them on Sunday. Mr. Editor, at the end of the season and the end of the harvest, I did better than any of my neighbors who observed Sunday and went to church. How do you explain that?" The editor's answer was brief. He wrote, "God doesn't make up His final account in October."[54]

---

54 Charles L. Allen, *The Sermon on the Mount* (Westwood, New Jersey: Fleming H. Revell, 1966), 149.

October 12

When my heart was grieved
and my spirit embittered,
it was senseless and ignorant;
I was a brute beast before you
(Psalm 73:21-22).

Asaph not only has a different perspective on the wicked, but he sees himself differently as well. What he had considered logical and true in verses 4-14, he now sees as senseless, ignorant, and "stupid" (LB). Discouragement distorts your self-image. An encounter with God restores a proper self-image.

One of the most helpful books I have read in my pastoral ministry is Robert McGee's *The Search For Significance.* He explains that many of us have a distorted self-image because we have believed Satan's lie that self-worth equals performance plus others' opinions. When we believe this lie, we become approval addicts or fall into the performance trap. He explains that God's answer is the doctrine of justification. In Christ, God has forgiven us and given us the righteousness of Jesus Christ. We are totally accepted by God. McGee identifies five ingredients needed for emotional healing in one's life: (1) honesty, (2) affirming relationships, (3) right thinking, (4) the Holy Spirit, and (5) time.[55]

---

55 Robert S. McGee, *The Search For Significance,* 2nd ed. (Houston: Rapha, 1990).

October 13

Yet I am always with you;
you hold me by my right hand.
You guide me with your counsel,
and afterward you will take me to glory.
Whom have I in heaven but you?
And earth has nothing I desire besides you.
My flesh and my heart may fail,
but God is the strength of my heart
and my portion forever
(Psalm 73:23–26).

When Asaph regained a biblical perspective, he not only saw the wicked differently and himself differently, he saw God differently as well. He grasped the unconditional promises of God. He listed three things he knew to be true no matter what happened. This is one of the greatest lists of the promises of God in the entire Bible. No matter what happens in your life, here are three things that God guarantees will happen. First, God will always be with you. Or, as Asaph phrases it: "I will always be with you." Second, God will guide you with his counsel. Whatever happens, God will give his child direction in life. Third, God will take you to glory. Here are the three unconditional promises that are always true for every Christian: God is with you, God will guide you, and God will take you to heaven!

Note that there is no indication that Asaph's condition changed. There was still the possibility that his flesh and heart would fail. He may still have faced financial problems and criticism. What was different? His attitude was transformed. That changed everything.

October 14

Those who are far from you will perish;
you destroy all who are unfaithful to you.
But as for me, it is good to be near God.
I have made the Sovereign LORD my refuge;
I will tell of all your deeds
(Psalm 73:27-28).

As the psalm ends, Asaph's thinking has cleared, because he is looking at life with the end in view. Discouragement and despair always come from looking at a tiny slice of life in the present. When you look only at today or this week, you may be discouraged. You must step back and see the sweep of God's plan from eternity to eternity. Those who are far from God will perish. Those who are near God will find him a refuge.

Asaph ends this psalm with a renewed sense of mission: "I will tell of all your deeds." He has found purpose and meaning in life—beyond himself and his circumstances—in the kingdom of God.

Your perspective on life makes all the difference in your spiritual health. You cannot choose the circumstances of your life, but you can choose your attitude in life. You can choose to be negative, to overgeneralize, and to accuse God of wrong. Or you can choose to humble yourself before God in worship and let him give you a proper perspective on life. The key to overcoming discouragement is worship—to renew the mind through an encounter with God and his unconditional promises.

October 15–21
Psalm 1: The Wise Life

October 15

Blessed is the man
who does not walk in the counsel of the wicked
or stand in the way of sinners
or sit in the seat of mockers.
(Psalm 1:1).

We have studied two psalms that describe what it is to be a fool or think as a fool. Now we will study two psalms that describe the way of wisdom. Psalm 1 is a fitting introduction to the book of Psalms, for it summarizes the basic viewpoint of the book. Some scholars even believe this psalm was written specifically as a prologue to the book.[56]

Psalm 1 contrasts the two choices in life: the way of the righteous and the way of the wicked. While popular philosophy indicates there is a wide range of choices concerning how one may live, the Bible repeatedly says there are only two real choices, the way of wisdom or the way of folly. Jesus emphasized there are two possible roads to travel in life: the road to destruction or the road to life (Matt. 7:13-14). He said every life produces one of two kinds of fruit (Matt. 7:15-20), and every person builds his or her life on one of two foundations (Matt. 7:24-27). Psalm 1 offers the same advice: there are only two real choices in life. You can live your way or you can live God's way.

Psalm 1:1 says that God's way is the best way. The first word in this psalm—and thus the first word in the book—is "blessed." Elsewhere in the Old Testament this word is translated "happy" five times in the NIV. The Psalms begin by declaring that not only is God's way the right way to live; it is also the happy way to live.

---

56 Delitzsch, *Psalms,* 1:82.

October 16

Blessed is the man
who does not walk in the counsel of the wicked
or stand in the way of sinners
or sit in the seat of mockers.
(Psalm 1:1).

The first characteristic of a wise person is the company he keeps. Your relationships are an indicator of your wisdom. The wise person does not walk in the counsel of the wicked. Those you "walk" with are the people you "hang out with" only a regular basis. They are your best friends, the ones who influence you. The wise person will walk with those who are walking in the same direction he wants to go. There may be a regression implied in the last three clauses of this verse. The person who walks in the counsel of the wicked may soon stand in the way of sinners and then sit in the seat of mockers.

This verse does not mean that a Christian should withdraw from relationships with non-Christians or even immoral people. Jesus was a friend of sinners. He was criticized by religious people because of his relationships with society's outcasts. However, Jesus prayerfully chose those who would walk with him on a daily basis. He chose those whose desire was to walk in the same direction he was going. Jesus said to guard against two extremes in one's friendships. First, he warned of contamination. He warned that salt must not lose its saltiness (Matt. 5:13). Second, he warned of isolation. He warned that light must not be hidden under a bowl (Matt. 5:14-16). The wise person will love everyone, will look down on no one, and will befriend those very different from him. The wise person will choose carefully those with whom he walks in close relationship.

October 17

But his delight is in the law of the LORD,
and on his law he meditates day and night
(Psalm 1:2).

The wise person is also identified by his thought life, specifically his attitude toward God's law. He delights in the Word. He meditates on the Word. The Bible is the key ingredient in spiritual growth.

There was a Kansas farmer who raised two sons. Both sons joined the Navy. The farmer's brother was a psychologist, and one day he came for a visit. At dinner that night, the farmer said, "You're a psychologist. How could a farmer living in the middle of Kansas, where there's almost no water, raise two sons who both love the Navy?" The psychologist said, "That's a good question. Let me think about it." That night he slept in the boys' room. The next morning he came downstairs and told his brother, "I think I've got an answer for you. Come upstairs with me." They walked into the boys' room, and the psychologist pointed to a picture on the wall. It was a beautiful seascape, and in the middle of the sea was a ship. The psychologist said, "The first thing you see when you walk in this room is this picture. If you lie down on the bed, it is the last thing you see at night and the first thing you see in the morning. Did the boys have this picture long?" The farmer said, "Yes, since they were about three years old." His brother replied, "If you think about a picture like that long enough, you might become a sailor."[57] If you think about the Bible long enough, you might become wise.

---

57 Scott Wenig, "Using Scripture in Our Lives," www.preachingtodaysermons.com (accessed October 9, 2009).

October 18

He is like a tree planted by streams of water,
which yields its fruit in season
and whose leaf does not wither.
Whatever he does prospers
(Psalm 1:3).

This verse describes the stability that results in the life of a person who guards his relationships and meditates on God's law. God promises three things to such a person: fruitfulness, endurance, and prosperity. He is compared to a tree planted by a stream. In desert areas—whether in the Middle East or the American West—there are very few trees except along streams. While neighboring hillsides may be barren, the stream banks are lush with vegetation. The moisture of the stream nourishes the trees through dry season and prolonged drought. The location makes all the difference.

Anchoring your life in the Bible and in relationships with other believers is like sending roots into the moist soil alongside a stream. These relationships will sustain you through dry times and seasons of spiritual drought. Where have you planted your life? Sink your roots deep into the Bible and into Christian friendships.

October 19

Not so the wicked!
They are like chaff
that the wind blows away
(Psalm 1:4).

The first half of this psalm has described the wise person; now the second half describes the foolish person. The first stanza ends in verse 3 with a description of the stability of the righteous. The second stanza begins in verse 4 with a description of the instability of the wicked.

The word picture portrays the winnowing of grain. After grain was threshed to remove the heads from the stalks, the grain was scooped up from the threshing floor and thrown into the air. The heavy grain fell back to the threshing floor, but the lightweight husk or chaff was blown away by the wind. The lives of the wicked are compared to the husk that blows away. Life apart from God's plan is unstable. The person who is not rooted in God is blown to and fro by the events and tragedies of life.

October 20

Therefore the wicked will not stand in the judgment,
nor sinners in the assembly of the righteous
(Psalm 1:5).

When I went to college, I found that there was a lot less supervision than in high school. Some college professors did not take attendance; there was no immediate consequence for missing classes. In some classes, the entire grade for the course was based upon two tests: a midterm and a final exam. No one monitored whether a student took notes each day or did the reading assignments. Some first semester students took advantage of their new freedom. They often skipped class and rarely opened the textbook. They were having a lot of fun! However, when it came time for the exam, they were unprepared. No amount of cramming could make up for weeks of negligence. The same professor who did not mind students missing class did not mind failing students.

Life is a lot like college. God has given us incredible freedom to live our lives as we choose. Each day we choose how we invest our time and resources. We pick our friends and our habits. However, there is a test at the end. Those who have not made wise choices will not pass the exam on judgment day. The choices you make each day matter. Every day you are becoming the person you will be for all eternity.

October 21

For the LORD watches over the way of the righteous,
but the way of the wicked will perish
(Psalm 1:6).

This psalm ends by contrasting the two ways to live life. Which road are you on? Imagine you are a railroad engineer. Imagine two sets of railroad tracks leaving a station. The two tracks are roughly parallel, and at several points they come close together, with a switch that allows a train to move from one set of tracks to the other. The one on the left is a smooth, new track with a gentle grade over high trestles. The one on the right is an older way. It is rough and follows the contours of the land with hard upward pulls and long descents. You have been advised to take the old set of tracks. It is reported that somewhere in the distance a trestle is out on the new tracks. However, you reason that you can see several switches ahead where you can change tracks if needed. You start out on the left tracks. At every switch you think about moving to the old tracks, but you can see no danger ahead. The ride is smooth, and you decide to wait until at least one more switch. With each passing mile you become more comfortable with your choice. Soon you begin to pass the switches with little thought of changing tracks. Things have gone well so far. You reason it would be more logical for the old tracks to have a problem than these new ones. You congratulate yourself on your wise choice and begin to whistle.

October 22–28
Psalm 127: The Wise Family

October 22

Unless the LORD builds the house,
its builders labor in vain
(Psalm 127:1a).

Psalm 127 is a wisdom psalm about family life. Your "house" is your family. When you get married, you establish a "house," whether you live in a rented apartment, a single-family dwelling, a tent, or an igloo. The wise couple enlists the Lord to be the architect and general contractor of the "house" they build.

How can you allow the Lord to build your house?

- Determine while you are single that you will only marry a person who is a believer in Jesus Christ (see 2 Cor. 6:14). This means you should not date a person who does not share your faith.
- Get good Christian premarital counseling prior to your wedding. Even some state governments recognize the value of premarital counseling. In Tennessee, your marriage license is much less expensive if you have had at least four hours of premarital counseling.
- View your marriage as a sacred covenant, not just a legal contract (Mal. 2:14).
- Ask God to be a third partner in your marriage. "A cord of three strands is not quickly broken" (Ecc. 4:12).
- Establish a habit of praying together as a couple even before you marry.
- Join a church where you can worship and serve God together.

October 23

Unless the LORD builds the house,
its builders labor in vain
(Psalm 127:1a).

Allowing the Lord to build one's house is not limited to the establishment of a new family. As your family grows and you mature, continue to consciously depend on God and seek to honor him in your family life. Have you dedicated your home to the Lord? It has been my privilege to participate in several home dedication ceremonies. When a family moves into a new home, they may invite other Christian friends over to help them dedicate their home to the Lord. This typically involves moving from room to room and praying in each area of the house, asking that the activities of those rooms may honor Christ and bring glory to him. The ceremony itself is merely symbolic; it is meaningless unless there is a daily effort by family leaders to foster kingdom values and disciplines inside that home.

We are building bigger homes than we used to build. According to the National Association of Home Builders, the average size home in the United States in 1970 was 1400 square feet. By 2004, it had risen to 2330 square feet. We are building bigger and more luxurious houses with more and more amenities. Let us remember that "unless the Lord builds the house, its builders labor in vain."

October 24

Unless the LORD watches over the city,
the watchmen stand guard in vain
(Psalm 127:1b).

The second part of verse 1 deals with the concern for security. How does one protect one's family, both physically and spiritually? As children make their way into the city, parents are concerned that they be secure from both physical harm and moral danger. Parents must do all they can to warn their children about the advances of strangers, the need for seatbelts, and the danger of drugs. At the same time, they must entrust their families to the care of God.

One of the most important ingredients in a wise family is prayer. No matter how vigilant you are to guard your family from danger, you cannot do the job alone. You must call upon the Lord to watch over your family and protect them from the Evil One. An important part of parenting is done on one's knees.

October 25

*In vain you rise early
and stay up late,
toiling for food to eat—
for he grants sleep to those he loves
(Psalm 127:2).*

Many families maintain incredibly hectic schedules. They fill their lives with a dizzying array of activities, thinking more activity will bring more joy in life. Parents feel pressured to enroll their children in every class, lesson, and sport offered lest their children somehow "miss out" or fail to keep up with other kids.

Other families work extra jobs to support an inflated standard of living. Stress, fatigue, and sleeplessness result from the pressured pace of life.

The problem is that many people lack a center to their lives. Find your meaning in life not from work or play but from a love relationship with God. He "grants sleep to those he loves." How do you make that relationship the center of your family life?

- Put God first in your weekly schedule. Determine to work no more than six days a week. Set aside time to worship God.
- Rest in God's love. Do the best you can and trust God with that which is left undone.
- Find your meaning in who you are and not in what you accomplish.

October 26

Sons are a heritage from the LORD,
children a reward from him
(Psalm 127:3).

The second stanza of this psalm talks about children. My wife has a degree in children's education. For a while she wrote a newspaper column that she called "Celebrate Children." That is what these verses do. They celebrate children as a wonderful gift from God, a gift to be valued and cherished.

Almost every parent needs to be reminded of this truth at some point in the parenting process. Parenting is an exhausting process. Feeding, bathing, and cleaning up after children is an unending cycle. Children are precious, but they are also naturally self-centered. Their most effective strategy in getting their way—whether as a toddler or a teenager—is often to simply wear down a fatigued parent. It is easy for parents to become focused on the problems and demands of parenting and lose sight of its joys and rewards. Parents need to remind themselves of the rewards of children.

- Step back and get the big picture. Parenting becomes tedious when you always focus on the minutia of life and the constant demands.
- Laugh. See the humor even in disasters. Laughter is great medicine.
- Enjoy the journey. They really will be gone before you know it.

October 27

Like arrows in the hands of a warrior
are sons born in one's youth
(Psalm 127:4).

Wise parents see their children as their greatest assets. They realize that the molding of their children is more important than the building of their careers or the pursuit of other ventures. Almost every young adult has dreams of making a mark upon the world. Many of us do not realize that the most lasting impact we will have on the world will be in the legacy of our children and their children after them. We think we will make our mark through the businesses we build, the books we write, or the politics we influence. Yet, after most of these things are forgotten, we will continue to impact the world through the generations that follow us.

Christian young adults want to make a difference in the world for the kingdom of God. What are the weapons of kingdom warfare? This psalm says our children are like arrows in the hands of a warrior. We influence our culture for Christ most by raising children who love Jesus and continue his kingdom purposes.

October 28

Blessed is the man
whose quiver is full of them.
They will not be put to shame
when they contend with their enemies in the gate
(Psalm 127:5).

In an agricultural culture, a large family is viewed as an asset. Children provide much needed volunteer labor to maintain the family economy. In modern urban culture, a large family is often viewed as a liability. We are often reminded of how many hundreds of thousands of dollars it takes to raise a child to age eighteen. We are overwhelmed with estimates of how much it will cost to send our toddlers to college some day. The Bible maintains that the value of children always outweighs their liabilities.

During the 1970s social experts worried about the dangers of overpopulation. Large families were frowned upon. Verses such as this one that celebrate the blessings of a family with several children were considered politically incorrect. In an ecology class in college, our professor asked each student to write on a piece of paper how many children he or she wanted to have. The average answer of our class was one child per family. The professor smiled with approval. We had bought into his views on the proper size for a family.

Later, when birth rates began to decline in Europe and other parts of the world, social experts began to entertain the opposite concern: the population of some affluent nations might begin to decline. This verse did not seem so outdated after all. It is amazing how Bible truth, deemed outmoded by one generation, can be rediscovered by the next generation to be fresh and relevant.

November

Thank God!

November is the month when we celebrate Thanksgiving. I have never felt that one day is an adequate amount of time to spend in giving thanks to God. I invite you to spend the entire month of November exploring what it means to live with a sense of gratitude to God. This month we will examine psalms of thanksgiving.

October 29—November 4
Psalm 100: Enter God's Presence with
Thanksgiving

October 29

Shout for joy to the LORD, all the earth.
Worship the LORD with gladness;
come before him with joyful songs
(Psalm 100:1-2).

Psalm 100 is one of the best-loved psalms in Christian history. It is a simple, straightforward call to give thanks to God. Its title is "A psalm. For giving thanks." This could mean that it was to be sung when a worshipper brought a thank offering to God at the temple. The Bible does not talk much about feeling thankful to God; it talks about giving thanks to him. Thanksgiving must be expressed to God. Thanksgiving is not an inner attitude but an active expression. After all, we don't call our holiday "Thanksfeeling Day." We call it "Thanksgiving Day!" The expression of thanksgiving transforms our attitudes.

How are we to express our thanksgiving? The first two verses of this psalm tell us how to give thanks to God.

Thanksgiving is to be expressed verbally. These verses admonish us to "shout for joy" and to sing "joyful songs."

Thanksgiving is to be expressed in corporate worship. While our culture tends to emphasize personal or family thanksgiving on Thanksgiving Day, the biblical call is to "worship" and "come before him." We are to gather with other believers and express thanksgiving.

Thanksgiving is to be expressed in all of life. The word worship is sometimes translated "serve." All of our service to God—all that we do in his name—should be viewed as an expression of thanksgiving.

October 30

Shout for joy to the LORD, all the earth.
Worship the LORD with gladness;
come before him with joyful songs
(Psalm 100:1-2).

All three lines of these verses emphasize the joyful nature of thanksgiving. Gladness and joy are to be trademarks of God's people. You cannot choose the circumstances of your life, but you can choose your attitude toward those circumstances. To give thanks is to choose to focus on the positive blessings in your life.

Helen Keller became blind and deaf at a very early age. We would think that a person who lived in continual darkness and silence might easily slip into pessimism and despair. Yet she wrote in her autobiography:

> For three things I thank God every day of my life: thanks that he vouchsafed me knowledge of His Works; deep thanks that He has set in my darkness the lamp of faith; deep deepest thanks that I have another life to look forward to—a life joyous with light and flowers and heavenly song.[58]

She claimed that so much had been given her that she had no time to think about what had been denied her.

---

58 Quoted in David E. Garland, *Colossians/Philemon, The NIV Life Application Commentary* (Grand Rapids: Zondervan, 1998), 78-79.

October 31

Know that the LORD is God.
It is he who made us, and we are his;
we are his people, the sheep of his pasture
(Psalm 100:3).

Thanksgiving springs from knowing and acknowledging that the Lord is the one true god. Nineteenth century English writer Harriet Martineau was an atheist. One day, enjoying the beauty of an autumn morning, she exclaimed, "Oh, I'm so grateful!" Her Christian companion replied, "Grateful to whom, my dear?"[59] Gratitude must have some person to whom it is directed. The person who does not know God has little rationale for thanksgiving.

It is said that when members of a certain African tribe want to express gratitude, they sit for a long time in front of the hut of the person who did the favor and say, "I sit on the ground before you." That captures something of the spirit of this verse. Know that the Lord is God. Sit on the ground before him.

---

59 Elizabeth Achtemeier, "Cause for a Common Thanksgiving?" *Preaching,* November-December 1990, 14.

November 1

Know that the LORD is God.
It is he who made us, and we are his;
we are his people, the sheep of his pasture
(Psalm 100:3).

When we know who God is, we know who we are. Because he made us, we belong to him and he provides for us. A failure to understand the work of God undermines a life of thankfulness. Such ignorance can cause us to think we are self-made. In the movie *Shenandoah*, Jimmy Stewart played a homesteader. At the first meal harvested from the land, he offered this blessing: "Lord, we cleared the land, tilled the soil, planted the seed, harvested the crop, and prepared the food. But we want you to know that we thank you anyway. Amen."

We will not live a life of thankfulness unless we focus on the ultimate source of our blessings. In Daniel Defoe's novel *Robinson Crusoe,* the shipwrecked sailor discovered grain growing by the entrance to his cave. He was overjoyed at this miracle and gave thanks to God. Then he remembered that he had shaken out a grain sack at that spot, and he stopped giving thanks for the grain.

Our efforts do not produce blessings. They are always secondary. Know that the Lord is God. It is he who made us, and we are his.

November 2

Enter his gates with thanksgiving
and his courts with praise;
give thanks to him and praise his name
(Psalm 100:4).

As a worshipper approached Solomon's temple, he came through a series of courtyards. The books of Kings appear to distinguish three courts around the temple: a "great courtyard" (1 Kings 7:12), a "middle court" (2 Kings 20:4), and an "inner courtyard" (1 Kings 6:36). It is assumed that a series of gates provided entrance into these courtyards.[60] This psalm admonishes the worshipper to express his thanksgiving in songs of praise as he makes his way through the courtyards and approaches the presence of God. Even though our worship is no longer based in an earthly temple, there is a great concept of worship here. We are to approach God through thanksgiving.

Often when I pray I try to begin my prayers with thanksgiving. Before I start asking God for things I need, I want to thank him for what he has already given me. Often I will pray with a blank sheet of paper before me. The first thing I do is jot down the things for which I am thankful: big things, little things, spiritual things, physical things. This is certainly not a legalistic formula for prayer. There are many times when urgent needs crowd to the front of my prayers, but in normal times, there is great value in entering his presence through thanksgiving.

---

60 Stephen Westerholm, "Temple," *The International Standard Bible Encyclopedia*, rev. ed. (Grand Rapids: Eerdmans, 1988), 4:762.

November 3

Enter his gates with thanksgiving
and his courts with praise;
give thanks to him and praise his name
(Psalm 100:4).

When the temple was rebuilt by King Herod, there was a series of clearly identified courtyards surrounding it. The outermost courtyard was the Court of Gentiles. This was the only place Gentiles could worship. A wall and a warning sign prevented them from going farther. Jews could go through a gate into the next courtyard, the Court of Women. Jewish women worshipped there. A wall prevented them from going farther. Jewish men could proceed through a gate into the Court of Israel. There they stood and worshipped. Still farther was the Court of Priests. Only Jewish men who were priests could enter that courtyard. The priests also entered the outer room of the temple when it was their turn to lead in worship. Only the high priest entered the inner room of the temple, and he could do that only once a year.

The death of Jesus on the cross changed all that. The veil separating the inner and outer rooms of the temple was torn in two at the moment of his death. His blood brought unprecedented access into the presence of God for all people. Now any person, man or woman, Gentile or Jew, clergy or laity, has unhindered access to the throne of God. We can approach him and talk to him with confidence. How much more should we enter his presence with thanksgiving!

November 4

For the LORD is good and his love endures forever;
his faithfulness continues through all generations
(Psalm 100:5).

The last verse in this psalm establishes the rationale for a life of thanksgiving. We give thanks to God because he is good. His goodness is revealed in his enduring love and faithfulness. We must never forget that goodness characterizes the very nature of God. As we struggle with the problems of evil and suffering in our lives, some are tempted to surrender the doctrine of God's goodness. If God is good, we reason, how in the world could he allow such bad things to happen to us? The person of faith, however, sees evidence of the unchanging love of God even in the midst of inexplicable suffering.

Martin Rinckart was a Lutheran minister in the 1600s. He was pastor at Eilenburg, Germany, during the Thirty Years War. Because Eilenburg was a walled city, refugees crowded into the town to seek protection. Sanitation and medical care were inadequate, and thousands of people died from the plague. For two years Rinckart was the only clergyman left alive in his city. He conducted thousands of funerals, as many as fifty a day according to his journals. Yet, during this dismal time in his life he wrote one of our greatest Thanksgiving hymns:

> Now thank we all our God with hearts and hands and voices,
> Who wondrous things hath done, in whom the world rejoices;
> Who from our mother's arms, has blessed us on our way,
> With countless gifts of love, and still is ours today.

November 5-11
Psalm 104: Thank God for His Creation

November 5

Praise the LORD, O my soul.
O LORD my God, you are very great;
you are clothed with splendor and majesty.
He wraps himself in light as with a garment;
he stretches out the heavens like a tent
and lays the beams of the upper chambers on their waters.
He makes the clouds his chariot
and rides on the wings of the wind
(Psalm 104:1-3).

Psalm 104 calls us to praise God for what he has made. The first three verses focus our attention on the handiwork of God in the heavens. As more people work and play indoors, we have lost some of our connection with the night skies. When I was growing up, my parents and I often sat outside on the porch on summer nights, because it was cooler there than in our non-air conditioned home. We would gaze at the moon, the clouds, and the stars. We lose a sense of God's majesty when we are no longer exposed to the heavens.

This psalm emphasizes the personal involvement of God in the skies. He wears the heavenly lights like a coat. He stretches out the starry sky like a tent. The clouds are his chariot as he rides the wind. God seems to take personal delight in his creation. So should we.

Go outside tonight. Wait a few moments for your eyes to adjust to the darkness. Look up at the skies. Contemplate the God who made them.

November 6

He makes springs pour water into the ravines;
it flows between the mountains.

He waters the mountains from his upper chambers;
the earth is satisfied by the fruit of his work
(Psalm 104:10, 13).

Some have noted that this psalm roughly follows the six days of creation. The psalmist rejoices in each stage of God's creative work. After marveling at the heavens, the psalmist praises God for the gift of water.

Living most of my life in the southeastern United States, I confess I have sometimes taken for granted the gift of water. Rainfall is plentiful, and our region is blessed with streams and rivers. In 2007-2008, however, our area experienced one of the worst droughts in decades. Reservoirs reached new lows. Many communities rationed water. Crop yields plummeted. The gurgling stream on my father's little farm went dry for the first time in anyone's memory. We gained a new appreciation for God's gift of water.

Water is one of our most critical resources. Today you will drink water from a water fountain at work, a glass at a restaurant, a bottle in your backpack, or a faucet in your home. As you do, will you pause to acknowledge that drink as a gift from God? Will you thank him for his wonderful provision?

November 7

He makes grass grow for the cattle,
and plants for man to cultivate—
bringing forth food from the earth
(Psalm 104:14).

Our lives are totally dependent on the amazing process known as photosynthesis. God has designed our world so that plants harvest minerals and water from the soil and sunlight, retrieve carbon dioxide from the atmosphere, and use these elements to produce green leaves. So far no other planet in this vast universe has been discovered to possess the exact formula of ingredients that make this life-sustaining process possible.

I enjoy gardening. Every spring I marvel at how God has designed a shriveled, dry seed to possess the genetic code to produce a plant true to its type. Even though I have seen it for decades, I am amazed at how quickly those seeds, warmed by the sun and swelled by moisture in the soil, sprout and explode through the earth. Today, would you thank God for the green plants he has created that make life possible?

November 8

How many are your works, O LORD!
In wisdom you made them all;
the earth is full of your creatures
(Psalm 104:24).

More than any other aspect of creation, this psalm celebrates the animals God has made. It talks about wild donkeys, storks, cattle, wild goats, coneys, and lions. I have always had an appreciation for animals, especially wild creatures. I grew up catching "critters"—salamanders and crayfish from our spring, and baby rabbits and box turtles from the hayfield. I still marvel at the beauty of wildlife. We have four types of bird feeders in our backyard: sunflower seeds attract cardinals and chickadees, thistle seeds invite finches, peanuts attract titmice and jays, and suet draws a variety of woodpeckers. I love to visit our national parks and see the variety of North American wildlife. I love to fish because it puts me in the midst of God's creation.

The psalmist is amazed at the magnitude and diversity of creatures upon the earth: "How many are your works, O Lord!" I believe this psalm must have been written in spring or summer, when the earth is teeming with an abundance of wildlife. Why did God make so many different species? The variety of creation reflects the creativity and complexity of the God who made these creatures. Evolution cannot account for the complexity of the earth's creatures. The intricate design of creation points to a wise designer.

November 9

There is the sea, vast and spacious,
teeming with creatures beyond number—
living things both large and small.
There the ships go to and fro,
and the leviathan, which you formed to frolic there
(Psalm 104:25-26).

While verse 24 celebrates God's land creatures, verses 25-26 celebrate his creation of sea life. I once had the opportunity to go snorkeling on a coral reef in the Gulf of Mexico. That experience revealed to me a whole new world of exotic creatures. In addition to testifying to God's complexity and wisdom, creation also points to his beauty. I am not sure everything in creation serves a function. I believe some of the colors and designs of creation simply reflect God's sense of beauty. Evolutionists find a function for everything. If there is beauty in creation that is not functional, it is damaging to their argument for evolution.

I believe there is even a sense of comedy revealed in God's creatures. Is there not a fish named the clownfish? Does not the seahorse reveal a sense of humor? The psalmist speaks of the mysterious leviathan. Is he a whale? An extinct sea creature? A dinosaur? Whatever, he is created to frolic in the sea. God seems to enjoy his creation. So should we.

November 10

These all look to you
to give them their food at the proper time.
When you give it to them,
they gather it up;
when you open your hand,
they are satisfied with good things.
When you hide your face,
they are terrified;
when you take away their breath,
they die and return to the dust.
When you send your Spirit,
they are created,
and you renew the face of the earth
(Psalm 104:27–30).

Not only did God create all living things, but he sustains them as well. They look to him for food, and he gives it to them at the proper time. God is still active in his creation. He holds everything together. He sustains an amazing balance in his creation. Often our attempts to improve on this balance have created more problems than they have solved. We brought kudzu from Japan to the southern United States, thinking it would be an ideal plant to control erosion. Now it engulfs native trees as well as telephone poles, buildings, and anything else in its path.

God has charged us with the task of managing his creation, but we fall far short of his expertise. We are still learning about the contributions of wind, wildfire, flood, and drought to the harmony he has built into his world. We stand in awe of his management skills.

November 11

May the glory of the LORD endure forever;
may the LORD rejoice in his works—
he who looks at the earth, and it trembles,
who touches the mountains, and they smoke.
I will sing to the LORD all my life;
I will sing praise to my God as long as I live.
May my meditation be pleasing to him,
as I rejoice in the LORD
(Psalm 104:31–34).

Some who love the natural world tend to identify the universe with God. They see God in the majesty of a redwood or the grace of an eagle in flight. They are right to see God in every creature, but they are wrong to worship the earth. Creation is a reflection of the Creator. The natural world is not an end in itself. It points us to the one who made it.

For all the magnificence of creation, it is not eternal. God alone is eternal. He is so far beyond his creation that it trembles when he looks at it. The mountains smoke when he touches them. The proper response is to worship the God of creation, the one who made it all. The psalmist vows as long as he lives to sing praise to God. Will you join him?

November 12–18
Psalm 105: Thank God for Your Heritage

November 12

Give thanks to the LORD, call on his name;
make known among the nations what he has done.

Remember the wonders he has done,
his miracles, and the judgments he pronounced
(Psalm 105:1, 5).

You will never develop a deep sense of gratitude to God without a sense of heritage. You need to sense how God has been at work in your history to bring you where you are today. You need to develop an appreciation of your heritage on several levels. First, you need an understanding of the work of God in biblical history. Second, you need a sense of how God has worked in church history and the heritage you have received in your local church. Third, you need to appreciate the work of God in your own family and your personal life to bring you to him and guide you into the present.

You may protest that your past has been hard and that there is little for which you can be grateful in your family's history. Either you are not looking deeply enough, or you are focusing on particular events without getting the big picture. You need to develop a sense of God's direction in your history. To do this you must spend time reviewing and remembering your heritage so that you can see the hand of God and praise Him. Psalm 105 will help you do that.

November 13

He remembers his covenant forever,
the word he commanded, for a thousand generations,
the covenant he made with Abraham,
the oath he swore to Isaac.
He confirmed it to Jacob as a decree,
to Israel as an everlasting covenant:
"To you I will give the land of Canaan
as the portion you will inherit"
(Psalm 105:8-11).

Psalm 105 retells the stories contained in Genesis (105:6-22) and Exodus (105:23-45). The psalmist reviews the heritage of Israel so that the people will develop a sense of gratitude for God's faithfulness. He begins with the stories of the patriarchs: Abraham, Isaac, and Jacob. The key word in this section is "covenant." God entered into a covenant with Abraham. God swore it to Abraham's son, Isaac, and confirmed it with his son, Jacob. He promised them the land of Canaan, and this psalm is about how he kept that covenant promise.

If you are a Christian, God has entered into a covenant with you. He has promised to save you from your sin, to be your God, and to take you safely to the promised land of heaven. You have promised to be his servant and to obey his commands. Think back to the time you entered into a covenant relationship with God through Jesus Christ. Recall how his grace was extended to you. Think about the circumstances in your life, the people involved, and how you felt. Recall your baptism. Offer a prayer of thanks to God for his salvation and the channels through which it was delivered to you.

November 14

When they were but few in number,
few indeed, and strangers in it,
they wandered from nation to nation,
from one kingdom to another.
He allowed no one to oppress them;
for their sake he rebuked kings:
"Do not touch my anointed ones;
do my prophets no harm"
(Psalm 105:12-15).

These verses review how God protected the patriarchs when they were still wandering aliens in the land they would later possess. The passage recalls Genesis 20, when Abraham and his wife Sarah were living in the territory of King Abimelech. Abimelech believed Sarah was Abraham's sister, so he intended to take her as his wife. God appeared to the king in a dream and said, "You are as good as dead if you take this woman. She is the wife of a prophet." With great fear Abimelech returned Sarah to Abraham, along with gifts of camels and sheep and a thousand shekels of silver.

Can you recall times in your life when God has protected you? God seems especially protective of his people in the early stages of their spiritual development, when they are "few in number" or "wandering from nation to nation." His protection is evident in the early history of the church, the early history of our nation, and often in the early years of a new believer's experience. It seems God guards us closely until we "get our legs under us." Do you recall evidence of God's spiritual protection in your life when you were at your weakest? Breathe a prayer of thanks for this heritage of protection.

November 15

*He called down famine on the land
and destroyed all their supplies of food;
and he sent a man before them—
Joseph, sold as a slave.
They bruised his feet with shackles,
his neck was put in irons,
till what he foretold came to pass,
till the word of the LORD proved him true
(Psalm 105:16-19).*

Verses 16-22 summarize briefly the story of Jacob's son, Joseph, recorded in Genesis 37-50. Joseph's brothers sold him into slavery. A caravan took him to Egypt, where he eventually rose to power as second only to Pharaoh. A famine came to the land of Canaan, and the family of Jacob had to migrate to Egypt to survive. There they found long-lost Joseph in charge of the granaries of Egypt. As the psalmist states, God "sent a man before them—Joseph." Even the sins of Joseph's brothers were molded into the plan of God to guide and bless his people.

Think of the times of trouble and conflict in your life. Can you see now how God used them to accomplish his purposes? Thank God for how he has turned your problems into blessings. If you cannot see any redemptive value in your struggles, is it possible that future events will yet reveal the hand of God in your past problems?

God sent Joseph to Egypt ahead of Israel. Whom has God sent to go before you to bless you? A parent? A pastor? A teacher? Thank God for that heritage.

November 16

He sent Moses his servant,
and Aaron, whom he had chosen.
They performed his miraculous signs among them,
his wonders in the land of Ham.

He brought out Israel, laden with silver and gold,
and from among their tribes no one faltered.
Egypt was glad when they left,
because dread of Israel had fallen upon them
(Psalm 105:26-27, 37-38).

The second half of Psalm 105 retells the story of the book of Exodus. It summarizes how the Israelites grew in number, how they came to be hated by the Egyptians, and how God sent Moses and Aaron to deliver his people. It surveys the plagues God brought upon Egypt to convince Pharaoh to release the Israelites: darkness, water turning to blood, frogs, flies, gnats, hail, lightning, locusts, grasshoppers, and the death of all firstborn. Finally, it describes how the Egyptians gave the Israelites treasure to convince them to leave!

God did not want the Israelites to forget where they had come from and what they had been through. That is why he reviews their history in great detail. Many of us are unfamiliar with the rich heritage of God's faithfulness in our past. Do you know the stories of people like William Tyndale who sacrificed their lives that we might have the Scriptures in our language? An awareness of this history will make you more grateful for your Bible. Have you read stories of the heroes who brought religious freedom to America? An awareness of this heritage will make you grateful when you choose where to worship this Sunday. Are you familiar with the history of your local church? If your church is fairly new, ask older members to tell you stories of its history. If your church has a written history, read it. It is dangerous to forget your heritage. Forgetfulness is the enemy of gratitude.

November 17

He spread out a cloud as a covering,
and a fire to give light at night.
They asked, and he brought quail
and satisfied them with the bread of heaven.
He opened the rock, and water gushed out;
like a river it flowed in the desert.
For he remembered his holy promise
given to his servant Abraham.
(Psalm 105:39–42).

This section describes how God guided and provided for his people during the exodus. God sent a cloud to guide them by day and a pillar of fire to guide them by night (Ex. 13:21-22). God fed them with bread that fell from heaven called manna. When they longed for meat, he sent them quail to eat. He provided water from a rock. The key word in this section is "promise." God kept his promises that he made to Abraham.

God has made promises to us under the New Covenant. He has promised to always be with us (Matt. 28:20). He has promised to give us peace even in the midst of trouble (John 16:33). He has promised us the counsel of the Holy Spirit (John 14:26). He has promised we will never perish (John 10:28). Think back over your life. Has God ever failed to keep his promises? You will be able to say with Joshua as he testified near the end of his life: "You know with all your heart and soul that not one of all the good promises the Lord your God gave you has failed. Every promise has been fulfilled" (Josh. 23:14). Thank God for his faithfulness in your life.

November 18

He gave them the lands of the nations,
and they fell heir to what others had toiled for—
that they might keep his precepts and observe his laws.
Praise the LORD.
(Psalm 105:44-45).

These verses span the history of Israel all the way into the book of Joshua. They recount how God gave them the land he had promised to Abraham. "They fell heir to what others had toiled for."

You too fall heir to what others have toiled for. You have a rich heritage of God's faithfulness that spans from eternity, through the history of Israel, through the ministry of Jesus Christ, through two thousand years of church history, through the heritage of your denomination or tradition, and through your local church. You have a personal heritage of faith that may be traced back through your family tree or through other faithful witnesses that God sent your way. An awareness of this heritage will help sustain you in times when you do not see immediate evidence of God's faithfulness and activity in your life. It will be bedrock that keeps you from sinking too far into the mire of despair. Get to know your heritage and thank God for it.

November 19–25
Psalm 106: Thank God for His Mercy

November 19

Praise the LORD.
Give thanks to the LORD, for he is good;
his love endures forever.

We have sinned, even as our fathers did;
we have done wrong and acted wickedly
(Psalm 106:1, 6).

Like the psalm before it, Psalm 106 is a psalm of thanksgiving that surveys the history of Israel. However, rather than focusing on God's faithfulness, this psalm focuses on Israel's unfaithfulness. The key word in this psalm is "sin." This psalm recounts Israel's heritage of failures.

This psalm prompts us to review our lives and heritage again, this time recalling the times we have rebelled against God, forgotten God, or failed to trust God. You may be thinking, "When we have confessed our sins and God has forgiven them, aren't we supposed to forget them? Why bring up painful memories?" God does not want you to remember your past failures with grief or guilt, but he does want you to remember them with gratitude. If you forget the depth of your sin, you will lose the depth of your gratitude. If you get "used to" being forgiven, your love for God will grow cold. John Newton wrote the famous hymn, *Amazing Grace*, because he never forgot where he came from. He chose for his epitaph: "Once an infidel and libertine, a servant of slaves in Africa, was by the rich mercy of our Lord, restored and pardoned." Psalm 106 will help you recall your sin, so that you will forever be grateful to him for his mercy.

November 20

When our fathers were in Egypt,
they gave no thought to your miracles;
they did not remember your many kindnesses,
and they rebelled by the sea, the Red Sea.
Yet he saved them for his name's sake,
to make his mighty power known.
He rebuked the Red Sea, and it dried up;
he led them through the depths as through a desert.
He saved them from the hand of the foe;
from the hand of the enemy he redeemed them
(Psalm 106:7-10).

The psalmist begins his survey of Israel's history during the exodus, as the Israelites were trapped between the pursuing armies of Pharaoh on one side and the waters of the Red Sea on the other. They did not remember the miraculous plagues God had sent only a short time ago to secure their release from Egypt. They rebelled against God (Ex. 14:10-12). Yet, God in his mercy saved his rebellious people. He dried up the Red Sea so they could cross and then swallowed Pharaoh's armies in its waters. The deliverance at the Red Sea became the landmark event in Israel's history. Her prophets and writers repeatedly took the people back to that day to recall their sin and God's mercy.

You need to recall your sin and God's mercy that saved you from it. You may be thinking, "I don't have a history of flagrant sin as Israel does. I became a Christian as a child. I never did anything terribly bad." Outside my office window is a redbud tree. Underneath it are redbud sprouts coming up through the bed of ivy. The seedlings are not as big as the tree, but they are genetically the same. Left alone, they will become the same size. I was saved when I was nine years old. I had never committed murder. Yet, within my life were the seedlings of rebellion. I am no less indebted to the mercy of God for his salvation than a murderer. Recall your salvation and thank God for his mercy.

November 21

But they soon forgot what he had done
and did not wait for his counsel.
In the desert they gave in to their craving;
in the wasteland they put God to the test.

At Horeb they made a calf
and worshipped an idol cast from metal.
They exchanged their Glory
for an image of a bull, which eats grass.
They forgot the God who saved them,
who had done great things in Egypt
(Psalm 106:13-14, 19-21).

The Israelites soon forgot the dramatic deliverance of God at the Red Sea. They lost their sense of gratitude in the desert. They began to complain about the steady diet of manna. They longed for some variety in their menu. They wanted meat! In his mercy, God sent them flocks of quail into their camp (Ex. 16:13). Later, while Moses was on Mount Horeb receiving the law of God, the people made a golden idol and began to worship it (Ex. 32:4). Amazingly, God did not give up on his forgetful, idolatrous people. Though in his wrath he disciplined them, yet in his mercy he continued to deliver them and guide them.

God's mercy to you did not end with your conversion. Can you recall times in your life when you have forgotten him and his salvation? Often new Christians are flush with joy and exuberance in their newfound freedom from sin and death. They are usually eager to learn and grow. Later, there is a tendency to forget God's goodness. This often comes in times of trial, the "wastelands" of life. Thankfully, God does not abandon us in these times. In his mercy, he continues to walk with us. Thank him for the tenacity of his mercy.

November 22

Then they despised the pleasant land;
they did not believe his promise.
They grumbled in their tents
and did not obey the LORD
(Psalm 106:24-25).

These verses refer to Israel's refusal to enter the promised land (Num. 14:1-2). Ten of the twelve spies sent to survey the land of Canaan brought back a fearful report about the powerful inhabitants of the land. The Israelites refused to believe God would enable them to conquer their enemies.

How would you have responded to these people if you were God? What would be your reaction to their grumbling after setting them free from Egypt, parting the Red Sea, feeding them in the desert, and enduring their idolatry? God had every reason to abandon Israel, except that he had made a promise to them. He sentenced them to wander forty years in the desert until the unbelieving generations were gone, then he once again led them to the promised land.

Can you recall times you have failed to believe God and obey his commands? Have there been times when you have grumbled against God? Is it not true that there have been many times in your life when God would have been justified in abandoning you? Yet, he has continued to show you mercy in spite of your resilient sin. Great is his mercy!

November 23

They did not destroy the peoples
as the LORD had commanded them,
but they mingled with the nations
and adopted their customs.
They worshipped their idols,
which became a snare to them
(Psalm 106:34-36).

With these verses the survey of Israel's failures moves into the books of Joshua and Judges. The Israelites did not completely drive out the inhabitants of Canaan as God had commanded. Instead they intermarried, compromised, and adopted the religion of their culture.

Think of times when you have compromised your Christian convictions and values, times when you caved to the enormous pressure of our culture. Have you conformed to the customs around you rather than transforming them? It is painful to recall the history of your compromise, but it enables you to comprehend the greatness of God's mercy. A jeweler often displays a diamond on a field of black velvet. The contrast of the dark background accentuates the sparkle in the diamond. The mercy of God shines against the dark background of our lives and causes us to marvel at its beauty.

November 24

Many times he delivered them,
but they were bent on rebellion
and they wasted away in their sin.
But he took note of their distress
when he heard their cry;
for their sake he remembered his covenant
and out of his great love he relented
(Psalm 106:43-45).

These verses summarize the book of Judges. A cycle of sin and repentance is repeated over and over in that book. The people of Israel turned from God. He sent enemies to discipline them. In their distress they repented and cried out to God. He heard their prayers and sent a judge to deliver them from their enemies. Their conditions improved, and they forgot God again and returned to their sin. The cycle soon repeated itself.

To read the book of Judges is to be amazed at the mercy of God. How many times would he deliver these brazen sinners? Surely, one thinks, he will get fed up with their persistent rebellion and their repeated failures. Yet, time after time, God responded and sent them a hero to deliver them: Othniel, Ehud, Shamgar, Deborah, Gideon, and many others. Why? "He remembered his covenant and out of his great love he relented."

How many times have you failed God? How many times have you promised God you would change only to slip into sin again? Aren't you glad God does not just give second chances or third chances? Aren't you glad he relates to you out of his great love for you?

November 25

Save us, O LORD our God,
and gather us from the nations,
that we may give thanks to you holy name
and glory in your praise.
Praise be to the LORD, the God of Israel,
from everlasting to everlasting.
Let all the people say, "Amen!"
Praise the LORD
(Psalm 106:47–48).

When I was growing up, I had two dogs: a little black dog named Snoopy and a big brown dog named Rebel. They had very different backgrounds. Snoopy was given to us as a puppy by a nice family that had pampered him. Rebel was a stray dog my dad brought home from the dump. He was hungry, raw-boned, and covered with mange. We fed him and treated his mange. He grew into a beautiful dog. Snoopy could be stubborn and finicky, but Rebel was extremely loyal and would gobble down any kind of food placed before him. I think the difference in the two dogs was that Snoopy felt he was entitled to be fed and cared for, while Rebel was forever grateful for the kindness that he had been shown. He never seemed to forget that act of mercy.

Our thanksgiving to God will be richer when we keenly remember what we have been and where we have come from. We are not entitled to the status we enjoy in his family. We were strays at the dump. God has shown us mercy. Let us give thanks to his holy name and praise him from everlasting to everlasting.

November 26—December 2
Psalm 107: Thank God for His Rescue

November 26

Give thanks to the LORD, for he is good;
his love endures forever.
Let the redeemed of the LORD say this—
those he redeemed from the hand of the foe,
those he gathered from the lands,
from east and west, from north and south
(Psalm 107:1-3).

This psalm focuses on thanking God for his rescue in our lives. God is a redeemer or rescuer. After the introduction in verses 1-3, there are four stanzas in this psalm. Each stanza gives an example of God helping people in times of trouble.

Stanza one: God rescues people lost in the desert (vv. 4-9). Some wandered in the desert. They were hungry and thirsty. They cried out to God. He led them to a city and satisfied their thirst.

Stanza two: God rescues prisoners (vv. 10-16). Some were chained in prison, doing bitter labor. They cried out to God and he gave them freedom.

Stanza three: God rescues the sick (vv. 17-22). Some were diseased and near death. They cried out to God and he healed them.

Stanza four: God helps sea travelers caught in storms (vv. 23-32). Some were tossed by the sea. They cried out to God. He calmed the storms.

God is a God of rescue and redemption. Recall instances of God's rescue in your life.

November 27

Then they cried out to the LORD in their trouble,
and he delivered them from their distress
(Psalm 107:6).

This is a common phrase repeated with only minor variation in each of the four stanzas (vv. 6, 13, 19, 28). Each of these four groups responded to their trouble by praying to God for deliverance. The way to access the help of God in times of trouble is to cry out to him. God hears and responds to fervent prayer. It is incredible that the God who made and sustains the entire universe notices the whimpers of individuals who are hurting. To cry out means to pray with urgency and passion and abandon. Are you in trouble? Why don't you cry out to God today? Amazingly, we are overwhelmed by trouble but do not cry out to God. He is a God who rescues!

It is not wrong to spiritualize these four situations. Jesus did that with bread (John 6:51) and imprisonment (Luke 4:18). You may not be lost in a desert, but your life may seem as dry as a desert and you may have no idea which way to go. You may not be in chains, but you may be in bondage to sin habits. Your body may be healthy, but your soul may be sick. You may not be in a storm at sea, but you may be experiencing the storms of life. Cry out to God!

November 28

Some sat in darkness and the deepest gloom,
prisoners suffering in iron chains,
for they had rebelled against the words of God
and despised the counsel of the Most High
(Psalm 107:10–11).

The amazing thing is that God helps us even when the trouble is our own fault. In the first and fourth stanzas, the trouble came through no fault of their own. But in the second stanza, the trouble came because they rebelled against God and despised his counsel (vv. 10-11). In the third stanza, they became sick because they were foolish and rebellious (v. 17). God still delivered them when they cried out. He helps us even in trouble of our own making. How gracious is that! Cry out to God!

November 29

Let them give thanks to the LORD for his unfailing love
and his wonderful deeds for men
(Psalm 107:8).

This is a second phrase found in each of the four stanzas (vv. 8, 15, 21, 31). When God rescues or redeems you, the proper response is to give him thanks. Recall God's acts and focus on them in your life.

This is what the Pilgrims did. Governor William Bradford refers to Psalm 107 in his account of the founding of Plymouth. They landed there on Monday, December 11, 1620. Some think they may have read this psalm on Sunday, their last day on the Mayflower.[61] Their first winter was terrible. Half of the 102 settlers died, including most of the women. When the harvest finally came in the fall of 1621, they held the first thanksgiving. They could have focused on their hardship and loss. Instead they focused on the rescue of God. So can you.

---

61 Boice, *Psalms*, vol. 3, 864.

November 30

Let them give thanks to the LORD for his unfailing love
and his wonderful deeds for men.
Let them sacrifice thank offerings
and tell of his works with songs of joy
(Psalm 107:21-22).

Thanksgiving must be expressed to God. The act of expressing thanks to God hones your focus and brings perspective to your life. The third stanza of this psalm describes two ways to express your thanks.

First, you can express your thanks to God by making sacrificial thank offerings. If you are grateful to God for his rescue, express it by giving an offering to missions so that others may experience rescue. Express your thanks by helping someone going through financial difficulty or by contributing to a hunger fund.

Second, you can express your thanks to God by singing with joy. God loves singing. The singing of hymns or praise songs is not a human invention in worship. It is the God-ordained way to express your thanksgiving to him. Whether your singing is part of a planned worship service or a spontaneous burst of praise as you drive to work, God delights in your song.

The writer of Hebrews encouraged these same two expressions of thanksgiving: "Through Jesus, therefore, let us continually offer to God a sacrifice of praise—the fruit of lips that confess his name. And do not forget to do good and to share with others, for with such sacrifices God is pleased" (Heb. 13:15-16).

December 1

Let them give thanks to the LORD for his unfailing love
and his wonderful deeds for men.
Let them exalt him in the assembly of the people
and praise him in the council of the elders
(Psalm 107:31–32).

The fourth stanza reveals a third way to give thanks. You express your thanksgiving to God by telling others of his rescue. Every believer has a testimony of redemption. Learn to tell your story clearly and succinctly, with warmth and enthusiasm. Do not focus on yourself but on the wonderful grace of God. Learn to tell not only the story of how you accepted Christ as your Savior but also the story of God's continued acts of grace in your life. Learn to tell what Christ has meant to you at the death of a loved one, when you lost a job, or when you went through a divorce. If you make yourself available, God will give you opportunities to connect with others who are going through these same crises in life. Learn to tell of God's work in positive experiences as well: how he enabled you to finish school, find your spouse, or find your place of ministry. Your story is powerful. If you are grateful to God, he wants you to share your story with other people. Do not be pushy or obnoxious with your story. Pray and watch for opportunities to share with those who are receptive.

December 2

Whoever is wise, let him heed these things
and consider the great love of the LORD
(Psalm 107:43).

In 1830 Alexander Duff and his wife were sailing to India as missionaries. They were taking 800 books, hoping to start a Christian college. Rounding the Cape of Good Hope, the ship struck ground. The surf beat it to pieces. Everything was lost, but all made it to shore safely. A sailor, walking along the shore looking for food and fuel, found two books washed up: a hymnal and a Bible. Both had Duff's name in them, and they were returned to the missionary. Duff at once opened the Bible to Psalm 107 and read it to the survivors.[62] He could have focused on the loss. He chose to focus on the rescue. So can you.

---

62 Boice, *Psalms*, vol. 3, 876.

December

Our Present and Future King

This month we will study a group of psalms called enthronement psalms. These psalms declare that God is king. They remind us that God is always in control. However chaotic life seems to be, God is on his throne. Some think that the enthronement psalms may have been read each year at a celebration of the anniversary of the king of Israel. At such times they would remind the king and the people that the Lord is the real king of Israel and that all authority is derived from him.

These psalms are appropriate to read in December, because some of them prophesy the coming of the Messiah, the future king. All of them find their ultimate fulfillment in the coming of Jesus Christ and his kingdom.

December 3–9
Psalm 93: The Lord Is King of Creation

December 3

The LORD reigns, he is robed in majesty;
the LORD is robed in majesty
and is armed with strength.
The world is firmly established;
it cannot be moved.
Your throne was established long ago;
you are from all eternity
(Psalm 93:1-2).

"The Lord reigns!" Three of the enthronement psalms (93, 97 and 99) begin with this dramatic declaration. It is a declaration that God is in control. He is on his throne. There will be times in your life when you are not sure of that. There will be times when it seems all is chaotic and your world is spinning out of control. Believe his Word in those times. He still reigns!

Psalm 93 specifically declares the Lord to be king of creation: "The world is firmly established." The evolutionary worldview is that our universe came into being by random forces and the chaotic collision of molecules. In this worldview, our sun may burn out or our solar system fall apart. The biblical worldview is that the cosmos was firmly established by God. "It cannot be moved." In times of disaster it may seem the world is coming apart. It is not. God promised in Genesis 8:22: "As long as the earth endures, seedtime and harvest, cold and heat, summer and winter, day and night, will never cease." We need not worry. God reigns over his creation.

December 4

The LORD reigns, he is robed in majesty;
the LORD is robed in majesty
and is armed with strength.
The world is firmly established;
it cannot be moved.
Your throne was established long ago;
you are from all eternity
(Psalm 93:1-2).

Note that the word "established" is used twice in this passage: first of the world, then of the throne of God. Behind the stability of creation is the stability of the throne of God. The reason our world is firmly established is because the throne of God is established. The throne of God has been established from eternity. His reign predates the origin of our universe. Our world had a beginning. The reign of God had no beginning and will have no end.

The rule of God is not an open question. It is not up for debate or discussion. There will be rebellions and attacks on his authority, but they will not succeed. There will be disasters and seeming chaos, but the reign of the Lord is never in question. Understanding that truth lends a security and stability to life. Our world is never out of control. Your life is never completely out of control. God is on his throne. It cannot be moved.

December 5

The seas have lifted up, O LORD,
the seas have lifted up their voices;
the seas have lifted up their pounding waves
Mightier than the thunder of the great waters,
mightier than the breakers of the sea—
the LORD on high is mighty
(Psalm 93:3-4).

Psalm 93 focuses on one particular aspect of God's creation: the seas and their storms. The psalms are poetry. Hebrew poetry does not usually include rhyme but instead features repetition. Every verse in this psalm except the last uses repetition for emphasis. The repetition in verse 3 sounds like the relentless pounding of destructive waves: "the seas have lifted up... the seas have lifted up...the seas have lifted up."

The seas often represent chaos in the Bible. The Israelites were generally not a sea-faring people. The seas were mysterious and threatening. Yet, the psalmist affirmed by faith that the Lord is mightier than the seas. Again in verse 4 he uses repetition to affirm the reign of God over the seas: "mightier...mightier...mighty." Whatever chaos comes your way in life, even when it seems to come in one relentless wave of trouble after another, remember: "mightier...mightier...mighty. " The Lord on high is mighty. If you ever find yourself in a storm shelter and you wonder where to turn in the Bible, read Psalm 93.

December 6

The seas have lifted up, O LORD,
the seas have lifted up their voices;
the seas have lifted up their pounding waves
Mightier than the thunder of the great waters,
mightier than the breakers of the sea—
the LORD on high is mighty
(Psalm 93:3-4).

Throughout the Bible God has shown his dominion over the oceans. God created the order of our world out of a chaotic, water-covered world. The Lord reminded Job: "Who shut up the sea behind doors when it burst forth from the womb...when I fixed limits for it and set its doors and bars in place, when I said, 'This far you may come and no farther; here is where your proud waves halt?'" (Job 38:8, 10-11). In Genesis it tells how God sent a flood to destroy the earth. Not only did rain begin to fall, but the "springs of the great deep burst forth" (Gen. 7:11). Later God reclaimed the world from the flood. The springs of the deep and the floodgates of heaven were closed (Gen. 8:2). In Exodus God parted the Red Sea. The water stood up in walls while the Israelites crossed on dry ground. Then the waters flowed back over the fleeing Egyptians (Ex. 14). In the Gospels, Jesus showed he is the King of creation by calming a storm on the Sea of Galilee. He rebuked the wind and said to the waves: "Quiet! Be still!" The disciples asked each other, "Who is this? Even the wind and the waves obey him!" (Mark 4:39, 41).

God did these miracles to help us understand our world is not random and chaotic. God is mightier than the seas. He is sovereign over creation, and he is in control.

December 7

The seas have lifted up, O LORD,
the seas have lifted up their voices;
the seas have lifted up their pounding waves
Mightier than the thunder of the great waters,
mightier than the breakers of the sea—
the LORD on high is mighty
(Psalm 93:3-4).

Still today, with all our sophistication, the seas can be terrifying. On December 26, 2004, there was an earthquake under the Indian Ocean. At 9.15 on the Richter scale, it was the third most powerful earthquake ever recorded. It lasted not for a few seconds as most earthquakes do, but for ten minutes. The entire planet vibrated a few centimeters. It caused a tsunami, a wave as much as one hundred feet high, that killed 275,000 people, making it one of the deadliest disasters in modern history. The seas literally "lifted up." In 2005 an ocean storm named Hurricane Katrina pounded the Gulf coast of the United States. The levees of New Orleans failed, and homes and lives were lost. Once again, the seas "lifted up."

Yet, in both the tsunami of 2004 and the hurricane of 2005, there were many who found the Lord to be mightier than the seas. One woman in Thailand told her story. She had been taught about Jesus but had not yet believed in him. When the tsunami hit, she and some friends ran to the highest spot they could find, a temple. As the waves lifted up, she called upon the name of Jesus. She received not only rescue from the waves but redemption from her sins. The Lord on high is mighty!

December 8

The seas have lifted up, O LORD,
the seas have lifted up their voices;
the seas have lifted up their pounding waves
Mightier than the thunder of the great waters,
mightier than the breakers of the sea—
the LORD on high is mighty
(Psalm 93:3-4).

This psalm gives us reassurance, but it also raises some questions. If God is in control of the oceans and their storms, why does he allow hurricanes and tsunamis? If they are not random, what is their meaning? What is God doing in these storms? I do not believe we can say they are God's judgment on the areas affected by these storms. Jesus will not allow us to say that. When some were talking about a terrible disaster in Jesus' day, he responded, "Do you think that these Galileans were worse sinners than all the other Galileans because they suffered this way? I tell you, no! But unless you repent, you too will all perish" (Luke 13:2-3). However, we go too far the other way if we say storms have no spiritual message. God is in control and speaking to us through his creation (Amos 4:6-13). He reminds us he is God and we are not. These storms are a revelation of his nature, a preview of his terrible judgment. They are a wakeup call to our world, a reminder to all people to bow to the king of creation.

December 9

Your statutes stand firm;
holiness adorns your house
for endless days, O LORD
(Psalm 93:5).

This psalm began by saying God's throne was established from eternity. It ends by saying his word endures into eternity: "What you say goes—it always has" (THE MESSAGE).

In the end there are only two worldviews, only two ways to look at life. The first worldview is that matter is eternal. It has always been here. Life evolved by blind chance, random processes, chaotic collisions. There is no meaning or rhyme to life. It is simply the adaptation of species and the survival of the fittest. Life has no value, no purpose, and no end. The second worldview is that God is eternal. He created everything that exists by his intelligent design. He established and ordered the world. He controls the world. His word stands firm. His purpose will be accomplished through the reign of his Son, Jesus Christ, our rightful king. This is a far better and a far more believable worldview.

December 10–16
Psalm 96: The Lord Is King of the Nations

December 10

Sing to the LORD a new song;
sing to the LORD, all the earth.
Sing to the LORD, praise his name;
proclaim his salvation day after day.
Declare his glory among the nations,
his marvelous deeds among all peoples
(Psalm 96:1-3).

Psalm 96 is another enthronement psalm. It proclaims in verse 10: "The Lord reigns!" The key words in this psalm are "nations" (which occurs four times) and "peoples" (which occurs three times). The theme is that the Lord is king of the nations.

This psalm begins with a three-fold call to sing a new song. The new song is that the glory of the Lord is to be proclaimed among all nations. In God's unfolding plan, we learn that God wants to bless not only his chosen people the Jews but all peoples, for he is God of all nations. It is especially in the Christmas story, the coming of Jesus into the world, that God begins to fulfill his plan to declare his glory among all nations.

December 11

For great is the LORD and most worthy of praise;
he is to be feared above all gods.
For all the gods of the nations are idols,
but the LORD made the heavens
(Psalm 96:4-5).

Do you believe these verses? Is the Lord to be feared above all gods? Are all other gods idols? This is not the popular view today. The message of this psalm is not politically correct. The politically correct view is that all religions are equally valid, that we all worship the same god. Christianity, however, is an exclusive religion. The Bible says that the Lord is superior to all other gods. That sounds arrogant, narrow-minded, and harsh to our pluralistic culture. Many are abandoning the teaching of this psalm. As we have increasing contact with people of other cultures and religions, we find them to be intelligent, friendly, kind, and sincere in their faiths. It sounds much more loving and kind to say that all gods are the same or all religions have part of the truth. But all religions cannot be equally true. Hinduism says when you die you are reborn; Christianity says you die once and then stand before God in judgment. Both cannot be true. Buddhists say there is no god; Hindus say there are many gods; Christians say there is one God. All cannot be right. We must consider the truth claims of each religion and evaluate them carefully. Our conclusion is a crucial one.

December 12

For great is the LORD and most worthy of praise;
he is to be feared above all gods.
For all the gods of the nations are idols,
but the LORD made the heavens
(Psalm 96:4-5).

Let us be clear that Christians believe in a hierarchy of ideas but not a hierarchy of people. That is, not all ideas are equal, but all people are. Christianity is superior to Islam, but Christians are not superior to Muslims. The gods of the Hindus are inferior to the God of the Bible, but Hindus are not inferior to Christians. The fact that we believe their gods are idols should not cause us to dislike them or insult them or in any way be cruel to them. It should have the opposite effect. We must treat people of all nations and religions with respect and honor and kindness and compassion. Christians must never make disparaging remarks about people from other religions or cultures. The fact that God is king of the nations means he has great compassion and love for all peoples. So should we.

December 13

Splendor and majesty are before him;
strength and glory are in his sanctuary
Ascribe to the LORD, O families of nations,
ascribe to the LORD glory and strength.
Ascribe to the LORD the glory due his name;
bring an offering and come into his courts.
Worship the LORD in the splendor of his holiness;
tremble before him, all the earth
(Psalm 96:6-9).

God wants all nations to worship him. God calls the nations to do five things. These are the five things God desires in worship. He wants all peoples to (1) come into his presence, (2) bring an offering, (3) tremble before him in reverence, (4) openly confess (or ascribe) that He is the Lord, and (5) honor him by living a holy life. That is true worship! One day people from all the nations will do these very things.

> After this I looked and there before me was a great multitude that no one could count, from every nation, tribe, people, and language, standing before the throne and in front of the Lamb. They were wearing white robes and were holding palm branches in their hands. And they cried out in a loud voice: "Salvation belongs to our God, who sits on the throne, and to the Lamb" (Rev. 7:9-10).

December 14

Say among the nations, "The LORD reigns."
The world is firmly established, it cannot be moved;
he will judge the peoples with equity
(Psalm 96:10).

God wants us to tell the nations that he is king. This is the foundation for our missionary efforts. We have a mandate from God to tell the nations of the world about him. This verse links missions to both creation and judgment. Because the Lord made the whole earth, the inhabitants of all the earth need to know him. Because he will one day judge the whole earth, all the peoples of the earth need to know him.

Perhaps God has given you a heart for a particular nation or people group. Perhaps he is calling you to invest your life sharing the good news with them. God calls individuals to specific tasks within his kingdom purposes. He called Jeremiah as a "prophet to the nations" before he was even born (Jer. 1:5). Jesus said he called Saul to "carry my name before the Gentiles" (Acts 9:15). Is God calling you to invest your life in a particular nation or area of the world?

Certainly God is calling you to support those who are taking his name to the nations. Would you commit to pray for a specific area of the world or a particular missionary family? This Christmas season, consider giving a generous offering to support those who are saying to the nations, "The Lord reigns."

December 15

Say among the nations, "The LORD reigns."
The world is firmly established, it cannot be moved;
he will judge the peoples with equity
(Psalm 96:10).

In 2003 after the liberation of Iraq, our church joined many others in collecting food boxes for the people of that nation. A person of another faith wrote a guest editorial in the *Tennessean* labeling this practice "spiritual bribery" and "covert coercion" and questioning whether proselytization was right or necessary. I wrote a response, part of which is printed here:

> Our church is collecting food boxes to send to the people in Iraq. We are sending these food boxes to the Iraqis because we have compassion for them, because our faith teaches us to help the hungry. Do we think it would be good if the Iraqi people also came to learn about Jesus and put their faith in him? Yes, we do. Our Scriptures teach that Jesus was sent to earth to be the Savior of all peoples. We make no attempt to hide that belief. Thus, we do not, as you suggest "use covert means to effect conversion."
>
> You raise the "pesky question of whether proselytization is right or even necessary." That depends on one's perspective, doesn't it? If you believe there are many paths to God and that all religions are equally valid, then evangelism is not necessary. However, if you believe (as our Scriptures teach) that "there is one God and one mediator between God and man, the man Christ Jesus," then evangelism is certainly right and necessary. We believe the very best thing we could offer the Iraqi people or the people of any nation is the good news that forgiveness of sin and reconciliation with God is found through Jesus Christ. I do not believe this evangelism should contain any element of coercion, no matter how subtle. I believe the Iraqi people should have the freedom to accept or reject the message of Christianity.

With respect and love, we must say among the nations, "The Lord reigns."

December 16

Let the heavens rejoice, let the earth be glad;
let the sea resound, and all that is in it;
let the fields be jubilant, and everything in them.
Then all the trees of the forest will sing for joy;
they will sing before the LORD, for he comes,
he comes to judge the earth.
He will judge the world in righteousness
and the peoples in his truth
(Psalm 96:11-13).

One day God will come to judge all the nations. On that day all creation—even the trees—will sing for joy! Here is the part of this psalm that relates to Christmas. In various times of Christian history it has been traditional to read this psalm on Christmas Eve. It says the king is coming to judge or rule all nations. This was partially fulfilled when Jesus was born king of the Jews. It will be completely fulfilled at his second coming. Then all creation will rejoice. The fields will jump and the trees will sing. Christmas celebrates both comings of Jesus. Have you ever gotten a Christmas card with a lion and a lamb on it? The lion and the lamb will not coexist in peace until his second coming, but that process of reconciliation began with his first coming. Someone needs to design a Christmas card with a singing tree!

December 17–23
Psalm 89: The King Who Will Rule Forever

December 17

I will sing of the LORD'S great love forever;
with my mouth I will make your faithfulness known through all
generations. I will declare that your love stands firm forever,
that you established your faithfulness in heaven itself.
You said, "I have made a covenant with my chosen one,
I have sworn to David my servant,
I will establish your line forever
and make your throne firm through all generations"
(Psalm 89:1–4).

I believe the miracles of the Christmas story are true. I believe in the virgin birth of Jesus. I believe a star moved through the sky to guide the wise men. I believe God became man. I do not believe every miracle story I hear. Why do I believe some miracles and not others? I believe the miracles of the Christmas story because God predicted the details of this story far in advance.

Predicting the future is a difficult task. On April 18, 2005, a panel of sports experts for ESPN predicted who would win the 2005 World Series. In October, 2005, the Chicago White Sox won the Series by defeating the Houston Astros. Not one of the experts predicted the winner. Not one expert predicted either of these teams would even be in the World Series. It is hard to predict the future.

God predicted many details of the Christmas story hundreds of years in advance. This week we examine one specific prophecy that helps us know the Christmas story is true.

December 18

I will sing of the LORD'S great love forever;
with my mouth I will make your faithfulness known through all
generations. I will declare that your love stands firm forever,
that you established your faithfulness in heaven itself.
You said, "I have made a covenant with my chosen one,
I have sworn to David my servant,
I will establish your line forever
and make your throne firm through all generations"
(Psalm 89:1-4).

Psalm 89 is a royal psalm that proclaims God is king. The theme is introduced in these first four verses. God swears to King David that he will establish his throne forever. He promises David that his royal lineage will last through all generations. The key word in this psalm, occurring nine times, is "forever."

That's quite a promise! It is difficult to predict the fate of world leaders. The most famous psychic of the twentieth century was Jeanne Dixon. She gained fame by predicting a Democrat would win the 1960 election and would die in office. Sure enough, John F. Kennedy was elected president in 1960 and was assassinated in 1963. But Dixon missed on all three previous presidential nominees and elections. She also predicted World War Three would begin in 1958, Russia and China would become one country in 1964, Fidel Castro would die in 1966, a cure for cancer would be discovered in 1967, the first woman president would be elected in 1980, and a comet would strike the earth in the 1980s. Even a broken watch is right twice a day! Predicting the future is a difficult task. Yet, God boldly predicted that David's line would last forever. This is a specific, verifiable, and improbable prediction. The king before David did not see even one generation of his descendants on the throne of Israel. Would David be any different?

December 19

I have found David my servant;
with my sacred oil I have anointed him.
My hand will always sustain him;
surely my arm will strengthen him.
No enemy will subject him to tribute;
no wicked man will oppress him.
I will crush his foes before him
and strike down his adversaries
(Psalm 89:20-23).

These verses elaborate the promise God made to David. The prophet Samuel anointed David with oil to indicate he was to be king (1 Sam. 16:13). The word "anointed" is the origin of the title "Messiah." The Hebrew word "Messiah" and the Greek word "Christ" both mean "anointed one." The Jews quickly saw that the promises in these verses were not only true of David but also were prophecies of his descendant, the Messiah, the Anointed One. The Messiah would be a descendant of David.

The very first thing the New Testament says about Jesus is that he is "Christ, the son of David" (Matt. 1:1). Matthew follows that statement with a lengthy genealogy to clearly establish that lineage (Matt. 1:2-17). When the angel appeared to Joseph, he addressed him as "Joseph, son of David" (Matt. 1:20). The New Testament presents Jesus as the fulfillment of God's promise to David that his line would be established forever.

December 20

He will call out to me, "You are my Father,
my God, the Rock my Savior."
I will also appoint him my firstborn,
the most exalted of the kings of the earth.
I will maintain my love to him forever,
and my covenant to him will never fail.
I will establish his line forever,
his throne as long as the heavens endure
(Psalm 89:26–29).

The psalmist continues to describe God's promises to David and to his descendants. Christians see in these verses a clear portrait of Jesus Christ. Jesus claimed to have a unique relationship to God and called him "Father" (John 3:35). He claimed to be the firstborn and only Son of God (John 3:16). He said he came to establish a heavenly, eternal kingdom (John 18:36).

When the angel appeared to Mary to announce the coming of Jesus, he said,

> Do not be afraid, Mary, you have found favor with God. You will be with child and give birth to a son, and you are to give him the name Jesus. He will be great and will be called the Son of the Most High. The Lord God will give him the throne of his father David, and he will reign over the house of Jacob forever; his kingdom will never end (Luke 1:30-33).

Jesus is the descendant of David promised in Psalm 89. Jesus is also the unique Son of God. The Father has appointed him king. His kingdom will never end.

December 21

If his sons forsake my law,
and do not follow my statutes,
if they violate my decrees
and fail to keep my commands,
I will punish their sin with the rod,
their iniquity with flogging;
but I will not take my love from him,
nor will I ever betray my faithfulness.
I will not violate my covenant
or alter what my lips have uttered.
(Psalm 89:30–34).

God warned that his promise did not mean there would be an unbroken line of David's descendants on the throne of Judah. If the kings that followed David failed to keep his commandments, he would discipline them severely. However, even their unfaithfulness would not negate his promise to David.

God makes some promises that are conditional. The personal fate of David's successors was conditional on their obedience to God. God makes other promises that are unconditional. He promised David's line would last forever no matter the failure of individual kings. God will accomplish his purposes for our world regardless of the actions of human beings. "If we are faithless, he will remain faithful, for he cannot disown himself" (2 Tim. 2:13).

December 22

But you have rejected, you have spurned,
you have been very angry with your anointed one.
You have renounced the covenant with your servant
and have defiled his crown in the dust.
You have broken through all his walls
and reduced his stronghold to ruins.

How long, O LORD? Will you hide yourself forever?
How long will your wrath burn like fire?
(Psalm 89:38-40, 46).

The descendants of David sat on the throne of Judah for fourteen generations. His royal lineage was unbroken for about 400 years, from roughly 1000 BC to 600 BC. However, many of these kings did not follow God's commands. Just as he had warned, God broke the line of Davidic kings. He allowed Babylon to conquer Judah and destroy her cities.

Psalm 89 was written after the fall of Judah. It mourns the destruction of the nation and longs for the restoration of the Davidic line. In anguish, the psalmist wonders how long this period of discipline will last.

Even after the exile was over and God allowed the people of Judah to return to their homeland from Babylon, God did not reinstate a Davidic king. For 600 more years the people of Judah would wait for God to fulfill his promise. This psalm expresses the longing of God's people for a Messiah. Charles Wesley captured this sense of longing in his carol, *Come, Thou Long-Expected Jesus*:

Come, Thou long-expected Jesus, Born to set Thy people free;
From our fears and sins release us; Let us find our rest in Thee.
Israel's strength and consolation, Hope of all the earth Thou art;
Dear desire of every nation, Joy of every longing heart.

December 23

Once for all, I have sworn by my holiness—
and I will not lie to David—
that his line will continue forever
and his throne endure before me like the sun;
it will be established forever like the moon,
the faithful witness in the sky
(Psalm 89:35-37).

With the coming of His Son Jesus to earth, God kept his promise that a descendant of David would forever rule over Israel. After a gap of 600 years, God sent us another Son of David. From the time of his birth, Jesus was recognized as a king. The wise men asked, "Where is the one who has been born king of the Jews?" (Matt. 2:2). Later Jesus rode a donkey into Jerusalem at Passover time, fulfilling the prophecy of Zechariah 9:9: "Shout, Daughter of Jerusalem! See, your king comes to you, righteous and having salvation, gentle and riding on a donkey."

Just before he entered Jerusalem, Jesus predicted that he would be lifted up from the earth (John 12:32). "The crowd spoke up, 'We have heard from the Law that the Christ will remain forever, so how can you say, "The Son of Man must be lifted up?"'" (John 12:34). These people knew the prediction of Psalm 89! They did not see how Jesus could fulfill it if he went back to heaven. They did not know that Jesus would be "lifted up" on the cross to save us, then "lifted up" into heaven at his ascension so that he could sit at the right hand of God and rule forever.

God has fulfilled his predictions of Psalm 89 exactly. He established David's line, then broke it because of the disobedience of his descendants, then reestablished it by sending Jesus, another descendant of David, to rule forever. God always keeps his promises.

December 24–30
Psalm 72: Gifts for the Perfect King

December 24

All kings will bow down to him
and all nations will serve him
(Psalm 72:11).

This is a psalm about the king of Israel. The title says it is a psalm "of Solomon." Either it was written for Solomon as he took the throne, or it was written by Solomon for his son's coronation. Either way, it quickly moves beyond the scope of any human king. No human king could be some of the things in this psalm. It points to the Messiah, the ideal king, the perfect King. It is fulfilled in Jesus. He is the only one who can do the things described in this psalm. These are Christmas promises. One day all kings will bow to him and all nations will serve him. Today we declare him our King as we celebrate his birth. Isaac Watts wrote:

Joy to the world! The Lord is come;

Let earth receive her King;

Let every heart prepare Him room,

and heaven and nature sing.

December 25

He will rule from sea to sea
and from the River to the ends of the earth.
The desert tribes will bow before him
and his enemies will lick the dust.
The kings of Tarshish and of distant shores
will bring tribute to him;
the kings of Sheba and Seba
will present him gifts
(Psalm 72:8-10).

What is the most widespread activity on Christmas Day in our culture? Certainly it is the giving and receiving of gifts. Not everyone will eat turkey or drink eggnog or sing carols, but in almost every home—certainly in every home with children—there will be some gift given or received. It is the central focus of Christmas in America. Some of you have been planning for months what you would give today. Some of you will go to the stores tomorrow to return your gifts.

Where did all this come from? What is the origin of this widespread custom? It came from Matthew 2:1-11. The Magi from the east came to Bethlehem to honor the newborn king of Israel. They gave to little Jesus gold and fragrant spices. Why did they do that? Where did that come from? Take a step back even farther. The origin of our gift giving today is Psalm 72:10. This psalm predicted that the perfect king would receive gifts from the ends of the earth. The place names reflect the four points of the compass from Israel: the (Euphrates) River to the north, the desert tribes to the east, Tarshish to the west and Sheba to the south. One day every knee will bow to Jesus.

Today we celebrate the birth of the perfect King. We give gifts in his honor. We give him our worship and love and gratitude.

December 26

Endow the king with your justice, O God,
the royal son with your righteousness.
He will judge your people in righteousness,
your afflicted ones with justice.
The mountains will bring prosperity to the people,
the hills the fruit of righteousness
(Psalm 72:1–3).

The perfect King will rule the earth with righteousness and justice. In our world today, leaders are often corrupt and unjust. Take heart! Jesus has come to set up his kingdom. One day his kingdom will come in its fullness, and he will rule with righteousness. He will bring "prosperity" to the people. The word "prosperity" is the Hebrew word *shalom*, which means peace, wholeness, and harmony. Henry W. Longfellow wrote,

I heard the bells on Christmas day their old familiar carols play,
And wild and sweet the words repeat of peace on earth goodwill
to men.

And in despair I bowed my head: "There is no peace on earth,"
I said,
"For hate is strong, and mocks the song of peace on earth, goodwill
to men."

Then pealed the bells more loud and deep: "God is not dead, nor
doth he sleep;
The wrong shall fail, the right prevail, with peace on earth,
goodwill to men."

God's gift to us of complete righteousness and peace has not arrived yet, but it was been shipped to us on Christmas morning. It is on its way! We can track it through God's Word. We rejoice at its coming even before it arrives.

December 27

He will endure as long as the sun,
as long as the moon, through all generations.
He will be like rain falling on a mown filed,
like showers watering the earth.
In his days the righteous will flourish;
prosperity will abound until the moon is no more
(Psalm 72:5-7).

The perfect King will rule forever. The death of a king in Israel was a time of uncertainty and fear. Even today throughout the world a change of leadership in government can be marked by upheaval and chaos. In the United States, we are blessed with a stable government and a smooth transition of power. Still, every four years is a time of change and adjustment in our leadership.

Those who know Jesus will never face such fear and uncertainty in their lives. Jesus has come to earth and the Father has installed him as King. His rule will never end; his administration will never change. Christmas marks a new beginning in our world. Our King has come. He will reign forever.

December 28

For he will deliver the needy who cry out,
the afflicted who have no one to help.
He will take pity on the weak and the needy
and save the needy from death.
He will rescue them from oppression and violence,
for precious is their blood in his sight
(Psalm 72:12-14).

The perfect King will rule with compassion. He will take pity on the weak and will care for the needy. Most rulers are concerned with pleasing those who are powerful and influential. The perfect King will be focused on the lowly. He will rescue them from all oppression and violence.

This Christmas season there are many Christians around the world who are imprisoned because of their faith. Others suffer economic or social persecution because of their love for God. As many of us enjoy freedom, we must remember to pray for these brothers and sisters: "Remember those in prison as if you were their fellow prisoners, and those who are mistreated as if you yourselves were suffering" (Heb. 13:3). We long for the day when there will be no such oppression and violence. "He who testifies to these things says, 'Yes, I am coming soon.' Amen. Come Lord Jesus" (Rev. 22:20).

December 29

Long may he live!
May gold from Sheba be given him.
May people ever pray for him
and bless him all day long.
Let grain abound throughout the land;
on the tops of the hills may it sway.
Let its fruit flourish like Lebanon;
let it thrive like the grass of the field.
May his name endure forever;
may it continue as long as the sun.
All nations will be blessed through him,
and they will call him blessed
(Psalm 72:15-17).

The perfect King will bless all nations, and all nations will call him blessed. This week people around the world have celebrated the birth of Jesus and have proclaimed him Savior and Lord. Our worship this Christmas is a small preview of the eternal celebration we will share together. Revelation 15:2-5 gives us a glimpse of what that will be like:

> And I saw what looked like a sea of glass mixed with fire and, standing beside the sea, those who had been victorious over the beast and his image and over the number of his name. They held harps given them by God and sang the song of Moses the servant of God and the song of the Lamb:

> "Great and marvelous are you deeds, Lord God Almighty.
> Just and true are your ways, King of the ages.
> Who will not fear you, O Lord, and bring glory to your name?
> For you alone are holy.
> All nations will come and worship before you.
> For your righteous acts have been revealed."

December 30

The kings of Tarshish and of distant shores
will bring tribute to him;
the kings of Sheba and Seba
will present him gifts
(Psalm 72:10).

Whenever you look at a Christmas gift or wear a Christmas gift, I encourage you to reflect on three gifts.

First, think about the gift of God's Son Jesus to you. That is the greatest gift you will ever receive. A foster child received a huge pile of gifts on Christmas morning. After he had opened them all, his beaming foster parents asked, "Which gift do you like the best?" He climbed onto the couch between his foster mom and dad and said, "I like you best." Our best gift is a person. Our best gift is Jesus.

Second, think about the gift of yourself to Jesus. In response to the gift of Jesus, we give ourselves. Once a church was receiving an offering for missions. One girl had been moved by the service, but she had no money to give. When the offering plate reached her row, she placed it on the floor, got up, and stood in it. The best gift you can give Jesus is yourself.

Third, think about the gifts that will be given to Jesus when his kingdom comes in fullness. God gives gifts so we can give back to him. He will give us a crown. We will lay it at the feet of Jesus. That will be our most joyous moment.

December 31

Looking Back and Looking Ahead

The last day of the year is a day to look back and a day to look ahead. First, look back over this year. We have studied 52 psalms together. If you have persevered through this entire study, congratulate yourself! Well done! Think back over this study. I do not expect that you will remember every psalm, but what sticks in your mind? There is some message here that was especially meant for you. When you hear the voice of God speaking to you through his Word, you must respond to it.

> Anyone who listens to the word but does not do what it says is like a man who looks at his face in a mirror and, after looking at himself, goes away and immediately forgets what he looks like. But the man who looks intently into the perfect law that gives freedom, and continues to do this, not forgetting what he has heard, but doing it—he will be blessed in what he does (James 1:23-25).

Second, look ahead. Where will you go from here? I encourage you to plan another in-depth study of a portion of God's Word in the year ahead. Since you have studied a book from the Old Testament this past year, I suggest you focus on a New Testament book (or group of books since some are brief) in the year ahead. The Christian must be a lifelong student of the Word of God. "Like newborn babies, crave pure spiritual milk, so that by it you may grow up in your salvation, now that you have tasted that the Lord is good" (1 Pet. 2:2-3). May God bless you in the New Year!

Scripture Index

81	**July 30-Aug 5**	**Ecclesiastes**	
89	**Dec 17-23**	4:12	Oct 22
90	Feb 19-25	5:2-6	July 14
91	**June 25-July 1**		
93	**Dec 3-9**	**Isaiah**	
96	**Dec 10-16**	25:9	Jan 17
98:8	Mar 8	28:16	Apr 7
100	**Oct 29-Nov 4**	38:5	Feb 23
101	**July 2-8**	40:8	Mar 23
103	**Feb 12-18**	40:26	Mar 7
104	**Nov 5-11**	40:31	Jan 17
105	**Nov 12-18**	55:12	Mar 8
106	**Nov 19-25**	59:2	Mar 1
107	**Nov 26-Dec 2**		
110:1	Mar 20	**Jeremiah**	
111:9-10	Sep 24	1:5	Dec 14
112	**Sep 24-30**	29:11	May 20
118	**Apr 2-8**		
119	**Aug 13-19**	**Ezekiel**	
	Aug 20-26	36:25-26	Jan 13
121	**June 18-24**	36:25-27	July 18
125	**June 11-17**	47:1-12	Sep 6
127	**Oct 22-28**		
128:1	Sep 26	**Hosea**	
130	**Jan 15-21**	13:2	Apr 27
138	**Mar 19-25**		
139	**Feb 26-Mar 4**	**Joel**	
139:2-3	May 20	2:13	Feb 12
141	**May 7-13**		
142	**May 14-20**	**Amos**	
148	**Mar 5-11**	4:6-13	Dec 8
150	**Mar 26-Apr 1**		
		Jonah	
Proverbs		4:2	Feb 12
20:26	July 8	4:8	June 21
21:31	June 9		
27:6	May 10	**Micah**	
		5:8	Aug 4

10:28	Nov 17
12:1-3	Mar 26
12:32	Dec 23
12:34	Dec 23
13:10	Jul 17
14	Aug 23
14:3	Aug 26
14:26	Nov 17
16:33	Nov 17
17:3	Mar 4
18:11	Feb 10
18:36	Dec 20
19:23-24	Apr 13
19:28-29	Apr 11
19:30	Apr 15
19:34	Apr 11

Acts

1:8	Aug 4
2:29-32	Apr 18
3:16	Mar 21
4:10-12	Apr 6
4:25-26	Apr 24
4:17	Mar 21
5:40	Mar 21
5:41	Mar 21
9:15	Dec 14
9:31	Sep 25
12:23	Mar 9
13:26-31	Apr 19

Romans

1:19-22	Oct 2
1:20	Aug 7
1:21-28	Aug 3
3:12	Oct 4
3:25-26	Feb 14
3:26	Aug 26
4:7-8	Jan 25

5:8	Feb 18
6:23	Feb 14
8:31-34	Sep 22
8:33-39	Aug 26
8:38-39	Feb 18
10:9	Mar 21
13:1	Aug 4
16:20	June 30

1 Corinthians

2:10-14	Aug 21
11:25	Feb 10
12:3	Mar 21
13	Aug 23

2 Corinthians

4:6	Sep 15
6:14	Oct 22
7:8-10	Jan 5

Galatians

3:7	Mar 18

Ephesians

1:7	Jan 21
2:14	Mar 18
4:30	Jan 13
6:17	Aug 23

Philippians

2:10-11	Mar 18
4	Aug 23
4:13	June 8
	July 3

Colossians

3:3	Sep 14
4:5-6	Mar 22

1 Thessalonians

4:3	Aug 4
5:18	Aug 4

2 Thessalonians

1:9	Sep 15

2 Timothy

2:8	July 17
2:13	Dec 21

Hebrews

1:5	Apr 26
2:10-11	Apr 14
2:14-15	Sep 12
5:5	Apr 26
10:22	Jan 11
10:25	Aug 4
12:1	June 14
12:2	Apr 21
	May 12
13:3	Dec 28
13:6	Aug 26
13:15-16	Nov 30

James

1:22	Aug 24
1:23-25	Dec 31
2:10	Feb 9
3:6-7	May 8
4:6	June 7
4:8	Mar 1

1 Peter

2:2-3	Dec 31
2:4-6	Oct 7
2:7	Apr 7
2:8	Apr 7
5:7	May 27
5:8	June 30

1 John

3:2	July 29
4:4	June 30

Revelation

2:27	Apr 26
5:11-12	Mar 6
5:13	Mar 8
7:9-10	Dec 13
12:5	Apr 26
12:9	June 30
14:1	Oct 7
14:9-10	Feb 10
14:10	July 28
15:25	Dec 29
19:15	Apr 26
19:16	July 22
20:6	July 28
21:2	Sep 6
22:1-2	Sep 6
22:4	Sep 15
22:20	Dec 28

Subject Index

C

D

LaVergne, TN USA
07 November 2010
203877LV00003B/2/P